The Ultimate Book of Fun Things to Do in Retirement

Volume 2

S.C. Francis

Into The Unknown
Publishing

Copyright © 2023 by S.C. Francis All rights reserved.

No part of this book may be reproduced in any form or by any electronic or mechanical means, including information storage and retrieval systems, without written permission from the author, except for the use of brief quotations in a book review.

Under no circumstances will any blame or legal responsibility be held against the publisher, or author, for any damages, reparation, or monetary loss due to the information contained within this book.

Please note the information contained within this document is for educational and entertainment purposes only. All effort has been executed to present accurate, up-to-date, and reliable, complete information. No warranties of any kind are declared or implied. Readers acknowledge that the author is not engaging in the rendering of legal, financial, medical, mental health, or professional advice. The content within this book has been derived from various sources. The author generated this text in part with GPT-3.5, OpenAI's large-scale language-generation model. All art was created by the author with A.I. The activities and information contained herein may not be suitable for your situation. You should consult a licensed professional before attempting any techniques outlined in this book. Each individual's health situation is unique; readers are urged to consult with their physicians or other medical professionals before attempting any activities outlined in this book.

By reading this document, the reader agrees that under no circumstances is the author responsible for any losses, direct or indirect, which are incurred as a result of the use of the information contained within this document, including, but not limited to, — errors, omissions, or inaccuracies.

The internet is always changing, and you may find that some of the links in this book no longer work. Visit www.funretirementbooks.com/v2-links to be updated as to any changes to the links in this book that have come to our attention since the last printing, or contact us at links@funretirementbooks.com to let us know about any problems you have had accessing any of the references in this book.

We hope you enjoy this book from Into The Unknown Publishing. Our goal is to provide high-quality, thought-provoking books that provide inspiration and confidence to step into life's new experiences. For more information on other books, please go to www.funretirementbooks.com. Thanks for reading!

ISBN: 979-8-9881451-3-4 (Paperback)

ISBN: 979-8-9881451-5-8 (Hardback)

ISBN: 979-8-9881451-4-1 (Ebook)

First Edition

Dedicated to my loving family,

whose unwavering support and encouragement have made this journey possible.

Contents

Your Free Bonus	vii
Preface	ix
Introduction	xi
1. Finding Meaning, Purpose, and Passions	1
2. Bucket List Travel	11
3. The Great Outdoors	65
4. Discover New Experiences	107
5. Social Opportunities	149
6. Arts and Crafts	167
7. Cookin' It Up	185
8. Games, Music, and Curiosity	197
9. Use Technology	223
10. Healthy Mind	243
A Final Word	271
Bibliography	277
List Index	279
Also by S.C. Francis	283

Your Free Bonus

As an additional BONUS to thank you for your purchase, I'd like to give you a gift.

The Senior's Quick Guide to ChatGPT:

This 20-page PDF will show you how to use the revolutionary (free) Artificial Intelligence (AI) ChatGPT to enrich your Golden Years.

Get the free gift now here:

www.funretirementbooks.com/v2bonus

Alternatively, scan the QR code below:

If you have any issues, you can email me at
Francis@FunRetirementBooks.com

Your Future Helper- ChatGPT

I'd like to ask for a favor before you start reading. If you find value in this book and Bonus Guide, it would mean the world to me if you'd leave a quick, simple review or rating on Amazon, Goodreads, or another site where you purchased it. It helps others find my books and motivates me to keep writing. Thanks for your support!

- S. C. Francis

Preface
live more

If I could live my life again, I'd toss caution to the wind and embrace every adventure. Fear wouldn't hold me back; I'd dive headfirst into the unknown, savoring every twist and turn.

I'd trade material possessions for meaningful moments. Laughter, heartfelt conversations, and sunsets with loved ones would take precedence over any wealth or possessions. Relationships would be my greatest investment, weaving a rich tapestry of connections.

And I'd nurture an insatiable curiosity, always hungry for new discoveries. Whether it's exploring far-off places or diving deep into knowledge, I'd be a lifelong learner.

If given another shot, I'd live a life of fearless adventures, cherished moments, deep connections, and unquenchable curiosity, knowing that these are the ingredients of a truly fulfilling existence.

Reflecting now, it's not the path I've taken but the moments I've cherished that defined my life. If I could live my life again, I'd live more.

Introduction

Retirement! For some, it's a much-anticipated time to finally kick back and enjoy the fruits of their labor. For others, it's a daunting transition to a new chapter of life that can be filled with uncertainty and fear. Whether you fall into the former or the latter category, one thing is certain: retirement is a time for reinvention, discovering new passions and interests, and pursuing the things that genuinely make you happy.

But where do you start? How do you fill your newfound free time in a meaningful, fulfilling, and enjoyable way? The Ultimate Book of Fun Things to Do in Retirement- Volume 2 is here to help. This book adds a wealth of new inspiration and insider tips that we couldn't fit into Volume 1. In these pages, you'll find hundreds more ideas to spark your imagination to help you plan an exciting, active, happy, healthy, and mentally sharp life after work.

Perhaps you've already retired and are at a loss for what to do with all this extra time, or you're simply looking for new, exciting ways to fill your days. Maybe you're approaching retirement and feeling apprehensive about the changes ahead. Whatever your situation, this book is designed to guide you through discovering what brings you joy and fulfillment and provide you with the tools and inspiration to pursue those passions enthusiastically.

Let's face it: Retirement can be a challenging time. It's not uncommon to feel a sense of loss or uncertainty when you leave the workforce, especially if your career has been a significant part of your identity. Retirement can also bring with it feelings of boredom, loneliness, or lack of purpose. But with the right mindset and a willingness to explore new avenues, retirement can be an incredibly enriching time in your life. This book is all about embracing that sense of adventure, trying new things, and finding joy in unexpected places.

Picture this: a life filled with passion, purpose, and endless possibilities. No longer confined by the constraints of a 9-to-5 job, you have the freedom to pursue your interests and explore new horizons. You wake up each morning excited for the day ahead, with a sense of purpose and direction that fills you with joy. You spend your days engaging in activities you love, connecting with others who share your passions, and feeling truly alive in a way you may not have experienced in years.

And the best part? This new chapter of your life is entirely within your control. You can shape your retirement in any way you see fit to create a life that is uniquely yours and reflects your values, interests, and passions. The Ultimate Book of Fun Things to Do in Retirement Volume 2 is here to guide you along that journey, providing you with a roadmap to a fulfilling and joyful retirement.

So, what can you expect to gain from this book? First and foremost, you'll discover an abundance of ideas for fun, engaging activities to pursue in your retirement. From creative hobbies to fitness and wellness pursuits to travel and adventure, there's something for everyone on these pages. You'll learn about the latest technologies that can help you stay connected with loved ones and make new friends, from social media platforms to online communities for retirees. You'll also find practical advice on making the most of your retirement years, from powerful attitudes to social connections to maintaining a healthy and active lifestyle.

Perhaps most importantly, this book is designed to inspire you to live your best retirement life. You'll find guidance on approaching retirement with a positive mindset and embracing this new chapter of your life with enthusiasm and purpose. To help you tap into your passions and discover new interests, encourage you to take risks and try new things, and guide you towards a truly fulfilling and joyful life.

As for me, your author, I have a deep passion for helping retirees make the most of their retirement years. I have spent countless hours researching and compiling the best and most engaging activities and hobbies for retirees. I understand the challenges that come with retirement, and I've also seen the incredible potential for growth, exploration, and joy that this time can offer.

So, if you're ready to take charge of your retirement and create a fulfilling, engaging, and joyful life, then this book is for you. Let's get started on this exciting journey together!

How to use this book

You're only as old as you feel. Henry Ford's famous quote says it best, "Whether you think you can or you think you can't, you're right." We either have a positive, optimistic attitude that empowers us to try new experiences or a closed, pessimistic outlook that confines us to a small, safe world without risks.

As you read, try to be open-minded about the new things to do in retirement. Look for activities with the potential to ignite your imagination and inspire you to pursue it as your next passion. Mark the activities you're interested in by dog-earing the page or noting the page number. Approach this book as a guide to action. Give something different a try, and if the activity doesn't suit you, cross it off your list and move on to the next one. With persistence, you'll eventually find an activity you love and embark on a new adventure.

While it's true that certain activities may not appeal to all retired individuals, age should not be a limiting factor in determining what one can do. I have excluded some activities that may be more suitable for a younger crowd but have included some physically demanding options for those in great shape who are up for a challenge. Furthermore, even though someone may not want to participate in certain activities, such as football, they can still enjoy the events as a spectator. Regardless of age, there are always different ways to get involved and stay active.

Some "fun things to do" are self-explanatory, while others have more detailed explanations, especially those that offer more benefits for seniors. Simple steps are provided to help alleviate the fear of the unknown when learning something new, and some entries have lists of additional resources, books, or products that may be useful.

Go for it! Simple Start Steps

I often hear, "I'd love to do that, but I don't know where to start." With motivation, I believe even the most daunting things can usually be achieved by breaking them into small manageable steps. Start by brainstorming and breaking down each step into simple action steps. The plan doesn't need to be perfect or complete—just a guide to get you started. The steps usually begin with finding information and taking action. Simple start steps are included for some things to do. This strategy works and can turn excuses into accomplishments.

Printed Book Website Links

To make exploring additional information on a topic easier, this book contains many links to websites, books on the subject, or products that could be fun or useful. To avoid cluttering the book with long, ugly websites, we've simplified accessing the websites with any of the three options below.

To access the website links on the printed version of this book, either;

1. Use a smartphone camera or QR scanner app on the Chapter Title QR code image and go directly to our website with all the links for the chapter. (Basically, the QR code is a shortcut, so you don't need to type the full web address in an internet browser. Just point your camera phone at the image, then tap the QR code on the screen).

Introduction xv

2. Go to www.funretirementbooks.com/v2-links for all the helpful links.
3. Or email us at links@funretirementbooks.com for a free PDF with easy access to all the clickable links.

All Website Links

So, if you're ready to start some new adventures in retirement, simply turn the page, and let's start with a simple strategy to help see the big picture.

Chapter 1

Finding Meaning, Purpose, and Passions

Before diving into the nearly endless ways to spend your retirement, let's step back from the trees and attempt to see the forest. Since Volume 1 went into depth on living purposefully, we'll only briefly go over the main points of it here in Volume 2 for the benefit of new readers.

As we age, time seems to mysteriously speed up. Before we can figure out what's happening, we wake up one day and we're really old. Suddenly, we realize that all the little things we spent our days doing have now become how we lived our life. When that day comes, we can either feel satisfied and fulfilled, having spent our time wisely on the things that were important to us or be filled with regret about having let time slip away.

Before we can attempt to spend our days on purposeful, meaningful pursuits that will lead to a fulfilling retirement, we must first define what we consider meaningful with the following simple exercise.

What's Important?

Please take a few minutes to create a personal list of the important things to you. Go ahead and pause reading now, and use the blanks below.

1. .
2. .
3. .
4. .
5. .
6. .
7. .
8. .
9. .
10. .

If you skipped over the self-reflection, please stop here and go back...

No really, give it a shot...

Okay fine, you can come back later and make your list. 🤓

Moving on... Perhaps a few things below made your "important things" list?

10 Common Things People Consider Meaningful or Important

1. **Family and friends:** Relationships with loved ones are often considered the most valuable and meaningful part of life.
2. **Personal growth and self-improvement:** Pursuing one's passions, developing new skills, and learning new things are often important to people.
3. **Accomplishments and achievements:** Reaching goals and achieving milestones, such as career success or personal accomplishments, can bring a sense of satisfaction and meaning to life.

4. **Making a difference:** Many people find purpose and meaning in contributing to society or positively impacting the world around them through volunteering, charity work, or other forms of service.
5. **Health and wellness:** Taking care of one's physical and mental health is often a priority for people who want to enjoy a long and fulfilling life.
6. **Financial security:** Having enough money to live comfortably and pursue one's goals and dreams is often a key part of a meaningful life.
7. **Spirituality or religion:** For some people, finding meaning and purpose comes from connecting to a higher power or spiritual practice.
8. **Travel and adventure:** Exploring new places, trying new things, and experiencing different cultures can bring a sense of excitement and fulfillment to life.
9. **Creativity and expression:** Many people find meaning in expressing themselves creatively, whether through art, music, writing, or other forms of self-expression.
10. **Nature and the environment:** Connecting with nature, protecting the environment, and promoting sustainability can be a source of meaning and purpose for many people.

Now, please take another moment and add your future aspirations, such as the "bucket list" things you'd like to do or accomplish, to your list of things you care about.

If you did this.... well done! If you haven't yet..... it's worth taking a little time later to look inward. Retirement is the perfect time to reflect and take inventory of what's truly important to you. Below are some common aspirations. Were any on your list?

. . .

1 5 Common "Bucket List" Items

1. Traveling to a specific destination or multiple destinations, such as all 50 states
2. Skydiving or bungee jumping
3. Running a marathon or participating in a triathlon
4. Learning a new language
5. Climbing a mountain or hiking a famous trail
6. Taking a hot air balloon ride
7. Writing a book or screenplay
8. Swimming with dolphins or other sea creatures
9. Seeing a famous landmark or Natural Wonder, such as the Grand Canyon or the Northern Lights
10. Attending a major event, such as the Olympics or a famous concert
11. Learning to play a musical instrument
12. Starting their own business or pursuing a passion project
13. Going on a safari or wildlife adventure
14. Volunteering abroad
15. Taking a cross-country train journey

Lastly, please prioritize your list by putting the most meaningful things to you at the top. To help prioritize, consider your regret at the end of your life if the item went unfulfilled or was neglected.

Put your list on a wall or somewhere you'll often see to remind you of what's important.

With this personal list of meaningful items, you now have a rudder to help guide your decisions on what to do with your time. Spend the most effort on the priorities at the top of your list, the things you care about most.

Follow your "things that are important to you" list, and you'll be living purposefully and spending time on meaningful endeavors, leading

to a fulfilling and joyful retirement because you'll be following your heart.

Energy

As the years go by, we may find ourselves with less energy than we once had. It can be easy to fall into the trap of complacency and feel like there's not much we can do about it. But the truth is, there are mindset strategies we can use to get up and start being more active, even when we don't feel like it.

First and foremost, we must recognize that our thoughts and beliefs have a powerful impact on our actions. If we believe that we are too old or tired to be active, we will be less likely to take action. Instead, we must cultivate a mindset of possibility and focus on what we can do. By shifting our thoughts and beliefs, we can create a sense of motivation and energy to propel us forward.

Another key strategy is to find activities that we enjoy and that align with our values and interests. When we engage in activities that we are passionate about, we are more likely to feel energized and motivated. Small steps can lead to big changes. By setting achievable goals and taking small steps each day, we can gradually build up our energy levels and create positive momentum in our lives.

Exercise is also very important. We should try to incorporate exercise into our daily routine. The hardest part is getting started, but once we do, being active creates more energy for us in the future. This doesn't have to mean running a marathon or hitting the gym every day. Instead, we can start with small, simple exercises like walking briskly or doing gentle yoga/ flexibility exercises. Not only will this help to get our blood flowing and increase our energy levels, but it can also improve our overall health and well-being.

Another essential element to creating more energy is prioritizing self-care. This means taking the time to rest, relax, and recharge our batteries when needed. Whether taking a nap, reading a book, or indulging in a favorite relaxing hobby, allowing ourselves to slow down and unwind can do wonders for our energy levels and overall outlook on life.

Ultimately, the key to making the most of our time on earth is to stay engaged, stay curious, and stay connected to the things that matter most to us. By adopting a mindset of possibility, focusing on what we enjoy, and taking small steps each day, we can create the energy and momentum we need to keep life from passing us by. So, let us embrace the adventure of aging and make the most of the time we have left!

Passion

Passion is an incredibly powerful force that adds depth, purpose, and meaning to our lives. It's that spark within us that ignites our soul and fuels our desires, driving us to pursue our goals with unrelenting fervor. Whether it's a hobby, a sport, or a personal interest, passion is what makes us feel truly alive.

When we find something we're passionate about, it can transform our lives in countless ways. It gives us a sense of purpose and direction, guiding us towards the things that bring us joy and fulfillment. We feel energized and inspired, motivated to work hard and push ourselves to new heights. We become more creative, productive, and resilient, able to easily overcome challenges and setbacks.

Moreover, passion can help us connect with others and build meaningful relationships. When we share our passions with others, we create a sense of community and belonging that can be incredibly fulfilling. It allows us to bond with others over shared interests and experiences, forging strong connections that can last a lifetime.

As we enter retirement, finding a hobby or interest that we're passionate about can be particularly valuable. It can help us maintain a sense of purpose and structure in our lives, keeping us engaged and active even as we age. It can also provide an opportunity to explore new things and discover new talents, keeping our minds sharp and our hearts full.

So, if you haven't already found something you're passionate about, this book is here to help! Don't be afraid to try new things and explore different interests. Whether painting, hiking, cooking, or learning a new language, there's no shortage of hobbies and activities to pursue. The key is to keep an open mind, follow your heart, and let your passion guide you toward a life filled with purpose, joy, and fulfillment.

10 Popular Things to Do in Retirement

Retirement is a time for exploration, growth, and enjoying life to the fullest. Before jumping into specifics, here are 10 popular things to do in retirement:

1. **Travel:** Now is the time to take that dream trip you've always wanted to go on. Whether exploring a new country, taking a road trip across the country, or visiting family and friends, travel is a great way to expand your horizons and create lasting memories.
2. **Learn:** Retirement is a great time to learn new skills or pursue a lifelong passion. Take a class at a local community college or university, learn a new language, or take up a hobby like painting or woodworking.
3. **Volunteer:** Giving back to your community is a rewarding way to spend your time in retirement. There are countless organizations and causes that need your help, whether volunteering at a local shelter, working with children or seniors, or helping out at a community garden.
4. **Exercise:** Staying active is important for both physical and mental health. Join a gym, take a yoga or dance class, or go on daily walks. Exercise doesn't have to be strenuous to be effective.
5. **Spend time with loved ones:** Retirement is a great time to reconnect with family and friends. Plan regular get-togethers, organize family trips, or just spend a lazy afternoon catching up over coffee or lunch.

6. **Pursue a passion project:** Have you always wanted to write a book, start a business, or build a garden? Retirement is the perfect time to tackle that passion project you've been dreaming about.
7. **Explore your community:** There's so much to discover in your own backyard. Take advantage of local museums, galleries, and cultural events. Join a club or organization that aligns with your interests, like a book club or hiking group.
8. **Relax:** After years of hard work, retirement can be a time to slow down and enjoy some relaxation. Indulge in a spa day, curl up with a good book, or take a leisurely bike ride.
9. **Focus on wellness:** Retirement is a great time to focus on your health and well-being. Schedule regular doctor and dentist appointments, eat a healthy diet, and take time for self-care like meditation or massages.
10. **Practice your faith:** Learning, worshiping, and getting involved at your church or other place of worship is a fantastic social and spiritual outlet in retirement.

With so many fulfilling and enriching activities to choose from, retirement can indeed be the best time of your life. Let's find your next passion!

Chapter 2

Bucket List Travel

There are few things as thrilling and life-affirming as travel. Exploring new cultures, savoring exotic foods, and making unforgettable memories are some of life's greatest joys. And when you're retired, you have the time, freedom, and resources to embark on the ultimate adventure: bucket list travel.

Whether exploring the ancient pyramids of Egypt, experiencing the majesty of the Great Barrier Reef, or strolling the historic streets of Paris, travel is about pursuing your passions and discovering new world wonders. These experiences stay with you for a lifetime and can enrich your life in countless ways.

But bucket list travel is more than just ticking off destinations on a list. It's about immersing yourself in new cultures, meeting new people, and expanding your horizons. It's about challenging yourself to step outside your comfort zone, embrace new experiences, and discover that you're capable of more than you ever thought possible.

So, if you're looking for an adventure, don't hesitate to start planning your bucket list travel. Whether you want to visit the enchanting castles of Germany, cruise the azure waters of the Mediterranean, or attend a traditional Japanese tea ceremony, the world is waiting for you. So bring an adventurous spirit, and a sense of curiosity and wonder, because your bucket list travel experience might just be the journey of a lifetime!

30 Ideas To Experience A World of Wonder

1. Take a cooking class in Tuscany and learn the secrets of making homemade pasta, fresh pesto, and classic Italian sauces.
2. Walk the ancient streets of Kyoto, Japan, and admire the stunning temples, tranquil gardens, and fascinating geisha culture.
3. Experience the breathtaking beauty of India's Taj Mahal, an architectural masterpiece often regarded as one of the most beautiful buildings in the world.
4. Climb to the top of a temple and watch the sunset on the hundreds of other glistening temples and pagodas in Bagan, Myanmar.
5. Explore the colorful streets and bustling markets of Marrakech, Morocco, and immerse yourself in the exotic scents, flavors, and sounds of North Africa.
6. Cruise the Norwegian fjords and marvel at the dramatic scenery of towering mountains, cascading waterfalls, and pristine glaciers.
7. Visit the breathtaking Greek island of Santorini, go island hopping, and soak up the Mediterranean sun while enjoying fresh seafood, local wine, and spectacular sunsets.
8. Embark on an African safari and witness the splendor of lions, elephants, giraffes, and other wildlife in their natural habitats.
9. Hike the stunning Canadian Rockies and marvel at the crystal-clear lakes, soaring peaks, and lush forests of this untouched wilderness.
10. Take a hot air balloon ride over Napa Valley and enjoy a bird's-eye view of the vineyards, rolling hills, and charming towns of Northern California.

11. Visit the ancient ruins of Machu Picchu in Peru and discover the secrets of the Incas while admiring the picturesque Andean scenery.
12. Enjoy a scenic train ride through the Swiss Alps and marvel at the gorgeous vistas of snow-capped peaks, emerald valleys, and quaint mountain villages.
13. Explore the vibrant city of Tokyo and immerse yourself in the colorful pop culture, cutting-edge technology, and delicious food of Japan's capital.
14. Sail the turquoise waters of the Caribbean and indulge in sun, sand, and sea while exploring charming ports of call and exotic islands.
15. Take a road trip through the American Southwest and marvel at the otherworldly landscapes of the Grand Canyon, Monument Valley, and Zion National Park.
16. Cycle the scenic routes of the Loire Valley in France and savor this picturesque region's delicious food, wine, and history.
17. Cruise the Danube River and explore Central Europe's historic cities and charming villages, from Budapest to Vienna to Prague.
18. Visit the unforgettable National Parks of Yellowstone and Grand Teton and experience the natural wonders of geysers, hot springs, waterfalls, and wildlife.
19. Discover Spain's rich history and culture, from the Gothic architecture of Barcelona to the flamenco music and dance of Andalusia.
20. Explore Cambodia's majestic temples and ancient ruins, including the iconic Angkor Wat, one of the world's largest religious monuments.
21. Walk the streets of Havana and immerse yourself in Cuba's colorful culture, music, and history, from the classic cars to the cigar factories.
22. Take a scenic helicopter ride over the Grand Canyon and witness the awe-inspiring natural wonder from a thrilling aerial perspective.

23. Visit the charming towns and stunning landscapes of New Zealand's South Island, from the glaciers and fiords to the hobbit villages and vineyards.
24. Explore the exotic wildlife and landscapes of the Galapagos Islands and discover the inspiration for Charles Darwin's Theory of Evolution.
25. Get a rail pass and travel unlimited through the heart of Europe and discover the complex history, art, and architecture of cities like Amsterdam, Cologne, and Budapest.
26. Set foot among the ancient ruins of Pompeii and experience the tragic history of the Roman town destroyed by the eruption of Mount Vesuvius.
27. Experience the picturesque canals of Venice by gondola and admire the romantic grandeur of this ancient Italian city.
28. Walk in the steps of Jesus within the walls of Jerusalem and see with your own eyes the places within the Bible.
29. Stay in a luxury hut above the beautiful blue waters of Tahiti and add some of their famous black pearls to your jewelry collection.
30. Cruise the glacial passages of Alaska, enjoying the awe-inspiring beauty of pristine wilderness and a diverse array of wildlife, from breaching whales to majestic bears.

And while you may have already compiled an impressive list of travel bucket list ideas, there's always room for more inspiration and adventure. So, in this chapter, we'll reveal some dream travel destinations and experiences to fuel your wanderlust and add even more excitement to your retirement years.

In addition, consider delving into travel resources such as books, blogs, and magazines, where you can uncover more must-see destinations and hidden gems you may have never even heard of before. Furthermore, reading about other travelers' experiences can provide valuable insights and tips for making the most of your adventures. From learning how to navigate public transportation in a foreign city

Chapter 2   15

to discovering the best local cuisine, experienced travelers' wisdom can help you travel more confidently and efficiently.

So don't hesitate to keep reading and exploring the world of travel. You might find that through the process of compiling your favorite locations to visit next, you'll find hours of enjoyment because you'll soon be able to experience the place for yourself. With every new idea and inspiration, you'll be one step closer to making unforgettable memories.

Chapter 2 Website Links

Travel Inspiration and Tips from Volume 1:
Visit the Seven New Wonders of the World - Travel to Help (10 ideas) - Plan a Trip Around the World - Travel for Adventure (33 ideas) - Travel for Food (51 ideas) - Travel to Famous Places (30 ideas) - Travel for Culture (10 ideas) - Travel for Nature and Beauty (20 ideas) - Travel for Unique Stays (40 ideas) - Travel for New Experiences (26 ideas) - Take a Cruise - Motorhome/ RV Travel - Visit a National Park - Attend the World's Largest Hot-Air Balloon Festival - Go to an Amusement Park - Visit Egypt - Live in a Foreign Country for at Least a Month

* * *

Travel for Relaxation
Find peace and tranquility

From luxurious spa resorts to peaceful beach getaways, travel offers endless options for relaxation and rejuvenation, especially for the newly retired. There's something truly rejuvenating about getting away from it all and immersing oneself in a new and peaceful environment. Whether it's the sound of waves crashing on the shore, the feeling of hot springs enveloping your body, or the tranquil ambiance of a spa resort, travel offers endless options for rest and relaxation.

Picture yourself lounging on a white sandy beach, sipping a refreshing cocktail as you soak up the sun. Or imagine yourself being pampered with luxurious spa treatments, letting your worries melt away as you indulge in a massage or facial. Traveling for relaxation offers a chance to escape the daily routine and focus on one's well-being.

Relaxation Travel Ideas:

Go on a tropical getaway- A tropical getaway is the ultimate destination for those seeking relaxation and rejuvenation. The warm sun, crystal-clear waters, and lush green landscapes create a peaceful and inviting atmosphere that promotes rest and rejuvenation. Whether lounging on the beach, soaking up the sun, or exploring the lush surroundings, a tropical destination is the perfect place to unwind and forget about the stress and monotony of daily life.

6 Popular Tropical Destinations

1. **Bali, Indonesia-** Known for its stunning beaches, lush rice paddies, and mellow culture.
2. **Maui, Hawaii-** Offering breathtaking scenery, world-class watersports, and many opportunities for outdoor adventure.
3. **Koh Lanta, Thailand-** Dazzling coastline, serene beaches, and laid-back nightlife await.

4. **Turks and Caicos**- Northern Caribbean islands known for their pristine, uncrowded beaches and clear turquoise waters.
5. **Maldives-** Islands of the Indian Ocean showcase a true tropical paradise with crystal-clear waters and abundant marine life.
6. **Seychelles-** An exquisitely beautiful collection of islands known for their exquisite beaches, lush forests, and unique wildlife in the Indian Ocean.

Visit a **Wellness Retreat-** Wellness retreats are destination getaways focused on holistic health and wellness. They offer a range of activities, services, and amenities designed to promote physical, mental, and spiritual well-being. From yoga and meditation to massages, healthy meals, and fitness classes, wellness retreats provide a comprehensive approach to relaxation and self-care. These retreats often occur in peaceful and scenic locations, such as tropical islands, picturesque mountains, or tranquil deserts, and provide an escape from the stress of daily life. They are designed to help guests disconnect, recharge, and rejuvenate and offer a unique opportunity for growth and self-discovery.

5 Popular Wellness Retreat Destinations

1. **Ubud, Bali-** A hub for wellness, known for its lush jungle, traditional healing practices, and vibrant cultural scene.
2. **Koh Samui, Thailand-** A tropical budget-friendly oasis with a thriving wellness scene offering yoga, massages, and more.
3. **Sedona, Arizona-** A desert oasis known for its captivating red rock formations, spiritual energy, and abundance of wellness retreats.

4. **Costa Rica-** A tropical paradise with a thriving eco-tourism and wellness industry, offering opportunities for adventure, rejuvenation, and relaxation.
5. **The Blue Mountains, Australia-** A scenic mountain range with numerous wellness retreats offering lovely views, fresh air, and peaceful surroundings.

Soak in a Hot Spring- Looking for a way to soothe your mind, body, and spirit? Soaking in hot springs offers several health benefits, including reducing stress, relieving muscle tension, and improving circulation. The warm water, combined with the natural minerals and nutrients found in the water, can soothe and heal both body and mind. In addition to their health benefits, hot springs offer a unique and peaceful escape from the stress of daily life. Surrounded by scenic landscapes, beautiful views, and serene atmospheres, hot springs provide the perfect setting for rest, relaxation, and rejuvenation.

4 Popular Locations for Hot Springs

1. **Japan-** With over 3,000 hot springs, Japan is known for its rich hot spring culture and history. Some famous hot springs include Hakone's onsens and Beppu's hot springs.
2. **Iceland-** With its captivating landscapes and natural hot springs, Iceland is a top destination for hot spring lovers. Soak in the famous Blue Lagoon or explore the hot springs of the Reykjanes Peninsula.
3. **United States-** The United States is home to many natural hot springs in Colorado, California, and Oregon.
4. **New Zealand-** From the geothermal pools of Rotorua to the hot springs of the Coromandel Peninsula, New Zealand is a must-visit destination for hot spring enthusiasts.

Take a Cruise- Cruises offer a wide range of amenities and activities to help you unwind and rejuvenate, including swimming pools, spas, fitness centers, and entertainment options. Whether you want to soak up the sun on a deck chair, treat yourself to a massage, or dance the night away, a cruise has something for everyone.

4 Popular Destinations for Cruising

1. **Caribbean-** The turquoise waters and pristine beaches of the Caribbean make it a top destination for cruisers. Visit popular islands such as the Bahamas, Jamaica, and the Dominican Republic.
2. **Mediterranean-** Sail the sparkling waters of the Mediterranean and explore historic cities, dazzling coastlines, and charming villages in countries such as Italy, Greece, and Spain.
3. **Alaska-** Cruise to Alaska and marvel at this breathtaking region's glaciers, fjords, and wildlife.
4. **Pacific-** From Hawaii to the South Pacific, the Pacific offers a range of destinations, each with its unique culture, landscape, and attractions.

Visit a National Park- Going to a national park is the perfect way to escape the hustle and bustle of everyday life and connect with nature. A national park's serene beauty and peaceful surroundings provide the ideal backdrop for relaxation and rejuvenation. Whether you want to hike through scenic trails, watch wildlife in their natural habitats, or sit and admire the breathtaking views, national parks have something for everyone.

. . .

5 Popular National Parks for Relaxation

1. **Yosemite National Park, California-** Famous for its massive granite cliffs and scenic waterfalls, Yosemite is a must-visit for nature lovers. Yosemite Valley is one of the park's most serene and picturesque areas. Relax beside the Merced River, listen to the gentle flow of water, and take in iconic views of El Capitan and Bridalveil Fall. Mirror Lake is another serene spot for reflection and relaxation.

2. **Yellowstone National Park, Wyoming, Montana, and Idaho-** Explore the geothermal wonders of Yellowstone, including geysers, hot springs, and bubbling mud pots. The Lamar Valley, with its expansive meadows and abundant wildlife, offers a tranquil setting for wildlife watching and reflection.

3. **Great Smoky Mountains National Park, Tennessee, and North Carolina-** Stroll through the rolling hills and verdant forests of the Great Smoky Mountains and experience the beauty of one of the largest protected areas in the eastern United States. Embrace serenity in Cades Cove, a picturesque valley renowned for its scenic beauty and abundant wildlife. Whether driving the loop road or enjoying a leisurely bike ride, you'll find tranquillity throughout this idyllic landscape.

4. **Rocky Mountain National Park, Colorado-** Marvel at the Rockies' majestic peaks and alpine lakes and breathe in the fresh mountain air. Bear Lake is a serene and easily accessible destination for relaxation. The crystal-clear lake is surrounded by towering peaks and offers a peaceful setting for picnics or short hikes.

5. **Zion National Park, Utah-** Hike through Zion's enchanting red rock canyons and dramatic cliff formations and relax in the tranquil beauty of the surrounding desert landscape. Unwind along the Riverside Walk, a gentle, paved trail that meanders into the narrows of Zion Canyon. As you wander, immerse yourself in the towering canyon

walls and the tranquil sounds of the Virgin River. The Emerald Pools area also offers a picturesque escape with its peaceful pools and cascading waterfalls.

Get Pampered at an All-Inclusive Adult Resort- With everything taken care of, from meals and drinks to activities and entertainment, you can truly unwind and focus on your well-being. You can enjoy a stress-free environment, be surrounded by like-minded people, and participate in various activities designed to help you relax and recharge. You'll find plenty of opportunities to unwind, from yoga classes and spa treatments to swimming and sunbathing.

5 Popular All-Inclusive Adult Resort Destinations

1. **Secrets Resorts, Mexico and the Caribbean-** Renowned for their stunning beachfront locations, luxurious accommodations, and endless amenities. Guests can indulge in gourmet dining at multiple on-site restaurants, enjoy top-shelf cocktails, and partake in activities like snorkeling, yoga, and nightly entertainment. The resorts are celebrated for their romantic ambiance, making them ideal for couples and honeymooners.
2. **El Dorado Spa Resorts, Mexico-** Synonymous with world-class spa experiences. These all-inclusive resorts offer guests access to top-notch wellness facilities and a wide range of spa treatments, from massages to hydrotherapy. The resorts also feature exceptional dining options with gourmet cuisine and beautiful beachfront settings for relaxation and romance.
3. **Couples Resorts, Jamaica-** Tailor-made for romantic getaways. Set in the lush landscapes of Jamaica, these resorts provide a tranquil and intimate atmosphere for couples. Guests can enjoy personalized service, including

excursions like snorkeling and sunset cruises, and the option to dine at various on-site restaurants offering Jamaican and international cuisine.
4. **Sandals Resorts, Caribbean-** Renowned for their exclusive focus on couples, offering the utmost in luxury and privacy. These resorts feature stunning overwater bungalows, private plunge pools, and direct access to pristine beaches. Guests can enjoy unlimited water and land sports, world-class dining, and premium drinks. Sandals is known for its exceptional service and the opportunity to explore multiple Caribbean destinations with one resort booking.
5. **Hedonism II, Jamaica-** An adventurous and carefree adults-only resort that caters to those seeking a lively and liberating experience. It's famous for its clothing-optional areas, themed parties, and an uninhibited atmosphere. The resort offers many activities, including water sports, entertainment, and a bustling nightlife scene, making it a unique and exciting destination for open-minded travelers.

Unwind by a Lake- A lake's tranquil surroundings and serene beauty create a peaceful, relaxing atmosphere. Lakes offer various activities for all ages and interests, whether you want to swim, fish, kayak, or sit back and enjoy the views.

5 Popular Lake Destinations for Relaxation

1. **Lake Tahoe, California, and Nevada-** Surrounded by captivating mountain scenery, Lake Tahoe is a popular boating, fishing, and outdoor recreation destination.
2. **Lake Geneva, Switzerland-** Enjoy the incredible views of the Swiss Alps and picturesque lakeside towns while relaxing on the shores of Lake Geneva.

3. **Lake Como, Italy-** Take in the breathtaking scenery and enjoy the relaxed pace of life in the charming lakeside towns of Lake Como.
4. **Lake Powell, Arizona, and Utah-** Explore the fantastic canyons and beaches of Lake Powell while kayaking, fishing, or simply lounging on the shores.
5. **Lake Louise, Canada**- Surrounded by the towering peaks of the Canadian Rockies, Lake Louise is known for its turquoise waters and picturesque setting.

Resources (Print book readers, see the end of the Introduction Chapter for 3 ways to access website links. Ebook readers can click on the link).

1. 14 Incredible Places to Visit if You Need Peace and Relaxation link
2. 22 Gorgeous Vacation Spots to Choose if You Just Want to Relax link
3. 16 of the World's Most Relaxing Places link

* * *

Travel for History

Step into the story

Visiting historic places is like taking a step back in time. It's an opportunity to explore the past and gain a new perspective on how people lived, worked, and played—a chance to immerse yourself in the culture of a bygone era. Whether you're visiting national landmarks, ancient ruins, or small-town sites with local significance, historical places offer a unique insight into our shared history.

You might find yourself standing in awe of the grandeur of a majestic castle or marveling at the engineering feats of an ancient aqueduct. You could be inspired by stories of courage and resilience while exploring monuments to those who served our country during wartime. Or you might enjoy strolling through centuries-old streets lined with traditional storefronts and homes that still stand today as reminders of our collective heritage.

No matter where your journey takes you, visiting historical places can bring about an appreciation for all that has come before us—a reminder that we are part of something larger than ourselves. From discovering hidden gems tucked away in small towns to seeing some of the world's most iconic monuments firsthand, there's no better way to gain insight into our past than by visiting historical places.

3 6 Historic Places to Visit

1. **Normandy Beach, France-** An iconic historical spot where brave Allied soldiers landed on June 6th, 1944, to fight for freedom. Visiting this site will allow you to pay tribute to the courageous men and women who made the ultimate sacrifice for their country.
2. **Berlin Wall, Germany-** Visiting the Berlin Wall is a must-do for history buffs, as it provides a unique glimpse into one of the most important political and cultural moments of the 20th century. Get a sense of what it was like during the Cold War era by exploring its remains and discovering stories of hope, courage, and resilience.
3. **Jerusalem, Israel-** A place of immense historical and religious importance, offering a unique opportunity to explore centuries of culture and tradition in one of the oldest cities in the world. Its ancient monuments, holy sites, and spiritual atmosphere make it an unforgettable experience for any history lover.
4. **Changing of the Guard, London-** Witnessing the Changing of the Guard ceremony at Buckingham Palace is a must-do for any history lover. It provides a glimpse into centuries-old British military pageantry that still lives on today.

5. **Black Taxi Tour, Belfast-** Take a journey through Northern Ireland's history with a black taxi tour and experience firsthand the rich culture and tumultuous past of this beautiful region.
6. **Panama Canal, Panama-** An iconic engineering feat that has changed the face of international travel and trade. It offers visitors a chance to explore its historic infrastructure and witness firsthand how it continues to shape global economics.
7. **Louvre Museum, Paris-** One of the world's most iconic and influential museums, housing some of the most celebrated works of art in history and making it a must-see destination for any art enthusiast.
8. **Terracotta Warriors, China-** The Terracotta Warriors of Xian are an incredible archaeological find. Visiting them is a unique opportunity to take a step back in time and explore an ancient civilization. As the largest clay army ever found, these warriors give us an unprecedented window into Chinese history.
9. **Rome, Italy-** A vibrant and mesmerizing city full of ancient wonders, from the iconic Colosseum to grandiose monuments like the Pantheon, making it one of Europe's most important tourist destinations - a must-see destination for any history buff!
10. **Climb Mt. Sinai, Egypt-** Take in the stunning views from the top, and you'll be standing where Moses received the Ten Commandments - a pivotal moment in history. Feel the spiritual power of this ancient landscape and discover what it meant to generations of people.
11. **Luxor, Egypt-** An iconic destination for history lovers, boasting a wealth of ancient monuments and temples from the Pharaohs' time, including the spectacular Karnak Temple complex and Luxor Temple. Here, you can explore 5,000 years of history in one unforgettable place.
12. **Beijing, China-** A city that has seen thousands of years of history and offers an incredible journey through time for those who visit. From the Forbidden City to the Great Wall,

Beijing has many iconic landmarks that will leave visitors in awe.

13. **Tokyo, Japan-** A vibrant city with centuries of culture and history where the past and present collide to create a unique experience that can't be found anywhere else in the world.
14. **Statue of Liberty, New York City-** An iconic symbol of freedom and democracy, representing hope and opportunity to millions of immigrants who have arrived in America over the past centuries.
15. **Mt. Rushmore, South Dakota-** A stunning testament to America's past, offering visitors a chance to experience a piece of history while viewing the famous faces of four legendary presidents carved into the mountain. It is an iconic landmark that symbolizes the strength and resilience of our nation.
16. **The Gateway Arch, Missouri-** Symbolizes St. Louis' role in the early days of America's westward expansion and is a testament to the courage and vision of its citizens who helped shape the United States.
17. **Washington DC-** Brimming with historical significance, from the White House to the monuments on the National Mall. It's a must-see destination for any history buff! Visitors can take in the free museums and centuries of American history to experience firsthand the power of democracy at its core.
18. **Williamsburg, Virginia-** Colonial America's political, economic, and social capital. Today, it serves as a living history museum that allows us to experience what life was like in the 18th century.
19. **The Henry Ford, Michigan-** An extensive history and innovation complex showcases historic buildings, artifacts, and exhibits related to American history and innovation, including one of the first mass-produced automobiles, the Ford Model T.
20. **Kitty Hawk, North Carolina-** Where the Wright Brothers made their first successful powered flight in

1903, achieving a milestone that changed the face of modern aviation. It is an unforgettable destination for all who visit to pay homage to one of humankind's greatest feats.

21. **Pearl Harbor, Oahu-** The site of one of the most decisive and devastating events in American history, making it an important spot for visitors to reflect on the courage and sacrifice that changed our nation forever.

22. **Hiroshima Peace Memorial, Japan-** A poignant reminder of the devastating impact of nuclear weapons and a call for peace.

23. **Brooklyn Bridge, New York-** Symbolizes the ingenuity and resilience of New York City, as it was the first bridge to connect Manhattan to its neighboring boroughs - a feat that many thought impossible. It stands today as a reminder of the city's past and an inspiration for future generations.

24. **Alcatraz Island, San Francisco-** Once home to the notorious prison that held some of America's most infamous criminals, Alcatraz Island is now a fascinating historical landmark and a must-visit destination for travelers worldwide. Experience the rich cultural history of this iconic island and delve into the stories of its past inhabitants as you explore its many sights.

25. **Hearst Castle, San Simeon-** An iconic historical landmark that offers an unforgettable journey through the opulent lifestyle of newspaper mogul William Randolph Hearst, set against the natural beauty of the California coast.

26. **Mesa Verde National Park, Colorado-** An archaeological wonder offering visitors a unique opportunity to explore the ancient dwellings of the Ancestral Puebloans who inhabited this area more than 700 years ago. It is remarkable historical evidence of a civilization that established and flourished in this area, providing insight into their lifestyle and culture.

27. **Versailles Palace, France-** A symbol of absolute monarchy and opulence, reflecting the grandeur of the French monarchy.
28. **Independence Hall, Philadelphia-** A living symbol of American democracy, where both the Declaration of Independence and the US Constitution were debated and adopted - making it an essential place to visit for anyone interested in American history.
29. **Great Pyramids of Giza. Egypt-** Captivating tourists with their mysterious history and grandeur for centuries, making them one of the most significant archaeological sites in the world.
30. **National Civil Rights Museum, Memphis-** This museum is a powerful reminder of the African American struggle for civil rights, standing at the site of Martin Luther King Jr.'s assassination and housing a comprehensive collection of artifacts that tell the story of the civil rights movement.
31. **One World Observatory, New York City-** At the top of One World Trade Center is the highest observation deck in the Western Hemisphere. It offers unparalleled views of New York City and beyond, paying homage to those who lost their lives during 9/11. It is also a symbol of hope, strength, and resilience for all those who visit.
32. **Tomb of the Unknown Soldier, Arlington-** A monument of immense historical significance, paying tribute to the heroes who have made the ultimate sacrifice in defense of their country. A solemn reminder that freedom comes at a great cost, it serves as an inspiration and a testament to the bravery of all fallen warriors.
33. **Harvard University, Massachusetts-** Harvard University, founded in 1636, is the oldest higher learning institution in the United States. It has been a cornerstone of American history and culture ever since, making it an essential destination for any student or lover of history.
34. **Castillo de San Marcos, St. Augustine-** This 17th-century fort symbolizes Spanish colonial rule in the United

States. It is the oldest masonry fortification still standing in the continental US. It stands proudly today, offering visitors a look into its history and lasting legacy.
35. **Auschwitz Concentration Camp, Poland-** Symbolizes the Holocaust, serving as a poignant reminder of the horrors of World War II and offering a powerful educational experience about the need to prevent such atrocities in the future.
36. **The Alamo, San Antonio-** A visit to the Alamo is like stepping back in time and gaining an intimate glimpse into a momentous event that forever shaped the history of Texas. Visitors are surrounded by the unique historical atmosphere while exploring this iconic site where American heroes fought bravely for independence.

Resources

1. 23 Must-See Historic Landmarks in the US link
2. 100 Most Beautiful UNESCO World Heritage Sites link
3. 18 Top World Heritage Sites link

* * *

Travel for Water Experiences

Dive into aquatic adventures

Traveling to have unique water experiences can provide a sense of adventure or tranquility. Exploring waterways by boat or in the water itself can offer a new perspective on the world and a chance to connect with nature in a peaceful and rejuvenating way. Whether it's gliding through the iconic canals of Venice on a gondola, taking in the gorgeous views of Halong Bay on a traditional junk boat tour, or snorkeling in the crystal clear waters of a Mexican cenote, there are countless opportunities to have unforgettable experiences on the water.

. . .

2 ३ Water Experiences Worth Traveling For

1. **Float in the Dead Sea-** At 1,407 feet below sea level, the Dead Sea, located between Jordan and Israel, is the lowest point on Earth. Ten times saltier than seawater makes it nearly impossible to sink, allowing you to lay back, relax, and enjoy the warm, mineral-rich waters and magnificent views of the mountains.

2. **Marina Bay Sands Hotel Rooftop Infinity Pool, Singapore-** Consistently ranked as one of the world's most spectacular pools, swimming in the 57th-floor rooftop infinity pool of the Marina Bay Sands Hotel is a bucket list experience. With stunning views of the city skyline and the bay, you'll feel like you're floating on top of the world as you take a dip in the refreshing waters.

3. **Halong Bay Junk Boat Tour, Vietnam-** Admire the towering limestone cliffs and tranquil waters while cruising on a traditional wooden sailing boat, taking in the breathtaking scenery and enjoying delicious seafood meals. It's a serene and unforgettable way to experience one of Vietnam's most iconic destinations.

4. **Snorkel the Great Barrier Reef, Australia-** Snorkel the Great Barrier Reef off the coast of Australia for a once-in-a-lifetime experience. Explore the vibrant coral and diverse marine life, including colorful fish, sea turtles, and even dolphins and whales in their natural habitat. It's an exciting underwater adventure that you won't forget.

5. **Spelunking in a Glowworm Cave, New Zealand-** Explore the mesmerizing beauty of a glowworm cave by spelunking in Waitomo, New Zealand. Admire the twinkling lights created by thousands of glowworms, illuminating the dark underground passages as you pass through the caves.

6. **SUP in Leigh Lake at Grand Tetons National Park, Wyoming-** Explore the stunning scenery of Grand Tetons National Park by stand-up paddleboarding (SUP).

Surrounded by the towering peaks of the Grand Tetons, take in the breathtaking views reflected off the mirror-glass surface in a peaceful and secluded environment.

7. **Caribbean Sailing-** Sail the turquoise waters of the Caribbean and discover its tropical islands and beaches. Explore secluded coves, relax on pristine sand, and experience the beauty and culture of this tropical paradise on a sailing adventure.

8. **See Niagra Falls from the Watery Bottom, New York-** Take a boat tour to admire the power and beauty of the falls up close, feel the mist on your face, and capture the unforgettable memories of this mighty natural wonder.

9. **Gondola Ride in Venice, Italy-** Experience the romance and charm of Venice by taking a leisurely gondola ride along the city's canals. Admire the splendid architecture, glide under bridges, and take in the dazzling views of this beautiful city while being serenaded by a gondolier.

10. **Snorkeling or Scuba in a Cenote, Cancun-** Snorkel or scuba dive in a Cenote, the unique sinkholes found in Mexico's Yucatán Peninsula. Explore the crystal-clear waters and admire the fantastic underwater landscapes, including caves, formations, and vibrant marine life. It's a once-in-a-lifetime adventure in the heart of Mexico's tropical jungle.

11. **Sail Indonesian Islands-** Sail Indonesia's spectacular islands on the luxurious Dunia Baru, a traditional Indonesian Phinisi vessel. Explore vibrant tropical islands while enjoying the ultimate in comfort and style. It's a unique way to experience Indonesia's beauty and culture.

12. **Milford Sound Tour, New Zealand-** Explore one of New Zealand's most stunning fiords on a tour boat. Admire the towering peaks, cascading waterfalls, and wildlife while taking in the breathtaking beauty of this natural wonder. It's a must-do experience in New Zealand.

13. **Free Ferry Manhattan to Staten Island, New York-** Take a free ferry from Manhattan to Staten Island

for gorgeous views of New York City's skyline, including the Statue of Liberty. Enjoy a peaceful and scenic ride while observing the hustle and bustle of the city from a different perspective. It's a fun and budget-friendly way to see NYC.

14. **Greenland Iceberg Tour-** See the massive icebergs of Greenland up close on a scenic tour by boat. Admire the dazzling beauty of the towering ice formations, including vibrant blues and greens, and learn about this Arctic wonder's frigid geography and wildlife.
15. **Kayaking in Thailand-** Explore Thailand's lush and tropical landscape through its scenic waterways. Admire towering cliffs, dense forests, and lively wildlife while paddling through serene and peaceful waters.
16. **Punt Down the River Cam, England-** Punting is a traditional English pastime where you relax and glide down the river in a flat-bottomed boat, using a long pole to propel yourself. Admire the traditional architecture, including famous colleges and bridges, as you glide down the picturesque Cambridge River.
17. **Greek Ferry-** Explore the Greek islands by ferry and travel from island to island, taking in the breathtaking coastline, crystal-clear waters, and charming villages.
18. **Waikiki Sunset Catamaran, Hawaii-** Sail into the sunset on a catamaran and experience the island's beauty from a new perspective. Admire the colorful sky and glittering ocean as you glide along the coastline, making memories to last a lifetime.
19. **Sail the Nile River on a Felucca, Egypt-** Sail on a traditional felucca sailboat and experience the rich history of this ancient civilization. Enjoy the tranquil desert scenery, passing temples and villages, as you float down one of the world's most famous rivers.
20. **Sail the Whitsundays, Australia-** An unforgettable island-hopping adventure. Explore crystal-clear waters, pristine white sand beaches, and lush tropical scenery as you travel from island to island in this tropical paradise.

21. **Explore the Amazon River-** Embark on an adventure and explore the Amazon River, the world's largest river by volume and home to diverse wildlife. Discover the complex ecosystems and immerse yourself in the natural beauty of the rainforest.
22. **SUP Yoga-** Stand-up paddle board (SUP) yoga is a fun yoga practice on a special paddle board floating on water. It is an excellent way to challenge yourself by maintaining balance and focus while also enjoying the calming effects of being on the water.
23. **Underwater Scooter-** An underwater scooter is a motorized device that allows you to explore the ocean depths easily and quickly. If you're looking for an exciting way to explore the ocean and its inhabitants, an underwater scooter can provide a thrilling adventure you will remember.

Resources

1. The 27 Best Water Sports To Try Around The World link
2. 10 Unique Water Activities to Add to Your Bucket List link
3. Top 10 Best Water Sports in Wonderful Place link

* * *

Go to an Amusement Park

Relive your childhood excitement

Visiting an amusement park can be a thrilling adventure for anyone seeking excitement and a burst of energy. The sound of laughter and screams, the smell of cotton candy, and the sight of towering roller coasters create a memorable experience.

Stepping into an amusement park is like stepping into a different world where anything is possible, and adventure is always just a ride away. It's a chance to let loose, forget about the worries of daily life, and be a kid again.

Amusement parks offer a unique form of entertainment for families, couples, and individuals of all ages. Whether you're seeking thrills, laughter, or a day filled with memories, amusement parks will surely provide them. From classic rides to the latest cutting-edge attractions, there's something for everyone. And with an abundance of games, food stands, and souvenir shops, the fun never ends.

Even if you decide to skip the extreme rides, there are usually plenty more attractions that will appeal to more experienced folks. So pack your bags, grab some friends or grandkids, and embark on an exciting journey to the nearest amusement park. Get ready to scream, laugh, and make memories that will last for years.

12 US Amusement Parks Best for Lucky Retirees

1. **Disney World, Florida-** With its iconic characters, world-class attractions, and magical atmosphere, Disney World is a timeless destination that appeals to people of all ages. Relive childhood memories amidst the enchanting atmosphere of the "Happiest Place on Earth."
2. **Universal Studios, various-** Take a nostalgic journey through iconic movies and TV shows, with thrilling rides and immersive experiences that let you rediscover the magic of the silver screen.
3. **Knott's Berry Farm, California-** This classic park is known for its thrilling roller coasters and old-fashioned atmosphere, offering an ideal blend of nostalgia and excitement for a fun-filled day out.
4. **SeaWorld, various-** Get up close and personal with awe-inspiring marine life, from majestic whales to playful dolphins, and dive into the wonders of the ocean with interactive exhibits and shows.
5. **Polynesian Cultural Center, Oahu-** Situated in Laie, Hawaii, it is a tropical destination for sunning snowbirds looking to immerse themselves in the rich heritage and traditions of Polynesian Islands like Hawaii, Samoa, Fiji,

Chapter 2 35

Tonga, and many others. This park offers hands-on activities, traditional dancing and music shows, and authentic cultural demonstrations.

6. **Six Flags Magic Mountain, various-** Experience an adrenaline rush on world-class roller coasters, ideal for the healthy young at heart seeking excitement and thrills in a fun-packed environment.

7. **Busch Gardens, various-** Immerse yourself in intricately designed lands that transport you to various corners of the world while enjoying thrilling rides and cultural experiences. It's an ideal choice for retirees seeking adventure within beautifully themed environments.

8. **Cedar Point, Ohio-** Discover heart-pounding thrills at the "Roller Coaster Capital of the World," where free spirits can indulge their love for excitement with a wide range of exhilarating rides.

9. **Dollywood, Tennessee-** Enjoy the best of both worlds with classic amusement park attractions and the soulful music and culture of the Smoky Mountains, creating a unique and heartwarming experience.

10. **Hersheypark, Pennsylvania-** Satisfy your sweet tooth with delectable treats while enjoying family-friendly attractions, making it a delightful destination for indulgence and quality time with loved ones. Be sure to stop by their free chocolate factory tour.

11. **Kings Dominion, Virginia-** Find entertainment in a variety of attractions, from thrilling roller coasters to live shows, providing a well-rounded and enjoyable experience for retirees.

12. **Disney's Epcot, Florida-** Celebrate human achievement, innovation, and global culture in a unique theme park that offers technology, history, and cultural experiences, appealing to the curious and adventurous fun-lover.

17 International Amusement Parks Worth Visiting

1. **Onsen World: Hakone, Japan-** Onsen World is the perfect destination for anyone seeking a serene escape from the hustle and bustle of city life. This stunning amusement park is located in the breathtaking Hakone area of Japan, famous for its natural hot springs and scenic beauty. Visitors can take a leisurely dip in the warm, therapeutic waters or relax and soak in the stunning views of the surrounding mountains. With a wide range of amenities, including traditional Japanese gardens, saunas, and outdoor baths, Onsen World is a truly immersive experience that provides the ultimate relaxation and rejuvenation.
2. **Tokyo DisneySea: Chiba, Japan-** This unique Disney amusement park has beautiful and intricate themes inspired by legends of the sea, its classic Disney characters, and its variety of thrilling and gentle rides. The park also offers various restaurants and lounges to rest and relax, making it a wonderful getaway for off-the-clock folks looking for a watery and magical experience.
3. **Europa-Park: Rust, Germany-** This park offers a nostalgic and enchanting atmosphere with European-themed attractions, including traditional carousels and charming restaurants.
4. **Tivoli Gardens: Copenhagen, Denmark-** A timeless classic in a peaceful and picturesque setting with lush gardens, beautiful fountains, and classic rides.
5. **Efteling: Kaatsheuvel, Netherlands-** Efteling transports visitors to a magical world with its fairy-tale-themed attractions, charming architecture, and enchanting lights.
6. **Disneyland Paris: Marne-la-Vallée, France-** An unforgettable experience with classic Disney attractions, top-notch dining, and exciting parades.
7. **Ocean Park: Hong Kong, China-** An exciting blend of marine life, thrilling rides, and Asian culture, offering

visitors a fun-filled day of adventure.

8. **Lotte World: Seoul, South Korea-** A sprawling indoor and outdoor theme park with exciting rides, various shows, and cultural experiences.

9. **Dreamworld: Gold Coast, Australia-** A range of exhilarating rides, animal encounters, and entertainment options for all ages.

10. **Parc Astérix: Plailly, France-** A whimsical park inspired by the famous French comic book featuring rousing rides and cultural experiences.

11. **Universal Studios Japan: Osaka, Japan-** Universal Studios offers a variety of exciting rides and shows based on popular movies and TV shows, including the Wizarding World of Harry Potter.

12. **Hong Kong Disneyland: Hong Kong, China-** Another classic Disney experience with stimulating rides, parades, and characters, all set against the stunning backdrop of Hong Kong.

13. **PortAventura World: Salou, Spain-** This Mediterranean-themed park offers various attractions, from heart-pumping roller coasters to tranquil gardens, making it an excellent choice for retirees seeking a balanced experience.

14. **Liseberg: Gothenburg, Sweden-** With its diverse attractions, from exhilarating rides to stunning gardens and world-class dining, Liseberg is a beautiful spot for prime-timers who appreciate excitement and relaxation.

15. **Happy Valley: Shenzhen, China-** Boasting a wide range of attractions, from loopy roller coasters to tranquil gardens, Happy Valley will put a smile on anyone's face.

16. **Parc Astérix: Plailly, France-** This Gaul-themed park offers a unique blend of thrilling rides, stunning landscapes, and cultural experiences, great for golden travelers looking for an immersive and exciting experience.

17. **Mirabilandia: Ravenna, Italy-** This park features many attractions, from white-knuckle rides to tranquil gardens and cultural exhibitions.

* * *

Travel for Festivals

Celebrate at events

Susan, a recently retired woman with an adventurous spirit, had always dreamed of venturing across the globe and immersing herself in diverse cultures. Retirement's newfound freedom and flexibility finally spurred her to turn those dreams into reality.

One of her initial journeys took her to the heart of Thailand for the enchanting Yi Peng Festival in Chiang Mai. Arriving brimming with excitement, she anticipated an exploration of the unknown and a chance to soak up the essence of a culturally different world.

As the sun dipped below the horizon, she became a part of an enchanting spectacle. Along with many others nearby, Susan inflated a large white candle-lit hot air balloon-like lantern symbolically filled with her hopes and dreams. Then, later that evening, she released hers along with the hundreds of other lanterns. They illuminated the sky. Their warm glow contrasted beautifully with the celestial tapestry of stars. Against the backdrop of distant mountains, ancient temples, and the chanting of orange-robbed Buddhist monks, Susan felt an overwhelming sense of wonder as she watched these lanterns ascend gracefully, carried away by the gentle embrace of the wind.

Following this magical event, Susan indulged in days of exploration, delving into the exotic sights and savoring the delectable cuisine that Chiang Mai had to offer. Upon her return home, she captivated everyone with vivid tales of her travels, unable to contain her excitement and the lasting impact of her remarkable experience. It was a poignant catalyst, inspiring her to chart a course for more adventures, each uniquely tied to special events. From the vibrant Holi Festival in India to the spirited Oktoberfest celebrations in Germany, Susan was determined to seize every opportunity retirement presented for unforgettable journeys and cultural immersion.

. . .

Why festivals?

Traveling to a domestic or international festival is an adventure worth taking. Festivals are exciting, vibrant celebrations that bring together people from all walks of life who share similar interests and passions. From Coachella in California to Carnival in Brazil, there is a wide variety of festivals around the world that are sure to spark joy, creativity, and memories you'll never forget. Pack your bags and prepare to join in the festivities.

23 International Events and Festivals Worth Experiencing

1. **Day of the Dead, Mexico (November 1st and 2nd)-** The Day of the Dead, or Dia de los Muertos, is a Mexican holiday that honors deceased loved ones. With colorful altars, intricate sugar skulls, lively music, and processions, it's a vibrant and joyful celebration of life and death, offering a unique chance to experience Mexico's rich traditions and culture.
2. **Oktoberfest, Germany (end of September to early October)-** A festival in Munich, Germany, celebrating beer and German culture. With massive beer tents, traditional food, and lively music, it's a must-visit event for those seeking to celebrate German heritage and taste the country's famous beer culture.
3. **Sapporo Ice Festival, Japan (February)-** A winter event held in Sapporo, Japan. It showcases awe-inspiring ice and snow sculptures that tower above visitors and are lit up in the evenings for an even more magical experience.
4. **Yi Peng Festival, Thailand (November)-** An event held in Chiang Mai that celebrates the Buddhist holiday of Loy Krathong. It is characterized by releasing thousands of lanterns into the night sky, creating a breathtaking spectacle of floating lights. The festival is a time for making wishes and celebrating traditional Thai culture.

5. **Nozawa Fire Festival, Japan (January 15th)-** A traditional Japanese festival in Nozawa Onsen in Nagano Prefecture. It is marked by a large, fire-filled procession through the town's streets, with participants carrying torches and performing dances. The festival is a symbol of renewal and purification, offering a chance to witness a display of traditional Japanese culture and join in a celebration of the arrival of spring.

6. **Nippon Domannaka Festival, Japan (late August)-** The Nippon Domannaka Festival, also known as the Middle of Japan Festival, is held in the city of Inazawa in Aichi Prefecture, Japan. The festival features a procession of locals dressed in traditional garb, carrying mikoshi (portable shrines), and dancing through the streets to the beat of taiko drums. The festival celebrates local history, culture, and community, offering an extraordinary chance to experience a traditional Japanese event.

7. **Songkran Festival, Thailand (April 13th to 15th)-** At this unusual event, also known as the Thai New Year Festival, people pierce themselves with objects such as skewers, knives, and spears. The festival is marked by water-throwing, dancing, and religious ceremonies. It symbolizes the washing away of bad luck and the start of a new year.

8. **Carnival, Brazil (February or March)-** The Carnival of Rio de Janeiro is known for its colorful parades, street parties, and samba dancing. The festival displays vibrant culture, music, and energy. It's one of the world's largest and most iconic celebrations, offering a once-in-a-lifetime experience for those seeking to immerse themselves in the rhythm and energy of Brazil.

9. **Harbin International Ice and Snow Sculpture Festival, China (late December to February)-** The Harbin International Ice and Snow Sculpture Festival is held in Harbin, showcasing magnificent ice and snow sculptures created by artists from around the world. Visitors can admire the intricate sculptures, participate in winter

sports, and enjoy various cultural activities in the frozen wonderland created by the festival.

10. **La Tomatina, Spain (August)-** La Tomatina is a strange festival held in the Spanish town of Buñol, where participants engage in a massive tomato fight. Crowds gather in the town's main square, armed with tons of overripe tomatoes, for an hour of enthusiastic and messy fruit tossing. La Tomatina is a lighthearted and fun celebration, offering a chance to participate in a unique and quirky Spanish tradition.

11. **Chinese New Year, China (January or February)-** The Chinese New Year, also known as the Spring Festival, marks the start of the Lunar New Year. The festival is widely celebrated in Shanghai, with events like dragon and lion dances, fireworks, and family gatherings.

12. **St. Patrick's Festival, Ireland (March 17th)-** St. Patrick's Festival in Dublin honors the country's patron saint and cultural heritage. The festival features a range of events such as parades, concerts, and traditional Irish dance, as well as a host of food and drink offerings. St. Patrick's Festival is a lively celebration of Irish culture and history, offering a chance to experience Ireland's unique traditions and festivities.

13. **Holi Festival, India (March)-** The Holi Festival in India is a colorful celebration marking the arrival of spring and the triumph of good over evil. Held throughout the country, the festival features events such as bonfires, prayers, and the throwing of colored powder and water, symbolizing unity and the spreading of love and joy. Holi Festival in India is a vibrant and joyful celebration, offering a chance to experience the country's rich Hindu culture and traditions and join in the revelry.

14. **Cherry Blossom Festival, Japan (March or April)-** The Cherry Blossom Festival, also known as hanami in Japan, celebrates the country's iconic cherry blossom trees in bloom. The festival, held throughout the country, features events such as picnics under the blooming

trees, outdoor performances, and traditional Japanese tea ceremonies. It's a gorgeous display of the country's natural beauty and cultural traditions, offering an uncommon and unforgettable experience.

15. **Fes Festival of World Sacred Music, Morocco (June)-** The Festival highlights the world's diverse musical traditions, spirituality, and cultural heritage. The festival features performances by artists from around the globe, showcasing traditional and contemporary sacred music and dance.

16. **Montreux Jazz Festival, Switzerland (July)-** The Montreux Jazz Festival in Switzerland features performances by some of the world's most renowned jazz musicians. Held in Montreux's picturesque town along Lake Geneva's shores, the festival offers a distinctive atmosphere, combining music, lakeside scenery, and Swiss alpine charm.

17. **WOMAD International Arts Festival, England (July)-** WOMAD is a music and arts festival held in Wiltshire, England. The event celebrates world music, arts, and dance, showcasing diverse performers and cultural traditions from around the globe.

18. **Mevlana Festival, Turkey (December)-** The Mevlana Festival in Konya features colorful and energetic dance performances, music, poetry recitations, and spiritual gatherings, attracting hundreds of thousands of visitors worldwide.

19. **World Sacred Spirit Festival, India (February or March)-** Held in Jodhpur, celebrating the local culture and traditions with music and dance performances. It is an excellent opportunity for travelers to immerse themselves in authentic Indian culture and experience the vibrant atmosphere of this captivating city.

20. **Semana Santa, Spain (April)-** Semana Santa is a Holy Week festivity in Spain. It's a beautiful, vibrant event full of processions and colorful decorations. It can be found in cities all over the country. It's a fantastic opportunity to

experience Spanish culture and tradition firsthand, making it an unforgettable experience for anyone visiting.

21. **Leeds & Reading Music Festival, England (August)-** Leeds & Reading Music Festival is a two-day music festival held in the UK. With multiple stages, a wide variety of musical acts, and plenty of food, drink, and entertainment options, it's the perfect place to hear great music and have a memorable experience.

22. **Dragon Boat Carnival, China (June)-** The Dragon Boat Carnival in Hong Kong is a spirited event that honors the city's traditions, featuring dragon boat races, performances, and fireworks. Tourists will delight in watching or participating in this exciting celebration of culture and entertainment set against the stunning backdrop of Victoria Harbour.

23. **San Fermin Festival, Spain (July 6th to 14th)-** The San Fermin Festival, also known as the running of the bulls, is held in Pamplona. It is a week-long celebration filled with traditional Basque culture, live music, and bull-running events. It's an exciting opportunity to experience Spanish culture firsthand and create special memories with friends or family.

28 US Events and Festivals Worth Experiencing

If you're looking to keep a little closer to home, there are some exciting events and festivals all over the United States worth visiting. Choose your favorite and start planning an exciting road trip!

1. **Great American Beer Festival, Denver (December)-** The iconic three-day event showcases over 4,000 beers from over 800 breweries across the United States. It offers beer lovers the chance to sample some of the best craft beers in the country. Whether you're looking for a unique beer-tasting experience or an opportunity to

mingle with fellow beer enthusiasts, this festival is not to be missed.

2. **Sundance Film Festival, Utah (late January to early February)-** The Park City event is an excellent opportunity to see some of the latest independent films from around the world and attend exclusive events with celebrities, filmmakers, and industry professionals.

3. **Mardi Gras, New Orleans (March or February)-** Mardi Gras in New Orleans is the ultimate carnival celebration in the US! Every year, millions of revelers descend on the city to join the parades and celebrations filling the streets. From incredible costumes and music to fantastic food and endless parties, Mardi Gras in New Orleans is an unforgettable experience that everyone should experience at least once.

4. **Coachella Music Festival, California (April)-** The Coachella Valley Music and Arts Festival, located in Indio, is one of the largest and most famous music festivals in the United States, featuring a diverse lineup of musical artists and attracting attendees worldwide.

5. **Independence Day, Boston (July 4th)-** Boston's Independence Day celebrations are a patriotic and historic event. The city's celebrations include a flag-raising ceremony, a reading of the Declaration of Independence, a patriotic concert, and a spectacular fireworks display over the Charles River.

6. **Comic-Con, San Diego (July)-** San Diego's Comic-Con is one of the world's largest and most popular pop-culture events. It brings together hundreds of thousands of fans, celebrities, artists, and exhibitors to celebrate comic books, movies, TV shows, and video games. Visitors to Comic-Con can attend panel discussions, meet their favorite celebrities, see exclusive trailers and previews, shop for unique merchandise, and experience the ultimate celebration of comic culture.

7. **Lollapalooza, Chicago (July or August)-** Lollapalooza is a legendary music festival in Chicago,

Illinois. It features a diverse lineup of musical artists across multiple genres, including rock, hip-hop, electronic, and alternative music. The festival also includes food and art exhibitions and a variety of interactive experiences while surrounded by the vibrant energy of Chicago's Grant Park.

8. **Burning Man, Nevada (late August)-** Burning Man is a week-long community, art, and self-expression festival held annually in Nevada's Black Rock Desert. The festival centers around creating and burning a giant wooden effigy, "The Man." It encourages attendees to embrace principles of self-reliance, inclusiveness, and participation. The festival creates a temporary city filled with elaborate art installations, performance art, music, and unique themed camps and gatherings, creating an immersive and transformative experience for all participants.

9. **Macy's Thanksgiving Day Parade, New York City (November)-** Featuring massive floats, marching bands, musical performances, and character balloons. It's a quintessentially American holiday experience, offering visitors an unforgettable way to kick off the holiday season.

10. **New Year's Eve in Times Square, New York City (December)-** Thousands of people gather in New York City to ring in the new year. With the iconic Ball Drop serving as the centerpiece of the festivities, revelers enjoy music, light displays, and fireworks show in the heart of the Big Apple.

11. **Rockefeller Christmas Tree Lighting, New York City (early December)-** A holiday event held at Rockefeller Center in New York City. A towering Christmas tree, decorated with lights and ornaments, is lit up for the first time during the ceremony, attracting thousands of visitors who gather to enjoy live music, street performers, festive food, and drinks.

12. **National Cherry Blossom Festival, Washington DC (late March or early April)-** A celebration of the arrival of spring and the beauty of nature, as thousands of cherry blossom trees lining the Washington DC Tidal Basin

burst into bloom in a stunning display of delicate pink and white petals, attracting visitors from around the world. The trees were a gift from Japan. It's a time of renewal, hope, and joy as the city comes alive with a vibrant cultural and artistic program, including parades, performances, and special events.

13. **New Orleans Jazz Festival, Louisiana (late April)-** A jazz music celebration in New Orleans that brings together musicians worldwide for a multi-day event with performances, food, and drinks.

14. **Sturgis Motorcycle Rally, South Dakota (early August)-** Bikers from around the US gather to celebrate motorcycle culture and non-stop entertainment. The festival offers a unique experience for motorcycle enthusiasts and those looking for a wild time in the heart of the American West.

15. **Maryland Renaissance Festival, Crownsville (late August)-** The Renaissance Festival recreates a 16th-century English village. It offers visitors a chance to experience live theater, music, food, arts & crafts, and games, attracting those interested in historical reenactments and immersive cultural experiences.

16. **Maine Lobster Festival, Rockland (late July or early August)-** The Maine Lobster Festival honors lobster cuisine and culture in Rockland, Maine. It features lobster-themed food, live music, a parade, and arts & crafts.

17. **Gilroy Garlic Festival, California (late July)-** Three-day food extravaganza held in Gilroy, California. It features a variety of garlic-infused dishes, cooking demonstrations, live music and entertainment, and arts & crafts vendors.

18. **Oshkosh AirVenture, Wisconsin (late July)-** Oshkosh AirVenture is a week-long celebration of flight, innovation, and technology held in Oshkosh, Wisconsin. It is considered one of the largest aviation events in the world and attracts over 500,000 visitors every year. The event features a large number of military and civilian aircraft, air

demonstrations, and displays. From vintage planes to state-of-the-art jets, there's something for everyone to admire and explore in this thrilling aviation wonderland.

19. **St. Patrick's Day Parade, New York City (March 17th)-** The St. Patrick's Day Parade in New York is one of the world's largest Irish heritage and culture celebrations, attracting hundreds of thousands annually. The parade features a colorful display of marching bands, dance troupes, and floats, as well as a variety of food and drink vendors.

20. **New York International Auto Show, New York City (April)-** Showcasing new vehicles and technology from the world's leading automakers. The event is attended by auto enthusiasts, industry professionals, and the general public and typically features interactive displays, live demonstrations, and test drives.

21. **Lantern Floating Hawaii, Honolulu (late May)-** The Honolulu event allows participants to release lanterns into the ocean to symbolize their wishes and hopes. People visit this event to participate in the moving and meaningful tradition and to enjoy the beautiful display of lanterns floating on the water.

22. **Sterling Renaissance Festival, New York (July)-** The Sterling, New York event commemorates the Renaissance era with historical reenactments, musical performances, food, and crafts.

23. **Albuquerque International Balloon Fiesta, New Mexico (early October)-** The Albuquerque International Balloon Fiesta is a world-renowned 10-day event held in Albuquerque, New Mexico, attracting balloon enthusiasts and spectators from all over the world. The festival features hundreds of hot air balloons in a stunning display of color and creativity, taking to the skies for mass ascensions and aerial competitions.

24. **Camden Windjammer Festival, Maine (early September)-** A nautical merrymaking in Camden, Maine. During the festival, visitors can enjoy wooden ship

tours, live entertainment, and a grand parade of sail, where colorful windjammers are showcased along the harbor.

25. **Austin City Limits, Texas (October)-** The Texas event features diverse musical acts from various genres, including rock, country, hip-hop, and electronic dance music. It attracts thousands of music lovers to the city. It is known for its unique combination of great music, delicious food, and a relaxed, fun-loving atmosphere.

26. **Bonnaroo Music Festival, Tennessee (June)-** A boot-scooting four-day music and arts festival in Manchester, Tennessee. It features an eclectic lineup of musicians from various genres, including rock, hip-hop, and electronic dance music.

27. **Sundance Film Festival, Utah (late January)-** An independent film festival held in Park City, Utah, that showcases new works by American and international filmmakers. It's attended by film enthusiasts, celebrities, and industry professionals, making it a premier event in the film world and an excellent opportunity to see new and innovative works of cinema.

28. **Halloween, New York City (October 31st)-** Halloween in New York City is a notable holiday event with various activities such as costume parties, haunted houses, and parades. The city is known for its elaborate and unique costumes and the famous Greenwich Village Halloween Parade, attracting thousands of participants and spectators yearly.

Resources

1. 99 International Events and Festivals for your Bucket List link
2. 15 Best Festivals In The US To Add To Your Bucket List link
3. Japan's Top 10 Fire Festivals link
4. 9 Best Holi Celebrations in India link
5. Best of America: 14 of the Best Events and Festivals link

Chapter 2   49

* * *

Visit Egypt

Feel like you're traveling back in time to when pharaohs ruled

Your camel slowly walks over the sandy dune, and you get your first glimpse of a massive structure built over 5,000 years ago. You've seen this wonder hundreds of times before but never with your own eyes. You imagine you've gone back in time to one of the most powerful kingdoms in the world, to when it was the cradle of civilization.

Why Egypt?

Few places on earth feel as unique, ancient, and iconic as Egypt. There are many well-preserved structures and relics to visit that transport you back to a time of Pharaohs and mummies, gods, and hieroglyphs. After an adventurous week or two of exploring ancient Egypt's temples, pyramids, statues, tombs, and world wonders, you'll feel connected to the past. The time you spend getting around modern Egypt, you'll feel the intensity of this unique Islamic culture. All in all, you'll return with memories and experiences that are impossible to have anywhere else on earth. Egypt is one of the few places you can come back from and say your vacation was a trip of a lifetime.

11 Unforgettable Things to Do in Egypt

1. **Great Pyramids at Giza (15 miles outside Cairo):** As you approach this iconic site, the colossal pyramids rise majestically from the golden sands like sentinels of time. Riding a camel around them is like stepping into a scene from an adventure novel. Make sure to venture inside one of the three pyramids to feel the ancient whispers and behold the architectural marvels within. In the shadow of the pyramids, the mysterious limestone

sphinx awaits, its uncanny gaze seemingly guarding the secrets of the past. Remember to return in the evening for the awe-inspiring sound and light show, where lasers and lights bring the pyramids and sphinx to life, illuminating their timeless history.

2. **Valley of the Kings (Luxor):** Visiting this archaeological wonder is like stepping back in time. The Valley of the Kings is a mesmerizing burial ground for pharaohs, their tombs adorned with intricate hieroglyphics and breathtaking artwork that narrate tales of their lives and beliefs. Walking through these exquisitely decorated tombs feels like a passage into the very heart of ancient Egypt.

3. **Karnak Temple (Luxor):** Prepare to be utterly astounded by the sheer magnitude of the Karnak Temple complex, the second-largest in the world. Enormous columns, hieroglyph-covered walls, and sprawling courtyards make this a place where time seems to stand still. The grandeur of this temple is nothing short of awe-inspiring.

4. **Luxor Temple (Luxor):** Stroll through history amidst giant seated Egyptian statues and magnificent obelisks that have stood for millennia. The Luxor Temple is a testament to the artistry and devotion of ancient Egypt, and you'll feel a profound connection to the past as you explore its hallowed grounds.

5. **Egyptian Museum (Cairo):** The museum is a treasure trove of Egypt's rich history, boasting an extensive collection of artifacts, including intricately detailed sarcophagi, mummies, and golden statues that glitter with the tales of long-forgotten dynasties.

6. **Cruise on the Nile (Luxor to Aswan):** Set sail on a multi-day river cruise aboard a small boat, tracing the same path that ancient Egyptians navigated for centuries. The gentle flow of the Nile will carry you past picturesque landscapes and historic sites, providing a unique perspective on Egypt's natural beauty.

7. **Abu Simbel (Near Aswan):** The colossal statues of Rameses II guarding the entrance to this great temple are a sight to behold. Stand in awe of the precision and scale of this magnificent monument that pays tribute to one of Egypt's greatest pharaohs.
8. **Hot air balloon ride (Luxor):** Soar high above Luxor's temples as the sun's first rays gently kiss the horizon. The views from your hot air balloon are breathtaking, offering a bird's-eye perspective of the Valley of the Kings and its surroundings.
9. **Scuba dive in the Red Sea:** Dive into the crystal-clear waters of the Red Sea, where a vibrant underwater world awaits. Explore stunning coral reefs and discover the remnants of ancient shipwrecks as you're enveloped in the colorful marine life that calls this area home.
10. **Hike to the top of Mount Sinai:** Embark on a pilgrimage to this sacred mountain, said to be the place where Moses received the Ten Commandments. The trek to the summit is a challenging but rewarding experience, and watching the sunrise from the top is a spiritual moment that will linger in your heart.
11. **Sail a felucca down the Nile (Aswan):** Climb aboard one of these traditional boats with canvas sails and let the Nile carry you along. It's a serene and timeless way to experience the river and connect with the rhythms of daily life along its banks.

How to visit?

Deciding to take a guided tour, explore independently, or combine both will largely depend on your budget and travel savviness. When my wife and I were young budget backpackers, we saved a small fortune by working out our plans when we got there rather than booking an organized package tour in advance. We used our hotel to set up small day tours and transportation to sites, but haggling and not feeling entirely comfortable was the cost. Some locations required an armed convoy (Abu Simbel), so independent travel in this region is not for the faint of heart nor for those flustered easily by cultural differences.

Go for it! Simple start steps:

1. Get ideas of what you'd like to see and do by researching online, in guidebooks, and by looking at suggested tour itineraries from travel companies.
2. Compare pricing to travel independently vs. with an organized tour.
3. Book an inclusive tour and/or start making independent reservations (flight, hotels, ground transportation).

Resources

1. How to visit the Pyramids of Giza link
2. Must-see Attractions in Egypt by Lonely Planet link
3. 11 Tour Companies to Visit Egypt with link

Products

1. Universal All-in-One Travel Power Adapter link
2. Inflatable Travel Pillow link
3. Passport Hiding Belt link

Books

1. Essential Egypt by Fodor's link
2. Egypt by Lonely Planet link
3. 1000 Facts about Ancient Egypt by National Geographic link

Pairs well with: A visit to Israel and Petra, Jordan. Photography. Videography.

You might also like: Istanbul, Turkey. San Fermin, Spain. Erg Chebbi, Morocco.

* * *

Travel for Animal Experiences
Get wild with animals

Retirement is a time when many people are looking for new experiences, and traveling to have animal encounters can be an exciting and fulfilling way to do that. There's nothing quite like the thrill of being up close and personal with nature's creatures, whether it's a majestic elephant in Africa or a playful otter in Alaska.

These kinds of animal experiences can be incredibly gratifying because they allow for a break from the routine of everyday life and offer a chance to connect with the world in a different way. There are plenty of new animal experiences to have. Whether it's having breakfast at a hotel with giraffes peering in from the windows, a quiet kayak tour through a wildlife sanctuary, a horseback ride through the countryside, or a swim with colorful tropical fish, animal experiences can offer a rejuvenating escape that brings new meaning and joy to life. Make Steve Irwin proud and get ready to have an animal encounter of a lifetime.

A Note About Ethical Animal Tourism

Ethical animal tourism involves interacting with and observing animals in a responsible manner that respects their welfare. Please consider the treatment of the animals and do not support companies that treat the animals poorly. Whenever possible, seeing an animal in the wild is preferred to seeing an animal in captivity.

61 Animal Encounters

1. Horseback ride in Jardin, Colombia
2. Spot rare penguins in Dunedin, New Zealand

3. See the penguin parade at Phillip Island Nature Park, Victoria, Australia
4. Camel ride around pyramids in Giza, Egypt
5. Have a bear encounter at Montana Grizzly Encounter Sanctuary in Montana
6. Amish horse buggy ride in Lancaster, Pennsylvania
7. Feed giraffes from your hotel at Giraffe Manor in South Africa
8. Take a mule ride down the Grand Canyon in Arizona
9. Release sea turtles in the Indonesia Island of Sumba
10. Sunbathe next to giant sea turtles in Oahu, Hawaii
11. See giant soaring Andean Condors in Colca Canyon, Peru
12. Bathe an elephant at an elephant sanctuary in Chiang Mai, Thailand
13. Go on a dog sled ride in Fairbanks, Alaska
14. Go on a reindeer sleigh ride in Finland
15. Swim with wild dolphins in Oahu, Hawaii
16. Snorkel or scuba with whale sharks in Cozumel, Mexico
17. Scuba at night with giant manta rays Kailua-Kona, Hawaii
18. Snorkel with seals in Cape Town, South Africa
19. See a wild sloth in a city park in Cartagena, Colombia
20. Help baby wildlife at Reteti Elephant Sanctuary in Kenya
21. Spot the elusive pink dolphin in the Amazon River at Leticia, Colombia
22. See the monkeys on the rock of Gibraltar in Southern Spain (UK-owned)
23. See snow monkeys relaxing in onsens at Jigokudani Nagano, Japan
24. See famous dancing horses in Jerez, Spain
25. Attend a rodeo in the USA
26. Get close to incredible sea life and giant tortoises in the Galapagos Islands of Ecuador
27. Ssee swarms of thousands of parakeet birds returning at sunset from the Amazon in Leticia, Colombia
28. See wild kangaroos in Australia
29. See the mountain gorillas of Rwanda

Chapter 2 55

30. Watch giant iguanas jump from trees into the water at John Prince Park Campground, Lake Worth, Florida
31. Look for manatees in Three Sisters Springs, Crystal River, Florida
32. Chill with penguins in Antarctica
33. Bike by many wild alligators on Shark Valley Loop of Everglades National Park, Florida
34. Witness a salmon run in Anchorage, Alaska
35. Take a float plane to go fly fishing on a lake in Alaska
36. See the elusive blue whale off Sri Lanka
37. Hear orangutans in Borneo
38. Take a river safari in Africa
39. See alligators jump out of the water at Gatorland Park in Kissimmee, Florida
40. See sacred animals like cows walking free in the streets of India
41. Take a humpback whale watching tour
42. Search for polar bears in Canada, Churchill, Manitoba
43. Go on a Big Five African photo safari (elephant, lion, leopard, buffalo, rhino)
44. See a giant panda in China- Giant Panda Research Center
45. Test your bravery cage diving with great white sharks in South Africa
46. Spot a Moose in Canada or Grand Teton National Park
47. Kayaking with Beluga Whales in Manitoba, Canada
48. Stay a safe distance from grizzly bears catching fish in the Yukon
49. Hear wolves in Canada
50. Hold a koala and pet a kangaroo at the Lone Pine Animal Sanctuary, Brisbane, Australia
51. See toucans in Brazil at Iguazu Falls Bird Sanctuary
52. Witness thousands of bats coming out of Carlsbad Caverns National Park, New Mexico
53. See giant bats hanging in trees in Cairns, Australia
54. Listen to elk calls in Rocky Mountain National Park, Colorado

55. Watch the Buffalo Roundup at Custer State Park, South Dakota
56. Photograph bison herds in Yellowstone or Grand Teton National Park
57. Enjoy the Bracken Bat flight experience with 20 million bats near San Antonio, Texas
58. Search for humpback and blue whales in a schooner boat around Iceland
59. See adorable lemurs in Madagascar at Andasibe National Park
60. Get close to cute Quokkas on Rottnest Island, Australia
61. Visit the world-famous San Diego Zoo

Resources

1. A Quick Guide To Ethical Animal Tourism link
2. Horseback rides in Colombia link
3. 9 Best Trips for Unforgettable Wildlife Encounters Around the World, According to Travel Experts link
4. How To Tell If An Animal Encounter Is Ethical link

***

Travel for Sporting Events

Become a superfan

Attending a sporting event is an unforgettable experience at any time, but the excitement is taken to another level during championship times, and the game becomes a once-in-a-lifetime opportunity. These are the moments when the best teams and players compete for the ultimate prize and showcase their talent on the biggest stage.

Whether it's the Super Bowl, World Series, or NBA Finals, the energy in the stadium is electric, with thousands of fans from all over the country gathering to support their teams. The atmosphere is lively, filled with cheering, shouting, and infectious excitement.

Chapter 2

Going to a championship game means more than just watching a game and paying a huge sum of money; it's a chance to be part of something special. The events become an opportunity to make memories with friends and family, try local cuisine, and immerse yourself in the culture of the city you are visiting.

10 Major Sporting Events in the US

1. **The Super Bowl-** The biggest event in American sports and a cultural phenomenon with a high price tag to match. It's a bucket-list event for many seasoned football fans.
2. **The Masters-** A golf tournament held at Augusta National Golf Club, known for its iconic course and history of great champions.
3. **The Kentucky Derby-** A horse racing event held in Louisville, known for its tradition, fashion, and mint juleps.
4. **The World Series-** The championship of Major League Baseball, offering a showcase of the best teams and players in America's national pastime.
5. **The NBA Finals-** The National Basketball Association championship series featuring the world's best players and high-stakes drama.
6. **The US Open Tennis Championships-** One of the four Grand Slam tournaments in tennis, held in New York and featuring top players from around the world.
7. **The NCAA March Madness Basketball Tournament-** The college basketball tournament, with 68 teams competing in a single-elimination format for the National Championship.
8. **The Indianapolis 500-** A legendary 500-mile race held at the Indianapolis Motor Speedway, featuring top drivers in the world of IndyCar racing.
9. **The Summer X Games-** An action sports competition featuring skateboarding, BMX, and other adrenaline-fueled events held in various cities across the US.

10. **The Ironman Triathlon World Championships-** A grueling endurance race held annually in Hawaii, featuring a 2.4-mile swim, 112-mile bike ride, and 26.2-mile run.

14 International Sporting Events

From passionate football (soccer) matches to local martial arts competitions, there are exciting international sporting events worth traveling for.

1. **Summer Olympics-** A prestigious international multi-sport event held every four years in different host cities worldwide. It showcases the world's top athletes competing in a variety of sports. It attracts visitors from around the world who come to experience the excitement, cultural exchange, and pride of their country's athletes.
2. **Winter Olympics-** Showcasing various winter sports, including skiing, snowboarding, ice skating, bobsledding, and more. It's an opportunity to witness top athletes compete in thrilling competitions and experience winter sports in stunning mountain destinations, making it a must-visit event for sports fans and winter enthusiasts.
3. **FIFA World Cup-** The most popular international football tournament held every four years. It features the best national teams from around the world competing in a month-long contest, with matches occurring in various venues across the host country.
4. **UEFA Champions League-** A club football (soccer) competition organized by the Union of European Football Associations (UEFA), featuring the best European teams. With top-tier talent, it's considered the most prestigious club competition in the world, showcasing a high-stakes knockout tournament format.

5. **Cricket World Cup-** An international cricket tournament that occurs every four years and features the best cricket teams worldwide. It's one of the most significant sporting events in the world. It draws massive crowds, offering an exciting display of the sport's talent and a unique chance to experience the passion and energy of cricket culture.
6. **Wimbledon-** The tennis tournament held in Wimbledon, London, is considered the world's oldest and most prestigious. With an exciting history and a tradition of hosting the best players, it's a must-visit event for tennis fans. It offers the chance to witness premier talent compete in a historic and picturesque setting.
7. **Le Tour De France-** A multiple-stage bicycle race covering over 3,000 kilometers throughout France. Perhaps the most famous cycling race in the world, it attracts millions of fans. It offers a chance to witness some of the best cyclists compete in a challenging and scenic tour of the French countryside.
8. **The Rickshaw Run-** The Rickshaw Run is an adventurous charity rally in India. Participants drive auto-rickshaws (similar to Tuk Tuks of South East Asia) over 2,000 km across India, from the West Coast to the East Coast, facing unique challenges and experiencing the incredible culture and diversity of the country. It's a once-in-a-lifetime adventure for thrill-seekers and culture enthusiasts.
9. **French Grand Prix-** A Formula One motor race held at the Circuit Paul Ricard in Le Castellet, France. It is considered one of the most exciting races in the F1 calendar. It draws thousands of fans each year, offering an incredible chance to witness high-speed action and next-level talent in the beautiful country surroundings.
10. **Royal Ascot Races-** A prestigious horse racing event in Ascot, England. It is known for its history, fashion, and tradition, attracting some of the world's best horses and jockeys, the Royal Family, and thousands of visitors

worldwide. It's a must-visit event for horse racing fans and those seeking a taste of English tradition.

11. **FIS Alpine World Ski Championships-** An international skiing competition held every two years and organized by the International Ski Federation. It features the world's best skiers competing in various disciplines, including downhill, slalom, and giant slalom, among others. With stunning mountain backdrops and unrivaled talent, it's a bucket list event for skiing enthusiasts.

12. **Rugby World Cup-** An international Rugby Union competition featuring the best teams worldwide, is held every four years. It's a celebration of the sport, with passionate fans and high-stakes matches, offering an unforgettable chance to experience the energy and excitement of rugby culture.

13. **French Open-** Also known as Roland-Garros, it is a yearly tennis tournament in Paris, France, one of the four Grand Slam tournaments. It offers a chance to witness the world's best players compete on the red clay courts of Roland-Garros.

14. **Muay Thai Boxing-** Muay Thai is a combat sport originating from Thailand that involves the use of punches, kicks, elbows, and knees. Often referred to as "the art of eight limbs," Muay Thai is known for its intense physical demands and passionate culture. It's an unforgettable event for martial arts fans and those seeking an exciting and unique cultural experience.

Resources

1. The Rickshaw Run link
2. Best Places to Experience Muay Thai in Thailand link
3. How To Visit The Olympic Games link

* * *

Travel for Disney

Feel like a kid again

Need a happiness boost? Just make a visit to the happiest place on earth, technically Finland. Or you could visit the other "happiest place on earth" Disneyland! Disney's parks, resorts, and cruises offer a magical and unforgettable experience for people of all ages. Whether it's reliving childhood memories at Disney World, exploring the wonders of Disneyland, or setting sail on a Disney cruise, you can expect to be surrounded by an immersive world of adventure, imagination, and pure magic. From exciting attractions and thrilling shows to luxurious accommodations and world-class dining, visiting Disney is a perfect opportunity to create new memories and celebrate life's special moments with friends and family. Get ready to feel like a kid again!

12 Disney Theme Parks Around The World

1. Magic Kingdom Park (Part of Disney World) - Lake Buena Vista, Florida, USA
2. Epcot (Part of Disney World)- Lake Buena Vista, Florida, USA
3. Disney's Hollywood Studios (Part of Disney World)- Lake Buena Vista, Florida, USA
4. Disney's Animal Kingdom (Part of Disney World)- Lake Buena Vista, Florida, USA
5. Disneyland Park - Anaheim, California, USA
6. Disney California Adventure Park - Anaheim, California, USA
7. Disneyland Paris - Marne-la-Vallée, France
8. Walt Disney Studios Park -Marne-la-Vallée, France
9. Hong Kong Disneyland Resort - Hong Kong
10. Shanghai Disney Resort - Shanghai, China
11. Tokyo Disney Resort - Tokyo, Japan
12. Tokyo Disney Sea- Tokyo, Japan

14 of Disney's Resort Hotels in the USA

1. Disney's Grand Floridian Resort & Spa, Lake Buena Vista, Florida
2. Disney's Polynesian Village Resort, Lake Buena Vista, Florida
3. Disney's Contemporary Resort, Lake Buena Vista, Florida
4. Disneyland Hotel, Anaheim, California
5. Disney's Paradise Pier Hotel, Anaheim, California
6. Disney's Grand Californian Hotel & Spa, Anaheim, California
7. Disney's Yacht & Beach Club Resorts, Lake Buena Vista, Florida
8. Disney's BoardWalk Inn, Lake Buena Vista, Florida
9. Disney's Coronado Springs Resort, Lake Buena Vista, Florida
10. Disney's Port Orleans Resort, Lake Buena Vista, Florida
11. Disney's Caribbean Beach Resort, Lake Buena Vista, Florida
12. Disney's All-Star Resorts, Lake Buena Vista, Florida
13. Disney's Star Wars Galactic Starcruiser, Lake Buena Vista
14. Disney's Fort Wilderness (RV Campground), Lake Buena Vista

13 Exciting Ideas for Visiting Disney

1. Behind-the-scenes VIP tour
2. Disney at Christmas
3. Backstage Magic Tour
4. Explore Frozen Ever After at Epcot
5. Learn to surf at Disney's Typhoon Lagoon
6. Book a Keys to the Kingdom Tour at Magic Kingdom
7. Glide above the park at Epcot

8. Embark on a Wild Africa Trek tour
9. Stay in a bungalow at Disney's Polynesian Village Resort
10. Visit during Halloween
11. Stay at the Cinderella Castle Suite at Magic Kingdom
12. Run a 5K, 10K, or marathon through Florida or California Disney Parks
13. Create memories with grandkids on a Disney-themed cruise ship

Adventures by Disney Trips

Adventures By Disney is a brand of guided group tours offered by the Walt Disney Company, designed for families and travelers who want to explore destinations around the world in a unique and immersive way. Adventures By Disney trips typically include activities, cultural experiences, and exclusive access to various destinations and landmarks, accompanied by experienced guides and an exclusive Adventure Group. These include expedition cruises, river cruises, private experiences, adult exclusives, and more.

Resources

1. Adventures by Disney link
2. 20 Fun Things to Do at Disney link
3. Guide To Disneyland Parks Around The World link
4. Disney Running Events link

Books

1. 100 Disney Adventures of a Lifetime: Magical Experiences From Around the World by Marcy Smothers link
2. The Unofficial Guide to Walt Disney World by Bob Sehlinger link
3. The Unofficial Guide to the Disney Cruise Line by Erin Foster link

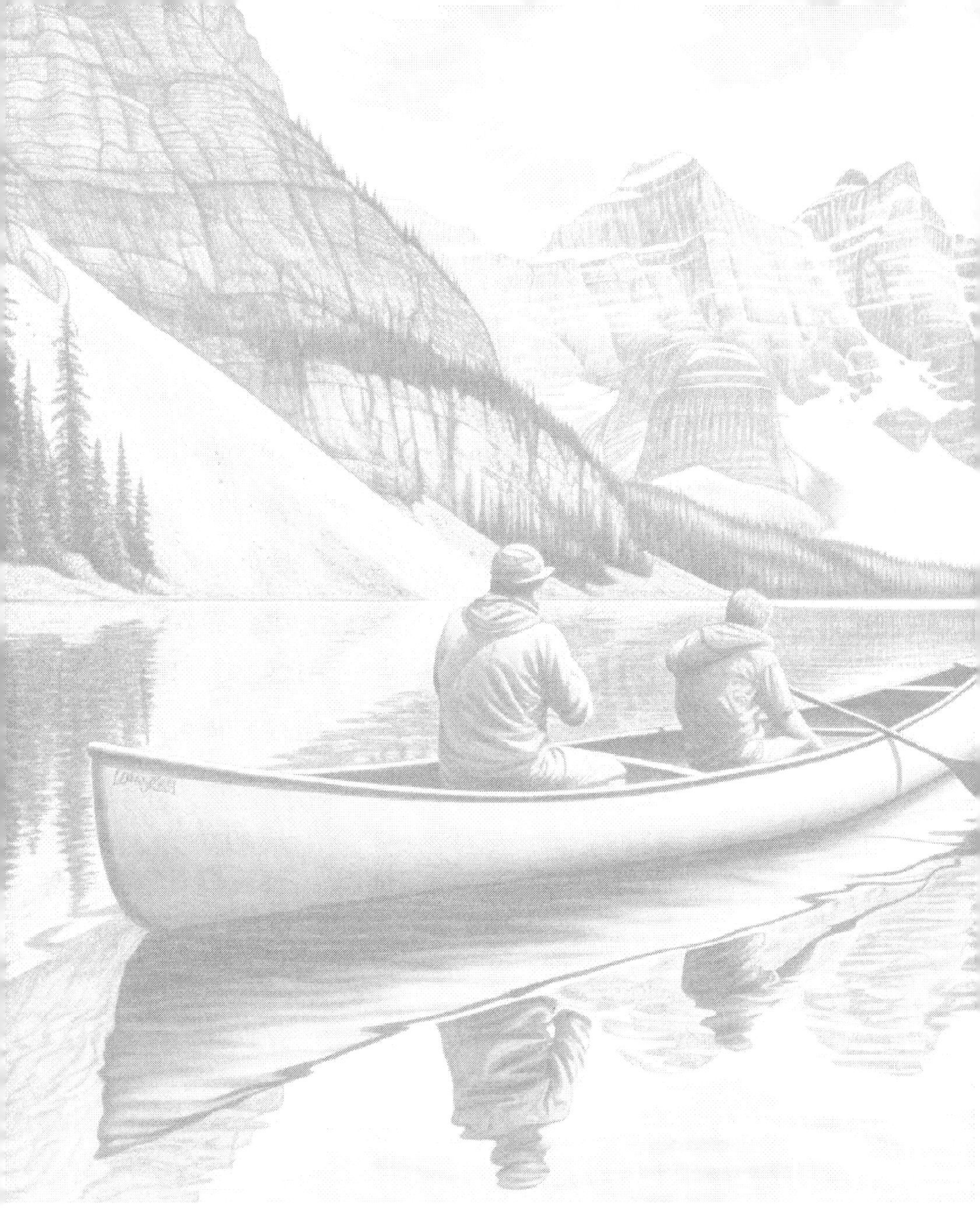

Chapter 3

The Great Outdoors

As we breathe in the fresh air and soak up the warmth of the sun, we are reminded of the undeniable benefits of being outdoors. Nature is a balm for the soul, and spending time outside has a way of lifting our spirits and calming our minds. Whether hiking in the mountains, going for a bike ride along a scenic route, or simply enjoying a picnic in the park, being outside can profoundly impact our mental and physical health.

Research has shown that spending time in nature can reduce stress, anxiety, and depression while improving overall well-being. The great outdoors's sights, sounds, and smells can help us feel more connected to the world and give us a sense of perspective. Whether we're marveling at the majesty of a towering redwood tree or watching a family of ducks paddle across a tranquil pond, the natural world has a way of reminding us of the beauty and wonder of life.

Along with the mental and emotional benefits, being outdoors can also positively impact our physical health. Activities such as hiking, biking, swimming, and gardening can all help improve our cardiovascular health, build strength and endurance, and promote weight loss. Spending time in the sun also helps our bodies produce vitamin D, which is essential for strong bones and a healthy immune system.

There are countless reasons to step outside and embrace the natural world.

50 Outdoor Fun Ideas

1. Take a walk in a nearby park or nature reserve.
2. Go for a bike ride on a scenic trail.
3. Have a picnic in the park or beach.
4. Play a game of frisbee or catch with friends or family.
5. Go birdwatching or nature spotting.
6. Take a hike in the mountains or a nearby hiking trail.
7. Rent a paddleboard and spend the day on the water.
8. Go on a camping trip in the wilderness.
9. Attend an outdoor concert or music festival.
10. Go on a photography walk to capture the beauty of nature.
11. Visit a botanical garden or arboretum.
12. Rent a convertible and take a scenic drive through the countryside or along the coast.
13. Go on a hot air balloon ride.
14. Attend an outdoor movie screening or drive-in theater.
15. Take a sunset boat cruise or yacht trip.
16. Go on a safari or wildlife tour.
17. Visit a local farmer's market or food festival.
18. Take a gardening class or workshop.
19. Go on a fishing trip or fly fishing adventure.
20. Attend a sporting event or game, like a baseball game or golf tournament.
21. Have a BBQ or outdoor party with friends and family.
22. Take an outdoor yoga or fitness class.
23. Go on a nature scavenger hunt with friends or family.
24. Attend a Renaissance fair or outdoor cultural festival.
25. Visit a nearby vineyard or winery for a wine tasting.
26. Go to a nature photography or painting workshop.
27. Attend an outdoor theater performance or Shakespeare in the park.
28. Go on a kayaking or canoeing adventure.

29. Attend an outdoor art show or craft fair.
30. Take a guided tour of local historical sites or landmarks.
31. Go on a geocaching adventure to find hidden treasures.
32. Attend an outdoor food and wine festival or street fair.
33. Take a scenic helicopter tour.
34. Visit a nearby beach or lake for a day of swimming and sunbathing.
35. Go on a river rafting or tubing adventure.
36. Take a guided stargazing tour or astronomy class.
37. Attend an outdoor beer or wine-tasting event.
38. Attend an outdoor jazz or music festival.
39. Take an outdoor cooking or grilling class.
40. Take a scenic train ride through the mountains or countryside.
41. Attend an outdoor book festival or literary event.
42. Go on a hot springs or natural spa adventure.
43. Attend an outdoor photography or art exhibit.
44. Attend an outdoor storytelling or poetry event.
45. Take an outdoor painting or art class.
46. Attend an outdoor science or technology event.
47. Take a guided fishing or fly fishing adventure.
48. Go on a nature or birdwatching hike.
49. Attend an outdoor fashion or design show.
50. Go on a scenic horseback riding adventure.

Chapter 3 Website Links

Outdoor Fun Ideas and Tips from Volume 1:
Outdoor Activities to Explore (58 ideas) - Ocean and Lake Activities (18 ideas) - Go Drone Fishing - E-biking - Play Shuffleboard - Motorhome/ RV Travel - Photography - Go Electric Hydrofoil Boarding - Take a Cruise - Visit a National Park

* * *

Play Pickleball

Serve up fun on the court

While some other hobbies can be enjoyed alone, pickleball is a social sport for all ages that brings people together. Grab a friend or three and hit the court, or take a few lessons and find a community of new active friends and teammates. It's easy to learn, doesn't cost much, isn't too physically taxing but still great for the body, and can become a regular exercise and social outlet. As one of the most popular sports in the country, many people get hooked, and it becomes their obsession.

What is pickleball?

Pickleball is a racket sport that combines many elements of tennis, badminton, and ping-pong. It's played outdoors and indoors on a badminton-sized court with a slightly modified tennis net. The rules are simple, but it can develop into a quick, fast-paced, competitive game.

How to Play Pickleball

The game can be played with two (singles) or four people (doubles), and there are five rules.

1. The ball must stay in bounds.
2. There must be one bounce per side.
3. Players must serve at the baseline.

4. Serves cannot land in the no-volley zone.
5. The game ends at 11, 15, or 21 points.

What's with the name?

In the summer of 1965 in Bainbridge Island, Washington, the game was created on a whim as a response to a challenge from a bored son. The father, Joel Pritchard, and his friend, Bill Bell, headed into the shed and pulled out what they could find: a wiffleball and table tennis paddles. They headed over to their badminton court and played the first game. Broken paddles became a problem, so they pulled in a handy neighbor, Barny McCallum, to construct more reliable handles. Together, they hashed out the rules, equipment, and the formation of this new unnamed game.

The name pickleball was suggested by Joel's wife, Joan. She explained the reference to leftover rowers who would race for fun in "pickle boat" crew race competitions. Like the leftover non-starter college rowers were thrown together for these races, she similarly felt the new game threw together elements of other sports (badminton, table tennis, wiffleball). The name stuck.

Some people believe the game was named after the Pritchards' dog, Pickles. But sweet little Pickles came a few years after the game was created.

Fun facts

- An estimated 400,000 people all over the world play pickleball.
- The typical pickleball paddle is larger than a ping-pong paddle but smaller than a tennis racket.
- The holes in the pickleball make it travel at approximately ⅓ the speed of a tennis ball.
- Players are called "Picklers," and those who have lost have been "Pickled."

- The 7-foot, non-volley zone directly in front of the net is called "The Kitchen."

Pickleball is now a worldwide sport. In a sleepy coastal town in South America last summer, I was surprised to come across a lively neighborhood commercial pickleball venue.

Go for it! Simple start steps:

1. Type in "pickleball lessons" in Google and find the location nearest to you.
2. Sign up for a class and learn the game.
3. Stay in touch with the other beginners, or get friends together and teach them to play.

Resources

1- US Senior Pickleball Association link

2- USA Pickleball link

3- Pickleball Magazine

4- How Pickleball Really Got its Name link

Products

1- Pickleball Paddle Balls Bag Set link

2- 12 Outdoor Pickleballs link

3- Pickleball Picker Upper link

Books

1- Pickleball Book For Beginners by Dennis Hall link

2- Smart Pickleball by Prem Carnot link

3- The Joy of Pickleball for the Senior Player by Mike Branon link

Pairs well with: Friends, warm days, tournaments

Practice Tai Chi

Create harmony between the mind and body

You might also like: Badminton, soft tennis, racquetball, table tennis

* * *

Practice Tai Chi

Create harmony between the mind and body

Tai Chi is a low-impact exercise combined with moving meditation originating in China. The health benefits for seniors, especially those with arthritis, are well-known worldwide.

"It integrates slow, intentional movements with breathing and cognitive skills like imagery" and "mindfulness on wheels" is how Harvard Medical School Guide to Tai Chi Author Peter M. Wayne Ph.D. describes it.

In a nutshell, it's an ideal mind-body practice combined with some basic athletic training.

Extensive Benefits of Tai Chi[1]

1. Decreased stress, anxiety, and depression.
2. Physical- better balance, power and strength, stamina, aerobic capacity, agility, flexibility, and speed of movements.
3. Enhanced immunity.
4. Improved cognition, mood, and focus.
5. Pain management and physical therapy for arthritis.
6. Effective recovery for cardiopulmonary conditions and COPD.
7. Significantly reduce chronic pain for conditions like fibromyalgia.
8. Improve neurological function for people with Parkinson's disease.
9. Enhanced sleep quality.

5 Main Styles of Tai Chi (in order of popularity)

1. **Yang-** The most popular form practiced today, characterized by gentle large-frame movements. Easy to learn and suitable for seniors.
2. **Wu-** Characterized by softness, it's an easy style for beginners.
3. **Chen-** The oldest form, characterized by alternating fast and explosive movements with slow and gentle ones.
4. **Sun-** The youngest form, it's known to have lively steps and a slightly higher stance. Good for arthritis.
5. **Hao-** A lesser-known style where the emphasis is placed on the internal force.

How do I learn?

- **In-person class-** YMCA, senior centers, martial arts schools, community centers, etc
- **Online classes-** Many free and paid online classes (see resources section below).
- **YouTube-** Search for Tai Chi, and many videos will pop up.
- **TV-** DVD/Blu-ray discs are available to learn on the TV.
- **Apps-** Many are available, such as Tai Chi Fit Strength.

Go for it! Simple start steps:

1. Watch a Tai Chi video on YouTube to understand the practice.
2. Search online for nearby Tai Chi classes and join.
3. Alternatively, take lessons online.

Resources

1. Best Online Tai Chi Classes link
2. Tai Chi for Seniors Online Info Guide link
3. 24 Tai Chi Movements link

Products

1. Tai Chi Fit Over 60 DVD link
2. Tai Chi for Beginners- 8 lessons DVD link
3. Tai Chi for Arthritis-12 lessons DVD link
4. Balance and Strength Exercises for Seniors -9 Practices DVD link

Books

1. The Harvard Medical School Guide to Tai Chi by Peter Wayne link
2. Tai Chi Illustrated by Pixiang Qiu link
3. Tai Chi for Beginners and the 24 forms by Dr. Paul Lam link

Pairs well with: Parks, meditation, physical therapy

You might also like: Yoga, water aerobics, dance instruction

* * *

Go on a Scenic Drive

Enjoy the outdoors from the road

Sometimes, you want to get out and enjoy some fresh air but don't feel like exerting yourself or can't get around easily because of an injury. Do what many motorcyclists do: go for a scenic drive just for fun.

Think about some nearby backroads you seldom take or find some spots with Google Maps that might have lovely views and head out with no particular destination other than to enjoy the natural surroundings. Be fully aware and actively search for and appreciate the beauty all around.

Explore a little. Find some out-of-the-way spots you never knew existed. Go down the roads you never had a reason to take but always wondered what was there. Make it about the journey and not the destination. You never know what you'll find and where you'll end up.

So, the next time you need to get out, consider taking the roads to nowhere rather than the road to the store.

Pairs well with: Convertible or electric car rental, your favorite music, ice cream stop

* * *

Learn Powered Paragliding

Soar with the birds on the simplest form of powered flight

If you've ever dreamed of flying as a child, now is the time to make your dreams come true. Powered paragliding (PPG), also known as paramotoring, is the simplest, easiest to learn, and least expensive way to achieve powered flight. Pure and simple: no plane, no windows, just you floating on air.

What is Powered Paragliding?

A form of ultralight aviation where a pilot wears a small motorized propeller backpack to give thrust to the paraglider (similar to a parachute but used for gliding). Launched by foot, typically in an open field, the pilot uses a handheld throttle to accelerate the propeller, the wing goes up, and within a few steps, you are lifted off the ground. Once airborne, there are two flight controls, left and right, via the glider's pull toggles and a handheld throttle to climb and descend.

. . .

7 Advantages of Powered Paragliding

1. **Easy to learn-** One of the easiest and safest forms of flight to master, and it offers an unrivaled personal flying experience.
2. **Low cost-** The most affordable way to achieve powered flight is typically $7,500 to $15,000 for the flight gear and instruction.
3. **Portable-** Pop it in the car and take it anywhere. No airplane hanger is required.
4. **License not required-** FAA Federal Aviation Regulation 103 specifies that ultralight vehicles, such as powered paragliding, do not require a license or certificate. However, you should not take off without professional instruction for your safety.
5. **Low and slow-** PPGs typically fly 100-2000 feet high and 25-30 miles an hour.
6. **Safety-** If the motor quits glide down to an open area to land.
7. **Open air-** With the wind on your face, fly free as a bird.

Go for it! Simple start steps:

1. Buy the Powered Paragliding Bible book and learn about the sport.
2. Google "powered paragliding/ paramotoring instruction/ lessons."
3. Contact several companies nearby to find the right one for you.

Resources

1. US Powered Paragliding Association link
2. How to Start Paramotoring link

3. Learn to fly FAQ's link

Products

1. Master Powered Paragliding 1- Ground Handling DVD link
2. Master Powered Paragliding 2- Advanced Launches DVD link
3. Master Powered Paragliding 3- Inflight Precision DVD link

Books

1. Powered Paragliding Bible by Jeff Goin link
2. Powered Parachute Flying Handbook by FAA link
3. The Complete Paramotor Pilots Book of Knowledge link

Pairs well with: Red Bull drink, GoPro camera, calm wind mornings

You might also like: Getting an airplane pilot license, motorcycle license, hang gliding or paragliding

* * *

Play Disc Golf

Walk through nature and throw for an ace

Disc golf, often affectionately referred to as frisbee golf, has been experiencing a remarkable surge in popularity among older generations, and it's not hard to see why. At its core, disc golf offers an alluring blend of simplicity and engagement. Its rules are refreshingly uncomplicated, making it an inviting sport for retirees eager to embark on a new adventure. One of its most appealing facets lies in its health benefits – it serves as a delightful form of exercise that's gentle on aging joints and muscles. This means you can stay active, enjoying the thrill of competition, without worrying about overexertion.

Moreover, disc golf is incredibly budget-friendly, requiring only a few discs to get started, and many courses are free to play. As you navigate the meticulously designed courses, you'll find yourself surrounded by the soothing embrace of nature. The serene atmosphere, the rustle of leaves, and the chirping of birds create the perfect backdrop for a leisurely round. But perhaps the most compelling aspect for retirees is the social dimension of the game. Disc golf provides a unique opportunity to forge new connections or strengthen bonds with friends and family. As you stroll along fairways and aim for those distant targets, you'll discover that disc golf isn't just a game; it's a gateway to memorable moments and lasting relationships.

What's Disc Golf?

It's similar to golf but played by throwing a flying disc into a basket.

5 Reasons Why Disc Golf is Better Than Ball Golf

- **It's faster-** Instead of 300-yard ball holes, disc holes are about 300 feet, making 18 holes take about half the time.
- **No tee times-** Show up and play.
- **No green fees-** Many courses are set up in public parks. It's just part of the fun there.
- **Equipment costs less-** You need three discs (a driver, a mid-range, and a putter) to play.
- **Easier to learn-** Forget figuring out how to use a bag of clubs with differing lengths and lofts, dealing with terrible ball lies, and reading the putting break. Just pick up and throw.

Did you know?

A hole-in-one in disc golf is called an ace.

. . .

Go for it! Simple start steps:

1. Buy some discs.
2. Google "disc golf courses" to find nearby places to play.
3. Show up and have fun.

Resources

1. The 17 Best Disc Golf Tips For Seniors [link](#)
2. Professional Disc Golf Association Seniors [link](#)
3. Disc Golf Rules [link](#)

Products

1. Disc Golf Set With 6 Discs and Bag [link](#)
2. Disc Golf Practice Basket [link](#)
3. Disc Golf Retriever Telescoping Pole [link](#)

Books

1. The Definitive Guide To Disc Golf by Justin Menickelli [link](#)
2. Zen and the Art of Disc Golf by Patrick McCormick [link](#)
3. Disc Golf Score Sheets [link](#)

Pairs well with: Sneakers, sunscreen, friends

You might also like: Golf, pickleball, tennis

* * *

Launch Model Rockets

See how high you can go

Who says getting old means growing out of playing with toys? Model rockets are a perfectly acceptable and exciting grown-up toy that can be enjoyed with all levels of mobility. Model rocketry hobbyists enjoy assembling different rockets, then launching them in fields, sometimes hundreds of feet in the air, to gracefully parachute back down. It's something the grandkids would enjoy as well.

The heart of model rocketry lies in the art of creation. Enthusiasts derive immense satisfaction from meticulously assembling rockets, where craftsmanship and attention to detail reign supreme. Each rocket becomes a miniature masterpiece, a testament to one's skill and imagination. It is a gratifying endeavor for those who appreciate precision and creativity.

However, the true magic of model rocketry ignites when the countdown begins, and the rocket is launched into the vast expanse of the sky. The sheer delight of witnessing your creation soar upwards, sometimes reaching dizzying heights hundreds of feet above, is a thrill. And when it descends, a perfectly timed parachute unfurls, guiding it back to earth with a gentle descent.

The best part? This is a hobby that transcends generations. It's something your grandkids would find fascinating and a brilliant way to bond over shared excitement, creating memories that bridge generations and time. So, who says growing older means leaving play behind? Model rockets remind us that the joy of play is ageless.

* * *

Landscape Painting

Capture nature's beauty on canvas

Whether you have an artistic side or want to develop your talents, landscape painting is a great way to spend quality time in nature. Like photography, lighting and composition are essential, so the painter must keep an eye out for the perfect vantage point to capture the natural beauty on canvas. Give it a shot. Beauty is in the eye of the beholder, after all.

. . .

3 Types of Landscape Paintings

1. **Impressionistic-** The natural scenery is accentuated with more saturation and creative feeling to invoke an emotional charge from the viewer.
2. **Representational-** A realistic painting that attempts to capture the essence of nature.
3. **Abstract-** A form of art that allows artists to alter the scene's reality to express their perceptions of the environment.

3 Types of Paint Used

1. **Acrylic**- Best for beginner painters
2. **Oil**
3. **Watercolor**

4 Steps to Landscape Painting

1. Sketch the landscape.
2. Paint wash the background colors of the landscape.
3. Paint the landscape from background to foreground.
4. Mix more colors and add them to the landscape from darkest to lightest.

Go for it! Simple start steps:

1. Watch a few online landscape painting tutorials.
2. Go to an art supply store and ask them what you need.
3. Search for a great outdoor spot and start painting.

Books

1. The Landscape Painters Workbook by Mitchell Albala link
2. Mastering Composition by Ian Roberts link
3. Carlson's Guide to Landscape Painting by John F. Carlson link

* * *

Play Lawn Croquet

Whack some wooden balls through little hoops

Croquet is an enjoyable pastime that combines elements of strategy, skill, and sociability. What makes croquet enjoyable is the blend of competitiveness and leisure it offers. Players must strategize their shots, carefully planning their moves to navigate through wickets while preventing opponents from doing the same. The physical aspect of the game, involving precise ball control and mallet technique, adds a layer of skill that can be both challenging and satisfying. Moreover, croquet is a social activity that encourages interaction and camaraderie among participants. It's often played in a relaxed outdoor setting, making it perfect for enjoying a sunny afternoon with friends or family.

The type of person who might enjoy playing croquet is someone who appreciates a mix of mental engagement and physical activity in their recreational pursuits. Individuals who enjoy strategic thinking, problem-solving, and friendly competition are likely to find croquet appealing. It can also be an excellent fit for those who prefer low-impact sports but still want to engage in an outdoor, physically stimulating activity. Furthermore, croquet is well-suited for people who value socializing and spending quality time with others while engaging in a leisurely yet engaging game. In essence, croquet is a versatile and enjoyable pastime that can be appreciated by a wide range of individuals who seek a balance of mental stimulation, physical involvement, and social interaction in their recreational activities.

. . .

Did you know?

Croquet was played in the Olympics in 1900 only.

How much does it cost?

Once you pick up a croquet set of 6 for about $50, head out to a lawn or park, and it's free.

Resources

1. How To Play Croquet [link](#)

Products

1. Croquet Set With Bag [link](#)
2. Croquet Set With Stand [link](#)

Books

1. Complete Croquet by James Hawkins [link](#)
2. Croquet The Sport by Jack R. Osborn [link](#)

Pairs well with: Friends, sunny afternoons, parks

You might also like: Golf, bocce ball, horseshoes

* * *

Care for a Garden

Grow something tasty

Gardening can be an incredibly enjoyable outdoor activity for a multitude of reasons. Firstly, it offers a direct connection with nature, allowing individuals to nurture and witness the growth of plants and flowers. This connection can be immensely satisfying, providing a sense of accomplishment as you see your garden flourish over time.

Gardening is also a great way to relax and relieve stress. The process of tending to plants, digging in the soil, and caring for your garden can be therapeutic and calming. Moreover, it's a creative outlet that allows for personal expression through landscaping choices and plant selection. For those who appreciate fresh, homegrown produce, gardening provides the opportunity to cultivate your own fruits and vegetables, enhancing the flavor and quality of your meals.

Gardening is a great choice for someone who has an appreciation for the outdoors, a love for nature, and a desire to engage with it on a personal level. Gardeners tend to be patient individuals who can relish the gradual growth and evolution of their plants. It's also a perfect hobby for those who enjoy working with their hands and don't mind getting a little dirty in the process. Gardening can appeal to individuals of various ages, from retirees seeking a peaceful pastime to families looking to bond over a shared outdoor activity. Ultimately, gardening is a versatile and fulfilling activity that can be enjoyed by anyone with a green thumb or a desire to cultivate beauty and life in their outdoor spaces.

6 Types of Gardens

1. Herbs
2. Vegetables
3. Flowers
4. Hydroponics (growing plants without soil)
5. Butterfly (plants that attract butterflies)
6. Container (grow in containers)

5 Benefits of Gardening

1. Exercise
2. Relaxing
3. Outdoors
4. Beautiful flowers to look at

5. The best-tasting food ever 😊

Go for it! Simple start steps:

1. Decide where to garden.
2. Search online for plants you might be interested in growing.
3. Learn how to grow, purchase supplies, and go for it.

Resources

1. 10 Top Gardening Tips For Beginners [link](#)
2. Benefits of Gardening For Seniors [link](#)
3. Vegetable Gardening For Beginners [link](#)

Products

1. 83 Piece Gardening Set [link](#)
2. Gardening Gloves With Claws [link](#)
3. Hydroponic Growing System [link](#)

Books

1. Vegetable Gardening Handbook by Old Farmer's Almanac [link](#)
2. The Healing Garden: Cultivating Herbal Remedies by Juliet Blankespoor [link](#)
3. The Flower Gardener's Bible by Lewis Hill [link](#)

Pairs well with: Cooking, sunscreen, lemonade

You might also like: Bonsai trees, knitting, baking

* * *

Rent a Kayak or Canoe

Reflect on water

There's something relaxing about being on the water. The tranquility of water has a uniquely calming effect. Extensive research has demonstrated that as little as 20 minutes immersed in a natural setting can significantly lower stress levels. Imagine starting your day with a serene kayak or canoe ride, gliding gracefully across the surface of a tranquil lake. Here, you are enveloped in a sense of profound serenity, where the water mirrors the world around it, casting reflections of nature's beauty. This meditative experience offers a precious opportunity to slow down the constant chatter of our minds and truly be present, which is pivotal for maintaining our mental well-being. And for those who prefer company on their journey, two-person kayaks provide an excellent avenue to share the experience with a friend, fostering connections while basking in the soothing embrace of nature's calmness.

Kayak or Canoe?

A kayak is generally smaller and streamlined, with riders securely seated in individual cockpits, wielding a double-sided paddle to make alternating strokes for precise control. In contrast, canoes are larger and more open, designed for multiple passengers who sit on benches or kneel, using a single-bladed paddle for a rhythmic and coordinated paddling style. The choice ultimately depends on your preferences, the type of experience you seek, and whether you plan to paddle solo or share the adventure with others.

Exercise

In addition to the relaxing benefits, getting on the water can provide an excellent opportunity to get the weekly CDC-recommended[2] minimum 150 hours of moderately intense exercise in a low-impact way.

. . .

5 Benefits of Kayaking[3]

1. Improves heart health.
2. Strengthens the upper body, core, glutes, and legs.
3. Low impact on joints.
4. Improved mental health from being outdoors.
5. It can help you lose weight.

Go for it! Simple start steps:

1. Search online for a nearby body of water suitable for kayaking or canoeing.
2. Purchase a lightweight, portable, inflatable kayak and necessary gear.
3. Go kayaking!

Resources

1. CDC Recommended Weekly Physical Activity link
2. 15 Best Inflatable Kayaks link
3. Travel and Leisure Best Kayaks link
4. How much physical activity do adults need link
5. 20 mins in nature reduces stress markers link

Products

1. Budget 1-Person Inflatable Kayak link
2. Budget 2-Person Inflatable Kayak link
3. Budget Electric Air Pump link
4. Waterproof Dry Bag link

Books

1. How to Paddle a Kayak by Scott Parsons link
2. Recreational Kayaking The Ultimate Guide link

Chapter 3 87

3. The Practical Handbook of Kayaking and Canoeing by Bill Mattos <u>link</u>

Pairs well with: Fishing, birding, dogs

You might also like: Paddleboarding, boating

* * *

Become a Street Performer
Build a crowd and entertain

Certainly not for everyone, but for those who enjoy the thrill of a good crowd, becoming a street performer could be right up your alley. It's simple: find a spot with good foot traffic (downtown, at a public gathering, open festival, or touristy area), then show off your talents by yourself or with friends.

5 Talents to Entertain

1. **Music-** Play your instrument or sing karaoke style.
2. **Art-** Get your Bob Ross "Joy of Painting" show on, spray paint some masterpieces, or create a sidewalk chalk masterpiece.
3. **Dance-** Get your wiggle on. You do you.
4. **Talents-** Do you have a talent like juggling or hula hooping?
5. **Other Entertainment-** Dog tricks, balloon twisting, caricatures, clowning, comedy, face painting, fortune telling, magic, puppeteering, living statues, and storytelling.

Over the years, I've stumbled upon some interesting sidewalk acts, from blindfolded juggling while tightrope walking between stop lights (not recommended), to break dancers, to frozen painted people suspended in a strange pose, to a group of seniors playing ukulele along a beach walkway. Have some fun, and maybe make a few bucks on the side!

Books

1. Busking for Beginners by Gerald Helsden link
2. Stories of a Street Performer by Whit Pop Haydn link

Pairs well with: Upside down hats, busy areas, social friends

You might also like: Face painting, balloon animals, concerts

* * *

Collect Things

Search for things that fit your collection

It's not entirely understood why people collect things, but who doesn't enjoy a good treasure hunt? One estimate suggests that 40% of American households engage in one form of collecting or another. Whether searching for seashells, looking for vacation magnets, or checking off bucket list experiences, collecting can be a fun motivator to get out and find what we're looking for.

Top 10 Most Popular Things People Collect

1. Stamps
2. Coins
3. Trading Cards
4. Music
5. Comic Books
6. Wine
7. Toys
8. Antiques
9. Classic Cars
10. Fine Art and Jewelry

More Things People Collect

New experiences, spoons, precious stones, sea shells, fridge magnets, shark teeth, sea glass, vintage movie posters, dolls, funko pops, vintage action figures, car miniatures, vintage tableware, autographs, bookmarks, rare books, dried flowers, plants, postcards, old magazines, oil cans, perfume bottles, tattoos, shoes, zip lighters, shot glasses, matchboxes, snow globes, old photographs, watches and clocks, crystal, animal figures (frogs, cats, etc.), guitar picks, fountain pens, Precious Moments figures, video games, arrowheads, antique weapons, cameras, sand, ticket stubs, bugs, jerseys, buttons, erasers, things of one color, taxidermy, guitar picks, fossils, and travel souvenirs.

Warning: Be prepared to have your collection grow when others find out about it. My friend liked frogs and had a few frog collectibles. Before long, he was receiving frog gifts at every opportunity (birthday, Christmas, etc.) until there was no longer space. He fell out of love with frogs, but they kept coming. He now hates frogs.

Resources

1. Tips for Starting and Enjoying a Collection link
2. How to Start a Collection and 50+ Manly Collection Ideas link
3. 246 Cool Things To Collect link

Products

1. Acrylic Collectible Display Case link
2. 12 Cube Display Organizer link
3. Lighted Corner Display link

Books

1. Kovels Antiques and Collectibles Price Guide by Terry Kovel link
2. The NextGen Guide to Car Collecting by Robert C. Yeager link
3. The Ultimate Guide To Sea Glass Collecting by Mary Beth Beuke link

Pairs well with: Display cases, lots of room, an accommodating partner

* * *

Build and Race Remote-Control (RC) Vehicles

Get an adrenaline rush with miniature vehicles

There is a world of fun and excitement to explore with remote-control RC vehicles. From RC cars of all types to boats, planes, helicopters, submarines, drones, and more, people of all ages enjoy the hobby of building, using, and even racing RC vehicles. It brings people out into the fresh air, can be done alone or with other enthusiasts, and helps build hand-eye coordination and stay mentally sharp. In the past, some gas-powered RC vehicles were loud and annoying. But today, with rechargeable electric motors, they are silent, clean energy fun. There are many leagues where adrenaline seekers can compete by racing their RC vehicles around tracks at speeds that can reach 60 mph! Building and modifying vehicle parts can be a stress reducer while tinkering with different aspects of the vehicle. For some, an RC vehicle is not just a toy. It's a passion.

10 Reasons To Race Remote-Control Vehicles

1. The thrill of racing and competition.
2. The technical aspects of building and tuning the cars.
3. The sense of control and precision when driving the cars.
4. The camaraderie and community of fellow racers.

5. The opportunity to race in a variety of conditions and environments.
6. The ability to customize and personalize their cars.
7. The satisfaction of overcoming technical challenges.
8. The hobby can help to learn about mechanics, engineering, and physics.
9. It's a great way to relieve stress and enjoy a fun and entertaining activity.
10. It's a relatively inexpensive hobby that people of all ages and skill levels can enjoy.

7 Types of Remote-Control Vehicles

1. **RC cars-** These are the most common type of remote-control racing vehicles. They come in different scales and styles, such as touring cars, drift cars, off-road buggies, and trucks.
2. **RC airplanes-** They can be flown in various conditions, from calm to windy.
3. **RC helicopters-** Similar to airplanes, these vehicles are flown remotely but are more maneuverable and capable of hovering in place.
4. **RC boats-** Race on water surfaces, like lakes, ponds, and swimming pools.
5. **RC trucks-** Similar to RC cars, but are designed for off-road use on rough terrain or mud.
6. **RC drifters-** Explicitly designed for drifting, a driving technique where the rear wheels slide while the front wheels stay pointed in the direction of the turn.
7. **RC bikes-** Remote control motorbikes are a new category of RC vehicles recently gaining popularity.

FPV (First Person View) Racing Drones

A new competitive hobby has become one of the most exciting forms of RC racing, FPV drone racing. Drone operators wear head-mounted display FPV goggles to see from a camera on the front of their racing drone in real time. They'll then navigate around the course of obstacles from the drone's point of view, giving the operator the sensation that they are flying without the risk of crashing and burning for real! The fastest drone wins. For a real rush of excitement, give it a try!

Resources

1. Radio Operated Auto Racing ROAR link
2. Is Remote-Control Car Racing A Sport? Link
3. 5 Types Of RC Cars You Need To Know link
4. Drone Racing: Everything You Need to Know link
5. Drone Racing League link

Products

1. DJI FPV Drone Combo link
2. RC Car link
3. RC Plane link

* * *

Coach a Team

Share your winning attitude

Playing sports is more than simply winning or losing. Good coaches teach positive values that transcend sports, build character, and benefit the players throughout their lives. Many youth leagues need more parents with free time or experience to coach all the players. Getting involved as a coach or assistant coach is a great way to share your knowledge of the game and teach skills they can use beyond the field.

Popular Team Youth Sports for Males

- Baseball- Played by 40% of American males as a youth.
- Basketball- 32%
- Football- 31%
- Soccer- 14%
- Track and field- 14%
- Wrestling- 9%
- Volleyball- 7%
- Tennis- 7%
- Swimming and diving- 7%

Popular Team Youth Sports for Females

- Volleyball- Played by 17% of American females as a youth.
- Basketball- 16%
- Softball- 16%
- Dance- 10%
- Cheerleading- 9%
- Track and field- 9%
- Tennis- 9%
- Swimming and diving- 8%

After college, my roommate and I thought coaching a youth basketball team would be fun. We asked the local youth league if they needed help and were assigned eight middle school-aged boys and girls to play for our team. I had experience with competitive high school basketball and dreamed of getting the kids into a top-notch winning team. We drilled fundamentals and practiced plays, but it all seemed to go out the window when gameday came around. I soon realized the kids didn't care if we won or lost but just wanted to have fun. For the rest of the season, our practices focused on having fun. Despite coming in nearly last place, it was a great experience connecting and sharing with these kids, many of whom I discovered had parents who weren't around often.

Go for it! Simple start steps:

1. Search for youth leagues near you.
2. Contact the organizer to see if additional coaches are needed.
3. Research and plan out practices for your team.

Resources

1. 6 Benefits of Coaching Team Sports link
2. How to Become A Youth Sports Coach link
3. Benefits of Coaching In Old Age link
4. American Youth Sports Statistics link

Books

1. Sports Psychology For Youth Coaches by Ronald E. Smith link
2. Every Moment Matters: How the World's Best Coaches Inspire Their Athletes by John O'Sullivan link
3. Coaching Basketball For Dummies by Greg Bach link

* * *

Go Sunbathing

Soak up the Vitamin D

Going outside doesn't need to be complicated to be beneficial. Soak up those healing rays and give your well-being a workout. Get some rest, relaxation, and rays. You've earned it.

. . .

7 Benefits of Sunlight[4]

1. **Improves your sleep-** The hormone melatonin helps you sleep and is produced by your body after dark. Research indicates that an hour of natural light in the morning helps regulate your circadian rhythm. The more sunlight you can get during the day, the better your body will be at producing melatonin when it's time to sleep.
2. **Reduce stress-** Melatonin also helps reduce stress reactivity.
3. **Maintains strong bones-** Our bodies produce Vitamin D when exposed to sunlight. Vitamin D helps our bodies maintain calcium and prevents brittle, thin, and misshapen bones.
4. **Weight loss-** Research suggests a link between getting outside for 30 minutes between 8a.m. and noon. There are more forces at work than just sunlight, but it's fun to think we could lose weight while sunbathing in the morning.
5. **Strengthens your immune system-** Vitamin D is critical to the immune system. Fight your risk of illness, infections, some cancers, and mortality after cancer with the sun.
6. **Fights off depression-** Sunshine boosts your body's "feel good" serotonin levels, improving your mood and helping you stay calm and focused. Natural light exposure might help fight seasonal affective disorder (SAD) typical during shorter winter sunlight days.
7. **Might give you a longer life-** A study[5] that followed 30,000 Swedish women for 20 years revealed that those who spent more time in the sun lived 6 months to 2 years longer than those who didn't.

How much time is needed for Vitamin D production?

Depending on your skin shade, Vitamin D is estimated to be produced between 5 and 30 minutes of exposure to the sun. Wearing sunscreen will reduce Vitamin D production, and it's thought that about 15 minutes is adequate for fair-skinned people. Of course, too much sunlight can harm your health (skin cancer and others), so be careful with your skin exposure.

Resources

1. Sunlight and Your Health link
2. What Are The Benefits of Sunlight? Link
3. A Guide To Sunbathing And Sunburning link

Products

1. Set of 2 Reclining Zero Gravity Lounge Chairs link
2. Cobra Portable Mist Stand link
3. Womens Sun Straw Hat link

Pairs well with: Cool beverages, beach, pool

You might also like: Meditation, yoga, hikes

* * *

Try Geocaching

Use GPS to search for hidden treasure

Geocaching is a type of treasure hunt where people look for caches or hidden stashes of objects. Participants use global positioning service (GPS) technology to find hidden treasures (low-cost trinkets or geocoins). Get outside, enjoy nature, and have fun in the process.

D**id you know?**

Chapter 3 97

- It's estimated that more than 3 million geocaches are located worldwide in 191 countries, even Antarctica.
- Drive-up caches are called "cache and dash."
- After GPS navigating to about 20-30 feet of a cache, you'll need to search around for the small hidden waterproof container (false rock, etc.) with the treasure.
- It's like an outdoor hide-and-seek game.

Say What? Shirts About Geocaching

- I'm not lost. I'm geocaching.
- I use multi-million dollar satellites to find Tupperware in the woods. What's your hobby?
- Found the cache! Now, where is the car?
- Geocachers- Just nerdy pirates.

Go for it! Simple start steps:

1. Download a geocaching app on your phone ("Geocaching" is the largest and free).
2. Open the app and view nearby geocaches on the map.
3. Go find it!

Resources

1. Geocaching app geocaching.com link
2. How to Geocache link
3. How to Get Started Geocaching link

Pairs well with: Water bottle, good shoes, umbrella

You might also like: Pokemon Go (GPS phone game), scavenger hunts, hiking

* * *

Barbecue

Perfect your smoked flavor

Grilling is a great way to cook healthier meals and enjoy the outdoors. No backyard is truly complete without a BBQ. Put some backyard BBQs on your to-do list. Your tastebuds and invited friends will thank you.

3 Reasons To Get Your Grill On

1. **Healthier-** Grilling meats and veggies helps retain more nutrients than baking or frying. Grease drips down from meats, so you'll consume less fat.
2. **Outdoors-** It's good to get outside.
3. **Social-** Mention you're having a BBQ, and chances are your friends will come running. Entertaining around the grill, possibly with a few beverages in hand, is a relaxing social connector.

BBQ Fun Facts

- 64% of Americans own a BBQ or smoker.
- The biggest BBQ pit is in Brenham, Texas. It's 76 feet long and can cook four to six tons of barbecue at once.
- BBQ meats need to rest before and after cooking. One rule of thumb is to rest for 8 minutes per pound after cooking to reabsorb the juices.
- The most popular food for BBQ is hamburgers.
- The majority of primary household grillers are male (66%).
- National BBQ Day is May 16th, but July 4th is the day most people BBQ.

- Grilling and BBQing have different definitions. Grilling cooks with the lid up, and BBQing involves putting the cover down.

BBQ Shirt Slogans

- I like pig butts and I cannot lie.
- I like bourbon and my smoker... and maybe 3 people.
- Stop staring at my rack.
- I just want to drink beer and smoke meat.
- Brisketarian... because briskets never disappoint.

Resources

1. 13 Pro Tips Every Beginner BBQer Should Know link
2. Top 10 Tips For Excellent Summer Grilling link
3. 100 Best Grilling Recipes For Summer link

Products

1. Propane Grill link
2. Charcoal Grill and Smoker link
3. Wireless Meat Thermometer link

Books

1. The Barbeque! Bible by Steven Raichlen link
2. Project Smoke: 7 Steps To Smoked Food Nirvana by Steven Raichlen link
3. The Ultimate Book of Grilling by Love Food link

Pairs well with: Beer, friends, sunshine

* * *

Visit a Winery and Relax Outside

Relax among the vines

Is there anything more relaxing than finding a quiet spot at a vineyard overlooking rows of grapevines, appreciating the complexities of an excellent local wine, and letting your thoughts softly drift from anything troubling? With age, we've learned the importance of slowing down and savoring the moment where we can. Instead of running around, caught up in our neverending little tasks and responsibilities, we now have the wisdom to sit down, reflect, and enjoy the little things. What's the rush? Visiting a vineyard during the week on a beautiful day can be a great place to lower your stress, enhance your well-being, and count your blessings. You could be at work, after all.

Did you know?

- Jesus turned water into wine when the host at a wedding ran out. -John 2
- Medical studies[6] show a link between drinking red wine and lowering the risk of the leading cause of disease and death in the US, coronary heart disease. It has been shown to raise good cholesterol (HDL) and keep bad cholesterol (LDL) from causing injury.
- Grapes are the most planted fruit all over the world.
- Red wine is rich in antioxidants. Antioxidants prevent cellular damage caused by inflammation and oxidative stress. Drinking red wine has been associated with a reduced risk of Alzheimer's and Parkinson's disease (related to oxidative stress).
- A ton of grapes can be produced into 720 bottles of wine. One acre of land produces about 3-5 tons of grapes.
- Red wine may improve gut health.
- Wine tasters swirl their wine in their glasses to release its aroma. Flavor is the combination of taste and smell.
- An occasional glass of wine may reduce the risk of depression.

- The top wine producers in the world are #1 Italy, #2 France, #3 Spain, #4 United States, and #5 Australia.
- Wine may promote longevity.
- Not all wines improve with age. 90% of wines should be consumed within a year of production.
- Oenophobia (fear of wine) is a real thing.

7 Top Wine Regions in the US

If you're fresh out of relaxing at your nearby wineries and ready to branch out for a short getaway, below is a list of the top wine regions to visit and savor in the US. Although 89% of the country's wine is produced in California, many other wine regions make a fantastic destination for a wine-tasting trip.

1. **Napa Valley, California-** The most famous region in the US, with over 500 wineries and 30 different grape varieties. Best known for Cabernet Sauvignon and Chardonnay, and the best time to visit this Mediterranean-like climate is during the growing season between May and September.
2. **Sonoma Valley, California-** 250 wineries and a diverse, beautiful landscape with a relaxed vibe make Sonoma County the second most famous region. It's best known for Zinfandel, Cabernet Sauvignon, and Syrah.
3. **Other California-** Santa Barbara, Lodi, Paso Robles, Edna Valley, San Louis Obisbo, and Escondido are excellent wine regions in California.
4. **Texas Hill Country, Texas-** A growing hotspot for wine tourism, the area offers charm and natural scenery. The German-settled town of Fredericksburg is a popular jumping-off spot for a wine getaway.
5. **Walla Walla, Washington-** This little area with 120 wineries on the Washington and Oregon border is rising as it's recently received several awards, such as "Wine Region

of the Year" and "America's Best Wine Region" by different publications.
6. **North and Central Virginia-** Known as the birthplace of American wine after colonists attempted to grow in the early 17th century, even the 3rd President Thomas Jefferson was into viticulture. An hour's drive outside the Capital, you'll find the most visited area known as "DC's Wine Country," with picturesque country roads, rolling hills, and historic towns to enjoy. America's oldest wine grape, Norton, is found here as well.
7. **Snake River, Idaho-** Just 30 minutes from Boise, this up-and-coming region has some great wines and, at 3,000 feet, some of the highest-elevation vineyards in the US.

Drink in Moderation

While there could be health benefits to occasional glasses of wine in moderation, excessive drinking (or at all for certain people) has well-known harmful effects and can be deadly. The Center for Disease Control CDC official guidelines defines moderate drinking as:

- 1 glass of wine (or less) per day for females.
- 2 glasses of wine (or less) for males.
- One glass of wine is 5 ounces of 12% alcohol by volume.

Other US standard drink sizes

- 12 ounces of 5% beer.
- 8 ounces of 7% malt liquor.
- 1.5 ounces 40% (80 proof) distilled spirits (gin, rum, vodka, whiskey, etc.).

Resources

1. Is Red Wine Good For You- Medical News link
2. How to Taste Wine link
3. The Best Wineries in the US link

4. The Best 12 USA Wine Regions link
5. Top 7 US Wine Regions To Visit link
6. CDC Dietary Guidelines For Alcohol link

Products

1. Electric Wine Bottle Opener link
2. Wine Set With Electric Opener, Electric Aerator, Vacuum Stoppers link
3. Jesus Touched My Water Funny Wine glass link

Books

1. Wine Folly: The Master Guide by Madeline Puckette link
2. Wine Simple by Aldo Sohm link
3. The Sommelier's Atlas of Taste by Rajat Parr link

Pairs well with: Cheese, a book, a friend

You might also like: Becoming a Sommelier, visiting a brewery, Harvest Host membership for free overnight RV stays at wineries

* * *

Learn Bushcraft

Escape city life and learn to survive in the wilderness

Bushcraft, also known as woodcraft, is the practice of basic skills necessary to live in the remote outdoors. A form of wilderness survival, it's something between a hobby and an ultra-minimalist philosophy. Think of the popular TV show "Naked and Afraid" (but with clothes), where contestants must survive for days in the wilderness with nothing. They need the skills to find food (hunting, trapping, foraging, tracking, fishing), build a shelter, start a fire, and source water. Other skills such as twine-making, wood carving, knots and lashing, tool and weapon making, natural navigation, medicine and health, and camp craft are necessary.

. . .

4 Reasons To Practice Bushcraft

- **To escape city life-** They usually feel city life is crowded, polluted, busy, unnatural, and draining.
- **Recharge in nature-** Remote outdoor places provide fresh air and a chance to connect with our natural ancestral way of life.
- **Learn new skills-** There are endless new skills related to living without our modern conveniences.
- **Free themselves from distractions-** Practicing skills such as carving puts bush crafters in a sort of meditative state where they are fully engrossed in the task at hand and free of distractions.

Resources

1. Bushcraft Training For Beginners link
2. Bushcraft 101: Tools and Skills You Should Know link
3. Bushcraft Academy Master Class link

Products

1. Firestarter Survival Tool link
2. Bushcraft Survival Shovel Ax Tools link
3. Survival Camping Hammock link

Books

1. Bushcraft 101: A Field Guide To The Art Of Wilderness Survival by Dave Canterbury link
2. Bushcraft Illustrated by Dave Canterbury link
3. Ultimate Bushcraft Survival Manual by Tim MacWelch link

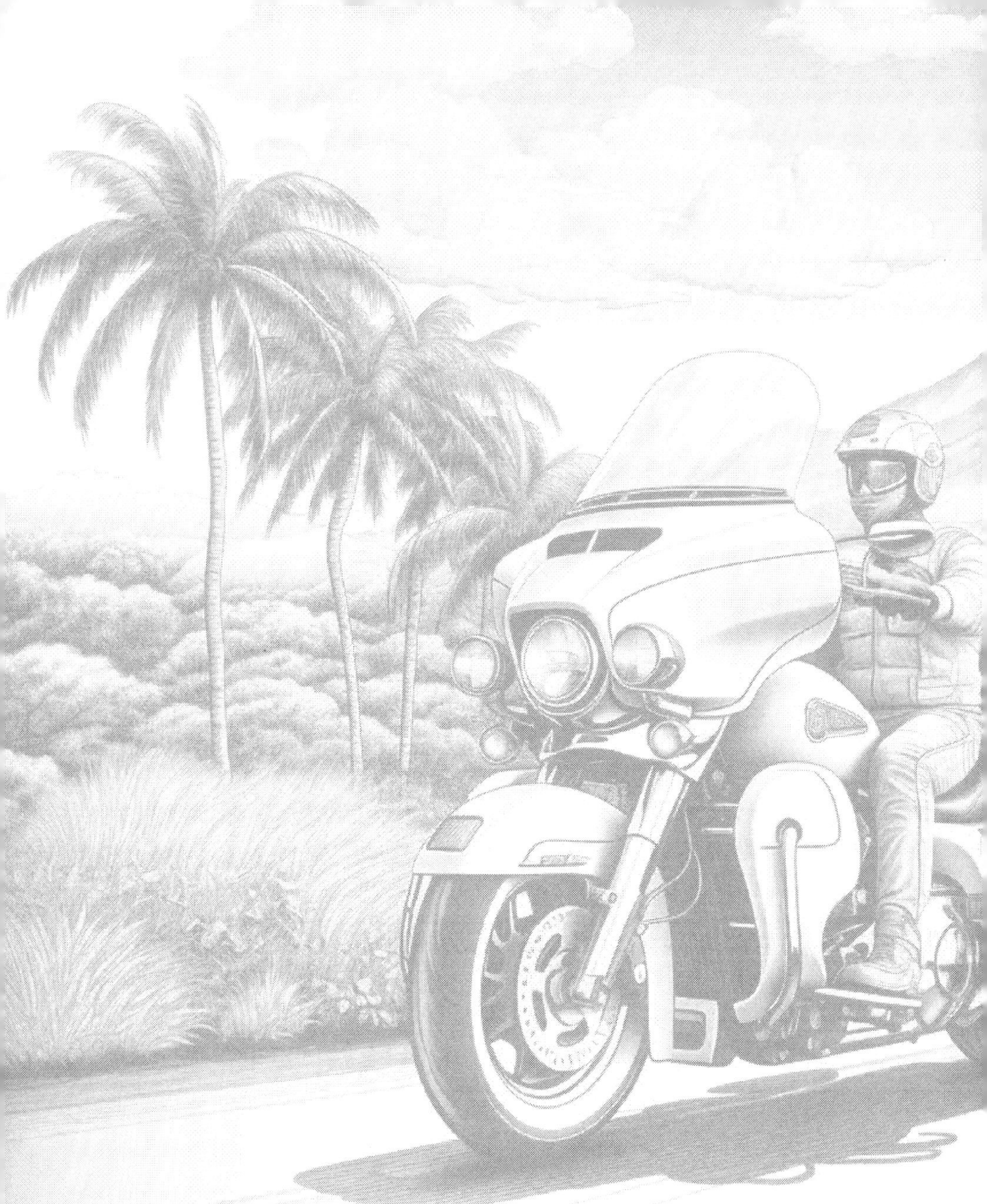

Chapter 4

Discover New Experiences

Trying new experiences is like embarking on a thrilling journey into the unknown, a journey where every step forward brings the promise of adventure and growth. It's like diving headfirst into a crystal-clear ocean, discovering a new world of beauty and wonder previously hidden from view.

Every new experience is like a puzzle piece that fits into the intricate fabric of our lives, painting a vivid and dynamic picture of who we are and who we are becoming. It's the spice that adds flavor to our existence, the fuel that ignites our passion and curiosity, and the spark that brings our dreams to life. So let us not shy away from the unknown but rather embrace it with open arms and an open mind, for it is in these moments that we come alive and experience the fullness of what life has to offer.

Chapter 4 Website Links

New Experience Ideas and Tips from Volume 1:
New Year's Eve Countdown in Times Square New York - Attend the World's Largest - Hot-Air Balloon Festival - Go Skinny Dipping - Run a Marathon - Eat at a Michelin - Star Restaurant - Volunteer - Attend a Symphony Orchestra - Skydive - Go to the Running of the Bulls - Houseboat on a Lake - Take a Brewery Tour - Learn to Scuba Dive - Live in a Foreign Country for at Least a Month - Visit a Japanese Onsen - Try Everything Once - Home Improvement Projects - Stretch Your Dollars

* * *

Take a Hot Air Balloon Ride

Float to the clouds and drift with the wind

A saying goes, "Only a surfer knows the feeling." The same could indeed be said about riding in a hot air balloon. It's really quite absurd when you think about it. You're attaching yourself to a balloon, standing outside in an open wicker basket, rising thousands of feet into the air, cannot steer, and have no idea where you might land. You'd think it should be only for the most daring Red Bull extreme sports cuckoos, but that's not the case.

Hot air balloon rides are deceptively calm and gentle. You'll drift in the wind, creating a quiet, peaceful stillness. Before you realize it, you're floating gracefully by the world below. You'll be so entranced by the unobstructed views that you might not even notice that your skillful pilot has climbed thousands of feet in the air. The horizon is so clear, along with the mountains you may have never noticed much while on the ground. Since the calmest winds are usually in the morning or afternoon, you may take in a beautiful sunrise or sunset as you blend with the colors of the sky.

Hot air balloon rides are a fantastic experience anywhere, but taking a ride while on vacation to enjoy the natural beauty of somewhere different adds a new level of scenery and excitement. Also, balloon rides can be relatively inexpensive if traveling in a country with a favorable exchange rate.

12 Famous Places to Take a Hot Air Balloon Ride

1. **Albuquerque, New Mexico-** The annual gathering of hundreds of hot air balloons, Albuquerque International Balloon Fiesta, is an opportunity to float among many other colorful balloons.
2. **Cappadocia, Turkey-** One of the world's most famous hot air locations. The unique rock formations and strange landscapes make for an unforgettable experience.
3. **Bagan, Myanmar-** The country in Southeast Asia has a treasure trove of intricate Buddhist temples that rise above the undeveloped natural treeline. There is no better way to sightsee than to drift from temple to temple.
4. **Serengeti, Tanzania-** Have an aerial safari, spotting lions, elephants, and zebras from one of the most popular places in Africa to balloon.
5. **Reims, France-** Drift over vineyards in the heart of Champagne country.
6. **Maasai Mara, Kenya-** The world-famous game reserve is home to many wildlife, including the rare black rhino.
7. **Wadi Rum, Jordan-** In the heart of the desert, 65 miles from the famous canyon carvings of Petra, the otherworldly sandstone landscapes are best viewed from above.

8. **Dubai, United Arab Emirates-** Soar above the tallest building in the world, the Burj Khalifa (2,717 feet), and see other modern skyscrapers rising from the surrounding desert.
9. **Teotihuacan, Mexico-** The archaeological complex of step pyramids is best experienced from the air.
10. **Napa Valley, California-** Float over famous wine country, then land and enjoy the fruits of the soil.
11. **Luxor, Egypt-** One of the best places to balloon in the world. Floating near the Nile River, you'll see temples, tombs, and statues. Our balloon pilot added an unexpected thrill at one point by going so low we had to rise to get over the 2 and 3-story homes. From a few feet above, we looked down and saw people going about their business on the undeveloped top floor.
12. **Others-** Loire Valley, France; Monument Valley, Utah; Atacama Desert, Chile; Vilnius, Lithuania; Yarra Valley, Australia; Chiang Rai, Thailand; Chianti, Italy; Queenstown, New Zealand.

More Info

- According to the FAA, balloon flights in the US are one of the safest forms of flight.
- US flights range from $150-300+ per person, but deals can sometimes be found on discount sites like Groupon and LivingSocial.
- Hot air balloons typically fly between 1,000 and 3,000 feet above the ground.

Resources

1. 7 Reasons Why a Hot Air Balloon Ride is A Must Have Experience link
2. 8 Reasons To Fly In a Hot Air Balloon link
3. How Dangerous Are Hot Air Balloon Rides link

Pairs well with: Binoculars, gloves, birthdays

You might also like: Powered paragliding, drones, harbor cruises

* * *

Climb Mount Fuji

See the world from the top of a sacred active stratovolcano

The iconic symbol of Japan, Mount Fuji, is the tallest mountain in the land. It's a perfectly symmetrical-shaped active volcano that can be seen for hundreds of miles on a clear day. For a few months each year during the trekking season, hundreds of thousands of people climb to the summit of this sacred mountain to enjoy a view they will never forget from 12,389 feet.

How to make it to the top?

Mount Fuji is easily accessible from Tokyo by 2-hour shinkansen (bullet train). During the hiking season from early July through early September, when the snow has melted from the peaks and the weather is best, up to 200,000 people make their way up this famous mountain. The hike is free and requires no hired guide because there are well-established trails. There are 4 hiking routes to the top, with the Yoshida trail being the most popular and accessible by public transportation. Each path has 10 stations or huts (many with food, water, and first aid) spaced along the route, and most treks begin at the 5th station. The Yoshida Trail 5th station starts at an elevation of 7,459 feet and takes about 6 hours to climb up and 4 hours to climb down by a separate path. Many people break up the hike with an overnight stay at the 8th hut (11,154 feet) and make an early morning hike up to watch the sunrise at the top.

How difficult is it?

The trail is primarily dirt and volcanic rock and requires no special skills. The high altitude makes the climb strenuous, so being physically fit and in good cardio is a must. Training should include endurance and strength training for the legs, as the descent will challenge different leg muscles to slow down.

Tips

Pick up a souvenir hiking stick on your way up and get it stamped at the stations as you ascend. There is a post office at the summit where you can mail a postcard to someone special. Altitude sickness can be a problem for some, no matter the level of fitness. A small bottle of oxygen can be purchased at huts along the way to give a little piece of mind if desired. An extra day exploring the beautiful nearby Hakone region is worth a visit.

From Defeat to Reminder

On clear days, I could see the towering volcanic peak from my balcony. When the climbing season opened, my girlfriend and I made our way to the 8th station hut to spend the night before a planned sunrise hike to the summit. It never happened. In the middle of the night, I woke from my tatami mat with shortness of breath and feeling like a fish in a fish bowl. Before long, instead of using my headlight to climb up the mountain, I was headed down in the darkness, puking along the way. The mountain had defeated me.

The following season, I returned alone, and instead of spending the night in the small, loud mountain hut, I went up all at once. I found that keeping active and my heart pumping sufficiently allowed enough oxygen in my lungs that I didn't feel the effects of altitude sickness this time. Because the hike was all in the daylight, it was easier to see the trail and more relaxing. There were many quite old Japanese folks slowly going up.

Later, on the way down, I met a single older man from the US who had become lost. He took the wrong route back and didn't know how we'd make it to his starting point, which was in a completely different area of the mountain. I offered to give him a ride when we got to the bottom together. We finally made it as the sun was setting. I learned he had cancer and only a year left to live. This hike was on his bucket list, and he decided to fly to Japan to conquer it alone. When I dropped him off, I could see the emotion in his eyes, having accomplished this dream. He was making the most of his remaining time on earth. I was reminded that day that life is short and to not put off to tomorrow what we can do today.

Go for it! Simple start steps:

1. Plan a trip to Japan and include a Mount Fuji hike.
2. Train for the climb with cardio and strength exercises.
3. Enjoy a journey of a lifetime with a bucket list experience!

Resources

1. Climbing Mount Fuji Guide link
2. Plan your Fuji Hike link
3. Japan Visit link

Products

1. Reusable Rain Poncho link
2. Hiking backpack link
3. Collapsible Water Bottle link
4. Rosetta Stone Learn Japanese Software link

Books

1. Japan by Lonely Planet link
2. Essential Japan by Fodor's link
3. Learn Japanese for Beginners by Yuto Kanazawa link

Pairs well with: JR Rail Pass, Hakone Kowakien Yunessun Hot Spring Theme Park, Lake Ashi (Hakone resort area with boat tours and mountain cable cars)

You might also like: Yosemite Half Dome Hike, Zion Angels Landing Hike, Marathon/ Half Marathon

* * *

Take a Ghost Tour

Get close to the supernatural

One activity that is sure to put you outside your comfort zone is taking a ghost tour. You'll be shuttled by an enthusiastic storyteller, spinning spooky tales of local historical events and the supernatural. It's a great way to see a city in a unique, darkly entertaining way, some say. If you're up for looking nervously into the shadows on tour and at home, ghost tours could be your thing. Or it could be a once-in-a-lifetime type of experience. Only one way to find out.

Resources

1. 10 Best Ghost Tours in The US link
2. Top 10 Ghost Tours for Halloween link
3. 15 of the Scariest Ghost Tours Around the World (and how to book) link

Books

1. Chasing Ghosts: A Tour Of Our Fascination With Spirits And The Supernatural by Marc Hartzman link
2. House of A Hundred Rooms: Tales The Ghost Tours Guides Do Not Tell by Keith J. Scales link
3. The Haunted Ghost Tour by Michelle Dorey link

Pairs well with: Halloween, travel, full moons

Chapter 4 115

★ ★ ★

Be a Member of a TV Audience

Get an up close and behind-the-scenes look at your favorite live show

Do you have a favorite game show or live show you watch regularly? Become one of the cheering audience and watch it being taped in person. If you're lucky, you may even be selected to come on stage and win prizes. Since most shows tape during the day, retired folk's flexible schedules make them a perfect candidate for joining the fun.

Popular Game Shows

- Jeopardy- Most popular TV game show in the US.
- The Price is Right
- Wheel of Fortune
- Who Wants to be a Millionaire
- Let's Make a Deal
- Family Feud
- Hollywood Squares
- American Idol
- The Voice
- America's Got Talent

Popular Talk Shows

- The View- One of the most-watched daytime talk shows.
- Live with Ryan and Kelly
- Dr. Phil
- The Ellen DeGeneres Show
- Today With Hoda & Jenna
- The Talk
- The Kelly Clarkson Show

Popular Other Shows

- Steven Colbert, The Late Show

- Seth Meyers, Late Night
- Jimmy Kimmel Live
- Saturday Night Live
- James Corden, The Late Late Show
- Jimmy Fallon, The Tonight Show
- Shows are primarily filmed in LA or New York City. Here's where you'll need to go.

LA Shows (in alphabetical order):

America's Funniest Home Videos, America's Got Talent, American Idol, American Ninja Warrior, Beat Shazam, Broke, Card Sharks, Celebrity Family Feud, Hollywood, Celebrity Name Game Conan, Dancing With the Stars, Disney's Just Roll With It, Dr. Phil, Family Feud, Food Fighters, Hollywood Game Night, Jeopardy, Jimmy Kimmel Live, Key & Peele, Let's Make a Deal, Lights Out With David Spade, Netflix's Family Reunion, Raven's Home, Real Time with Bill Maher, So You Think You Can Dance, The Carmichael Show, The Doctors, The Ellen Show, The Kelly Clarkson Show, The Late Late Show with James Corden, The Masked Singer, The Neighborhood, The Price is Right, The Talk, The Upshaws, The Voice, Wheel of Fortune

NYC Shows (in alphabetical order):

All In With Chris Hayes, Always Late with Katie Nolan, America's Best Dance Crew, America's Got Talent, Best Time Ever with Neil Patrick Harris, Full Frontal with Samantha Bee, Good Morning America, GMA3- Strahan & Sara & Keke, The Daily Show with Trevor Noah, Last Week Tonight with John Oliver, Late Night with Seth Meyers, Live with Kelly and Ryan, Rachel Ray Show, Tamron Hall, The Chew, The Crew, The Late Show with Stephen Colbert, The Dr. Oz Show, The Tonight Show starring Jimmy Fallon, The View, The Voice, The Wendy Williams Show, TODAY

How to Get Tickets

Chapter 4 117

Believe it or not, shows actually need audiences to fill the seats, and most give out free tickets or even pay you to attend. Score! Some even provide free stuff and giveaways to sweeten the deal. For talk and game shows, go to the show's website for information on how to get tickets (see resource #1 below for links to shows or do an online search). These can be difficult to come by, so you may need to book 1-3 months in advance, but not always. On a trip to New York, we walked by where they filmed the David Letterman show and scored tickets to return later that day for the taping.

5 Main Show Ticket Resources

1. 1iota- link
2. Onset Productions- link
3. On Camera Audiences- link
4. Audiences Unlimited- link
5. Applause Store- link

Be a Contestant

Are you a trivia whizz and ready to become the next game show superstar? Search online to become a contestant for your desired show. There are usually eligibility rules and an application to fill out. Next thing you know, you could be getting a call and a free flight to appear on the show!

Resources

1. How To Become An Audience Member Of a TV Show link
2. How To Get TV Show Tickets In Los Angeles link
3. How To Attend Live TV Tapings In LA link
4. How To Appear On A Game Show link

Pairs well with: Patience, Hollywood Walk of Fame, NYC NYE Celebration

You might also like: Being an extra in a movie, Trivial Pursuit game, sporting events

* * *

Go Off-Roading

Get your adrenaline pumping from a big kid toy

Ready for a little off-road thrill and excitement? Jump on a grown-up toy and feel the power. There are many fun ways to hit the dirt trails and get deep into some rugged natural terrain, from renting and controlling your own quad ATV to joining a group tour with a purpose-built dirt monster. You're missing out if you've never hit the backroads or sand dunes with an all-terrain vehicle.

6 Types of All-Terrain Vehicles

1. **Quad ATV (All-Terrain Vehicle)-** Like a motorcycle but with four wheels. It can seat up to two people.
2. **UTV (Utility Task Vehicle)-** Sometimes called side-by-side vehicles (SSV) because these little open-door buggy-like vehicles hold 2-6 passengers seated side-by-side in rows. They are general-purpose vehicles that can be used for work or pleasure.
3. **Sandrail-** Custom-built buggy-like off-road vehicles for fun in sandy terrain. They usually have a stretched-out, longer look with fat tires for pushing through soft sand and steep dunes.
4. **Dune Buggy-** Similar to other side-by-side off-road vehicles but slightly larger, faster, and more built for desert terrain.
5. **Off-Road Motorcycle-** Spiked tires and made for getting radical.

Chapter 4 119

6. **4X4 Vehicles-** These could be land rovers, trucks, jeeps, or larger purpose-built vehicles that can handle rugged terrain demands.

Try them all!

Try a tour of each type of vehicle and find your favorite. Riding up and down steep giant sand dunes in a sandrail is like a thrilling roller coaster where you can explore deep into the unique landscape not possible any other way. I've taken a few sandrail tours, but by far, the best was a Sunset Sandboarding Tour in Huacachina, Peru, by Tony SandRider. The 2.5-hour private tour was less than $30 US dollars and one of the most fun activities I've ever done with the family.

4X4 tours climb over impossible boulders and traverse buttcheek-tightening vertical sections. ATVs and UTVs can be great for getting around on trails and exploring the area without as much of an emphasis on being a thrill ride. Moab, Utah, is a beautiful place to rent an ATV and explore the dirt roads and slick rock on your own. Dirt motorcycles are best for those that have 9 lives. Always inquire into how physically challenging the tour is to find out if it's a good fit for your personal health situation.

Go for it! Simple start steps:

1. Search for off-road tours in your next vacation destination or near your home.
2. Compare prices, services offered, and company reviews.
3. Go and get your heart pumping!

Resources

1. Types of Off-Road Vehicles link
2. 16 Amazing Off-Road Destinations in the US link

3. 7 of the Best Off-Road Adventures in the US link

You might also like: Mountain biking, hiking, camping

* * *

Go Whale Watching
Search for giants

If you've never set out to search for elusive sea giants like the humpback whale, add it to your list of new experiences to have and roll the dice on your luck. At best, it's a thrill as you watch whales jumping, spouting (blowing water and air high into the air), and slapping the water with their giant tail fins. At worst, it's two hours of seasickness and the launching of lunch (hopefully overboard). Whether you find whales or not, it's a great excuse to get onto the water and enjoy the beautiful ocean and shoreline scenery.

Top 10 Places in the US for Whale Watching

1. **San Juan Islands, Washington-** Orca Whales, Gray, Minke, Humpback. Mid-April to Early October.
2. **Juneau, Alaska-** Orca and Humpbacks. April to November.
3. **Monterey Bay, California-** Gray, Blue, and Humpbacks. All Year.
4. **Bar Harbor, Maine-** Minke, Fin, and Right Whales. Mid-April to October.
5. **Cape May, New Jersey-** Blue, Finback, Humpback, Minke, North Atlantic Right, Pilot. March to December.
6. **Cape Cod, Massachusetts-** Fin, Minke, Humpback Whales. April to October.
7. **Glacier Bay, Alaska-** The whales to spot are Blue Whales, Minke, Orca, and Humpback. Peak Whale Watching Season: June to August.

8. **Maui, Hawaii-** Humpback Whales. December to April.
9. **Long Island, New York-** Sperm, North Atlantic Right, Blue, Sei, Fin, Humpback, and Minke Whales. July to Early September.
10. **Virginia Beach, Virginia-** Humpback Whales. December to March.

Resources

1. 15 Best Places In The US To Whale Watch And When link
2. Top 19 Best Whale Watching Places In The World link
3. 12 Interesting Facts About Whale link

Books

1. National Geographic Secrets of the Whales by Brian Skerry link
2. Spying on Whales: The Past, Present, and Future of Earth's Most Awesome Creatures by Nick Pyenson link
3. Handbook of Whales, Dolphins, and Porpoises of the World by Mark Carwardine link

Pairs well with: Travel, sun lotion, zoom cameras

You might also like: Swimming with wild dolphins, Hawaii, scuba diving

* * *

Take an Aerobatic Biplane Ride

Feel alive in the sky

When terrestrial roller coasters aren't exciting enough, take things up to the clouds for a real thrill. Dawn your old-time aviator goggles and pop your head out into the wind. You're about to have an aerobatic biplane ride of a lifetime. After climbing to a safe height, your pilot sitting behind you asks if you're ready. You nervously nod. Game on. He starts the smoke trail generator. The pilot somehow slams on the brakes, and you start flipping and spinning unnaturally. "Oh, shoot, this is a bad idea" runs through your head. Your plane recovers from the dive, and you're suddenly barreling at breakneck speeds into a graceful arc straight up to what feels like the moon.

Eventually, gravity wins, and you completely stop in the air, facing straight up. "Oh, crud" is the newest unsettling word that comes to your mind. Smoke from the tail streamer engulfs you as you realize you're in freefall. The pilot makes a control stick adjustment, and you're flipped over, racing straight down at the earth. The horizon spins and flips as you look around. The pilot continues to do giant loops, aileron rolls, and thrilling aerobatics. You relax and let go of all fear. A massive grin fills your face for the rest of your flight. After you land, your body tingles and the excitement stays with you for many hours. You've just had the thrill of your life.

Pairs well with: Birthdays, special occasions, sunny days

You might also like: Theme parks, getting a pilot's license, hot-air balloon ride

* * *

Go to a Parade

Watch people and floats go by

There's something about the excitement of a good parade. It's a joyous celebration of a holiday or special event. People line the streets from all over the world to see giant cartoon balloons, flower floats, marching bands, dazzling costumes, equestrian riders, dancing, and even bare breasts. Whatever your fancy, there's a parade somewhere with a crowd waiting for you to join the fun. Give it a go, and you'll know if it's one and done or more to come.

. . .

The 14 Most Popular Parades in the US

1. **Macy's Thanksgiving Day Parade** (New York, New York)- Nearly 100 years old and billed as the world's largest parade with 2 to 3 million spectators. Expect 16 giant cartoon balloons, many marching bands, and a Santa finale.
2. **Rose Parade** (Pasadena, California)- Held on New Year's Day since 1890, it now contains elaborate flower floats, dancing, marching bands, and equestrian riders. Initially conceived by residents who wished to showcase the mild Southern California winters. A founder announced, "In New York, people are buried in the snow. Here, our flowers are blooming, and our oranges are about to bear. Let's hold a festival to tell the world about our paradise." The word apparently got out over the 130+ years of the parade's existence as the Los Angeles metropolitan area is the second in the US with about 12.5 million residents.
3. **Mardi Gras** (New Orleans, Louisiana)- The over-the-top celebration and parade began in 1837. Costumes, beads, drinks, and two weeks of purple, green, and gold parades.
4. **Gasparilla** (Tampa, Florida)- Established in 1904, hundreds of thousands of spectators now line the streets of Tampa in January to watch this pirate-themed parade of more than 100 elaborate floats, marching bands, and 50 different krewes (groups).
5. **St. Patrick's Day** (Chicago, Illinois)- Claiming to be the world's largest St. Patrick's Day Parade (New York also claims), as many as two million people celebrate with Irish dancers, bagpipes, floats, and even a dyed green Chicago River.
6. **Chinese New Year** (San Francisco, California)- The oldest and largest celebration of its kind outside of China. Feed the energetic lion dancers (with money) for good luck as they move to the beat of the drum, gong, and symbols.
7. **National Cherry Blossom Festival** (Washington, DC)- 3,000 cherry blossoms were gifted to the nation's

capital as a symbol of peace in 1912. Today, during peak blossom time in March and April, people enjoy the delicate pink and white flowers and an entertaining parade with over 1.5 million spectators.
8. **Pride** (New York, New York)- A massive rainbow-colored civil rights celebration for LGBTQ+.
9. **Philadelphia Mummers** (Philadelphia, Pennsylvania)- Every New Year's Day, the streets of Philly are packed with up to 10,000 musicians and costumed performers in a celebration that dates back to 1901.
10. **Fourth of July** (Alameda, California)- One of the biggest Independence Day Parades in the nation, 170 floats and 2,500 red, white, and blue participants celebrate good old America.
11. **St. Paul Winter Carnival** (St. Paul, Minnesota)- In response to visiting journalists who said Minnesota was brutally unlivable in the winter months, this winter carnival and celebration of ice and snow was the response in 1886.
12. **Seminole Hard Rock Winterfest** (Fort Lauderdale, Florida)- Boats decorated in lights are the main event of this aquatic parade that entertains up to a million spectators.
13. **Bud Billiken Parade** (Chicago, Illinois)- The largest African-American parade in the nation. The event began in 1929 and is a fundraiser for local youth.
14. **Armed Forces Day Parade** (Bremerton, Washington)- What began in 1948 to honor a local Medal of Honor recipient, the event is now the largest Armed Forces parade in the nation, with an estimated 20,000 spectators.

Resources

1. 12 Epic Parades In The US link
2. Best Parades In The World And Where To Find Them link
3. 20 of the World's Best Carnivals link
4. History of Mardi Gras link

You might also like: State fairs, sporting events, festivals

Eat a New Orleans (or Disney) Beignet

Enjoy a famous sweet treat

Not all new experiences need to be death-defying. Sometimes, it's the new little things that can sweeten your life. One such treat is the famous New Orleans Beignet. It's much more than a simple little fried piece of square dough sprinkled with powdered sugar. Served fresh and hot, it's a piece of pastry perfection. Brought to New Orleans in the 18th century by French colonists, it stayed popular among the Creole-influenced local cuisine. Cafe du Monde is the most famous bakery in New Orleans, serving beignets since 1862.

Everything seems to taste better when it's challenging to find. The travel aspect of these little pastries makes them even tastier. Give them a try on your next visit to New Orleans and be sure to try the Mickey Mouse shaped beignets at Disney's Port Orleans Hotel Resort French Quarter cafe. We sampled both on a recent RV road trip, and the family verdict was that Disney made the best!

4 Other Similar Pastries to Try

1. **Malasada-** Popular in Hawaii and with Portuguese influence, the fried ball of dough served hot with sugar on the outside can be filled with haupia (coconut custard), chocolate, or custard. Leonard's Bakery is the most famous.
2. **Churro-** Originating in Spain and Portugal and popular in Mexican cuisine, the long fried strip of dough can be dipped in chocolate or caramel and sprinkled with sugar or cinnamon.
3. **Zeppole-** An Italian fried donut ball made out of creme puff dough. Topped with powdered sugar and can be filled with custard, jelly, cannoli-style pastry cream, or a butter and honey mixture.

4. **Funnel Cake-** Originally associated with Pennsylvania Dutch and German immigrants who brought this pastry style over in the 17th and 18th centuries. The pancake-like batter is poured into hot oil through a funnel to create an overlapping mass of fried joy.

Resources

1. 100 Most Popular Fried Donut Foods Around The World link
2. What Fried Donut Looks Like Around The World link
3. Photo Proof That Nearly Every Culture Makes A Version Of Fried Dough. Because It's Delicious link

Products

1. Cafe Du Monde Beignet Mix link
2. Cafe Du Monde Coffee Chicory link
3. Mickey Mouse Shaped Cutter for Cookies, Sandwiches, Beignets link

Books

1. French Pastry 101: Learn 60 Beginner Friendly Recipes by Betty Hung link
2. Pastry Love by Joanne Chang link
3. Flour: Spectacular Recipes From Boston's Flour Bakery and Cafe by Joanne Chang link

Pairs well with: Chicory coffee, Mardi Gras, exploring New Orleans

You might also like: Po boy sandwich, gumbo, muffuletta sandwich

* * *

Take an Overnight Train Journey

Rock, roll, and clickity-clack all night long

Just when you think it's hard enough to sleep when it's dark and quiet, it's nothing compared to sleeping on a train. The motion, the noise, the adventure! It could be a new experience that forces you to get out of your comfort zone.

Unlike in the US, trains are the preferred method of long-distance travel in many places of the world. High-speed Japanese Shinkansen bullet trains race around the country at 200 mph. Without the airport waiting times, it can be more efficient than flying. In developing nations, it's a cost-effective way of moving around the country for the ordinary person.

Train travel lets you see the country you're traveling through, leaving the traffic and squished bus seats behind. An overnight ride with a sleeping area will give you the time and space to relax and take in the journey. As a bonus, you'll save a night in a hotel. While luxury trains are fine if your budget allows, don't be afraid of the ordinary trains, where you might be thrown into the mix with everyday local folks. It makes for a most memorable experience.

Some of my most memorable travel moments were on overnight trains. As a young budget backpacker, I convinced my parents to take an overnight local train from Singapore to Kuala Lumpur with my wife and me. The ride was so loud, with many locals talking over the already loud train sounds, bumpy as all get out with a fair share of "hold-on-to-your-seat" moments, and only a curtain to close off our two-level berths from the hall. Completely out of our comfort zone and with the look of "What have you gotten us into?" from my parents, we all couldn't stop laughing at the absurdity of the chaos all around us.

Another time, on an overnight train in Egypt, we sat in amazement as people jumped into the upper overhead bin space to sleep and read the Quran out loud. And finally, the most memorable overnight train was in India when I got stuck in the bathroom in the middle of the night, and no one could hear my screams for a very long time because it was too loud. Okay, perhaps I'm not selling the overnight train ride thing with some of those experiences. But it's the way to go if you're looking for a bit of adventure and possibly getting out of your comfort zone!

9 Top Train Journeys in the World

1. **The Glacial Express:** Zermatt to St. Moritz, Switzerland
2. **The Mandovi Express:** Mumbai to Madgaon, India
3. **The Tokaido Shinkansen:** Tokyo to Osaka, Japan
4. **The Riviera Railway:** Cannes, France to Ventimiglia, Italy
5. **The Venice Simplon-Orient-Express:** Venice, Italy to London, UK
6. **The Trans-Mongolian Express:** Ulaanbaatar, Mongolia to Beijing, China
7. **The Qinghai-Tibet Railway:** Xining to Lhasa, China
8. **The Sunset Limited:** New Orleans to Los Angeles, USA
9. **The Rupert Rocket:** Jasper to Prince Rupert, Canada

9 Top Train Trips in the USA

1. **Durango to Silverton, CO:** Narrow Gauge Railroad. Winding between 14,000' peaks, this scenic 45-mile wild west experience has been rolling since 1882.
2. **Denver to Moab:** Rocky Mountaineer "Rockies to the Red Rocks" trip. Two days of luxury from the Rocky Mountains to the southwest.
3. **LA to Seattle:** Coast Starlight trip. The 1,377-mile scenic coastal route takes in the best of the west.

4. **Williams to the Grand Canyon:** The Grand Canyon Railway. A historic 2-hour 15-minute ride through breathtaking scenery from Williams, Arizona, to the South Rim.
5. **Chicago to Portland:** Empire Builder. Forty-six epic hours along much of the same route Lewis and Clark took to discover the west coast.
6. **Anchorage to Fairbanks:** Alaska Denali Star. 350 miles through the heart of Alaska's rugged wilderness.
7. **Bryson City, NC:** Great Smoky Mountains Railroad. Take in the fall colors with this adventurous 4.5-hour Nantahala Gorge excursion.
8. **Bretton Woods, NH:** Mount Washington Cog Railway. Jump on this antique train with sweeping views as it chugs up to the highest point in the Northeast (6,288 feet).
9. **Napa Valley, CA:** The Napa Valley Wine Train. Let your eyes take in the lush rows of vines while your mouth sips some wines. This rolling restaurant serves lunch and dinner in an antique vintage style.

15 **Eurail Passes**: Eurail offers a range of passes for non-European residents, allowing unlimited travel within multiple European countries or a single country. Some options include:

1. **Eurail Global Pass:** Offers unlimited travel in multiple European countries over a specific period.
2. **Eurail Select Pass:** Allows travel in a specific group of countries.
3. **Eurail One Country Pass:** Provides unlimited travel within a single European country.
4. **InterRail Passes**: InterRail is for European residents and offers similar options to Eurail but is specific to European countries.
5. **Swiss Travel Pass**: Provides unlimited travel on Switzerland's excellent rail network, as well as access to

buses, boats, and trams. It also includes free admission to many museums.
6. **German Rail Pass**: Offers unlimited travel on Germany's extensive rail network, including high-speed trains. It also covers certain bus and ferry services within Germany.
7. **France Rail Pass**: Allows unlimited travel on the French national rail network, including TGV (high-speed trains), Intercités, and regional trains.
8. **Benelux Pass**: Covers travel in Belgium, the Netherlands, and Luxembourg, offering flexibility and unlimited train travel within this region.
9. **BritRail Pass**: Designed for travelers exploring the United Kingdom, this pass allows unlimited travel on the British rail network, including England, Scotland, and Wales.
10. **Eastern European Passes**: Various passes are available for exploring Eastern European countries like Hungary, Poland, Czech Republic, Slovakia, and others.
11. **Scandinavia Pass**: This pass covers travel in Norway, Sweden, Denmark, and Finland, offering great flexibility for exploring the Nordic countries.
12. **Spain Pass**: Ideal for travelers exploring Spain, this pass offers unlimited travel on the Spanish rail network, including high-speed AVE trains.
13. **Italy Pass**: Provides unlimited travel in Italy, allowing you to explore the beautiful country by train.
14. **Balkan Flexipass**: Covers travel in several Balkan countries like Bulgaria, Greece, Montenegro, Serbia, North Macedonia, and Turkey.
15. **Global Passes**: Some passes offer global coverage, allowing travelers to explore multiple countries across Europe with a single pass.

Resources

1. These are the Best Train Journeys in the World link

Chapter 4   131

2. Readers' Choice Best Trains in the World link
3. The Man in Seat Sixty-One (Train Riding Resource) link

Books

1. Amazing Train Journeys by Lonely Planet link
2. Around the World In 80 Trains by Monisha Rajesh link
3. Trains: The Worlds Most Scenic Routes by Publications International LTD link

Pairs well with: Cheese and wine, binoculars, ear plugs/ music

You might also like: Cruising, group tours, unique Airbnb stays

* * *

See the Northern Lights
Become captivated by colorful dancing waves in the sky

The colorful skyward spectacle, known as the Northern Lights or Aurora Borealis, has captivated humanity since the beginning. Like something out of a fairytale, green, purple, and red waves dance across the dark northern sky. The natural phenomenon happens when the sun's energized particles impact our atmosphere's magnetic field. It's a bucket list-worthy event for many wanting to see the celestial show with their own eyes.

Did you know?

- The best place to see the Northern Lights is within the 1,500-mile radius of the magnetic north pole, including Norway, Finland, Sweden, Canada, Alaska, Russia, Iceland, and Greenland.
- Unpredictable strong solar winds called geomagnetic storms can move the Northern lights much further south, even into the US.

- The dark northern skies outside summer are best for viewing this year-round phenomenon, usually peaking around the spring and fall equinoxes (March and September).
- There is a Southern Lights, but its remoteness makes it much more difficult to see.

Resources

1. The Northern Lights: What they are and how to see them link
2. Northern Lights, Explained link
3. 12 Best Places to See The Northern Lights Around The World link

Books

1. The Northern Lights: Celestial Performances of The Aurora Borealis by Daryl Pederson link
2. Spirits in the Sky: Northern Lights Photography by Paul Zizka link
3. Aurora: In Search Of The Northern Lights by Dr. Melanie Windridge link

Pairs well with: Dog sled rides, ice hotels, hot chocolate

You might also like: Visiting the seven wonders of the world, cruising, climbing Mt. Fuji

* * *

Go Ax-Throwing

Feel like a Viking

When delicate little darts don't cut it, try ax throwing. Seriously, it's a thing. There are businesses dedicated to ax throwing. You'll first learn the proper technique from an onsite coach, then stand behind a line and let it fly toward the bullseye. Groups of two or more compete for the highest score after five throws. If you can tap into your warrior ancestry and get good, you might enjoy competing in ax-throwing leagues. Some locations even offer a ninja package where you can throw knives, throwing stars, metal playing cards, and even a tactical throwing shovel!

6 Similar Throwing Sports

1. Knife throwing
2. Archery
3. Darts
4. Slingshot
5. Wood Chopping- Attempt to cut or saw a log quickly.
6. Lumberjack- Many events, including log rolling, chopping, pole climbing, and power saw cutting.

Resources

1. Ax Throwing 101 link

Pairs well with: Drinks, friends, bottled-up anger

You might also like: Bowling, billiards, table shuffleboard

***

Learn to Fly

Follow in the Wright Brothers' footsteps

When the Wright brothers made the first controlled powered aircraft flight in 1903, they ushered in a new age for humankind. Conquering the sky has revolutionized and shrunk our world, allowing us to travel in hours, which previously took months. With a bit of bravery and determination, you can gain your pilot's license and do what was impossible for most of history- fly!

. . .

Why fly?

I learned to fly because, like many others, I had dreams of flying like a superhero when I was young. The freedom to take to the sky and go wherever I wanted was incredibly enticing. While soaring with only a cape and superpowers was just a fantasy, looking down on the world as a pilot was an achievable reality. You don't have to be from Krypton to experience the thrill of being in control as you rise above mountains, come close to puffy white clouds, or gaze forward into the unlimited horizon at sunset. Just become a pilot.

How it Works

The US national average private pilot's license cost is about $10,000. You'll need a minimum number of flight hours and instruction time before being eligible to take a written, oral, and flight test to gain your license. The major cost is the airplane rental fee of about $100-150 an hour (depending on the aircraft type) and the hourly instructor fee of about $50. You'll also need a pair of headphones, a flight computer, maps, a flight logbook, and books to study.

Besides physically learning how to operate the plane, you'll learn about meteorology, aerodynamics, airspace classifications, Federal Aviation Regulations (FARs), flight planning, and more. If you'd like to dip your toe in before diving into flying, pick up the colorful and well-written Jeppesen Private Pilot Manual textbook and see if you're interested in the topics.

Did you know?

- There are over 160,000 certified pilots in the US.
- No license or certification is required to fly an ultralight aircraft.
- More than 650,000 aviation enthusiasts attended the world's greatest week-long airshow, EAA Airventure, in

Oshkosh, Wisconsin, in 2022. It's an amazing spectacle, I highly recommend.
- Commercial Aviation is much safer than driving. General Aviation is roughly as safe as riding a motorcycle.

Go for it! Simple start steps:

1. Google search for flight schools near you.
2. Read reviews and contact your top three locations.
3. Visit the schools to learn about them and do a fun introductory flight.

Resources

1. How much do flying lessons cost? link
2. Federal Aviation Regulations Pilots Portal link
3. King Schools Study Guides Videos Courses link
4. EAA AirVenture, the ultimate Airshow link

Products

1. Aviation Headset link
2. Flight Bag link
3. Vintage Aviator Hat and Goggles link

Books

1. Jeppesson Private Pilot Manual link
2. Pilot's Handbook of Aeronautical Knowledge FAA-H-8083-25B link
3. Airplane Flying Handbook: FAA-H-8083-3C link

You might also like: Getting a helicopter license, gyrocopter flying, remote pilot certification

***

Visit a Mosque and Different Places of Worship
Peak into different cultures' holy places

One of the best parts of travel is experiencing the unfamiliar. When we head into the unknown, it broadens our life experience, seeing how people from all over the world live differently from us. Cuisine, sports, art, language, values, architecture, and religion are exciting cultural differences to explore and discover in every new country.

Visiting the local places of worship is a great way to broaden our minds, get a glimpse into a new culture, and learn about potentially unfamiliar traditions and practices. It's always fascinating to me to learn about local religious celebrations, see important relics, and view some of the most opulent buildings and works of art you'll see anywhere. There are centuries-old churches in Europe that will take your breath away. Buddhist temples worldwide vary widely by region, from Japan's traditional wooden structures with giant golden statues inside to Thailand's pointed, elaborate golden buildings and colorful insides, and everything in between. There are Hindu temples, Jewish synagogues, Islamic mosques, and many more exceptional religious buildings to explore.

Going inside a mosque is a foreign experience for many of us Westerners. It usually means we'll be visiting an Islamic country with very different cultural practices. We'll hear an enchanting call to prayer blasting from loudspeakers out of each mosque's tall minaret tower to all areas of a city five times a day. Women will wear a head covering and many other cultural differences. It will grow your comfort level as you learn about a culture that is very different from ours.

3 Istanbul, Turkey Mosques

Istanbul is often considered the crossroads of Eastern and Western culture. It was inhabited and made the capital of some of the most famous empires throughout history. First came the Greeks, then the Romans, then the Ottoman Empire, before finally gaining independence. Their mosques are some of the most beautiful and historic in the world.

1. **Blue Mosque-** An Ottoman-era historical imperial mosque completed in 1616.
2. **Hagia Sophia-** This mosque was originally a Greek Orthodox church from 360 AD until the conquest of Constantinople by the Ottoman Turks in 1453. It served as a mosque until 1935, when it became a museum.
3. **Süleymaniye Mosque-** This second-largest mosque in Istanbul was completed in 1557.

Major Religions of the World Fun Facts

- 85% of the world's population identifies with a religion. The most popular religions in 2020 are Christianity (2.38 billion), Islam (1.91 billion), Hinduism (1.16 billion), Buddhism (507 million), Folk Religions (430 million combined traditional African religions, Chinese folk religions, and both Native American and Australian aboriginal religions), Other religions (61 million combined catch-all that tracks smaller faiths such as Shintoism, Taoism, Sikhism, and Jainism), Judaism (14.6 million), Non-religious (1.19 billion).
- Countries with the highest percentage of non-religious populations are China, Estonia, the Czech Republic, Japan, Denmark, France, Hong Kong, Macau, Norway, Sweden, and Vietnam.
- Countries whose populations are at least 93% Christian: Vatican City, Pitcairn Islands, American Samoa, Armenia, Barbados, East Timor, El Salvador, Greece, Kiribati, Malta, Marshall Islands, Micronesia, Papua New Guinea, Paraguay, Peru, Romania, Samoa, San Marino, Tonga, and Venezuela.

- Countries whose populations are at least 95% Muslim: Maldives, Mauritania, Saudi Arabia, Afghanistan, Algeria, Comoros, Iran, Iraq, Kuwait, Libya, Morocco, Pakistan, Somalia, Sudan, Tunisia, Turkey, and Yemen.
- Countries with the highest percentage of Buddhists: Cambodia, Thailand, Burma/Myanmar, Sri Lanka, Laos, Mongolia, and Bhutan.
- Countries with a large number of Hindus: India, Nepal, Bangladesh, Indonesia, Pakistan, Sri Lanka, United States, Malaysia, United Kingdom, and Mauritius.
- About 3 out of 4 Americans are religious, and over 80% of Americans 75 and older are Christian.

Resources

1. 21 of The Most Beautiful Sacred Sites That Every Traveler Should Visit link
2. 26 Stunning Churches, Mosques, And Temples Around The World link
3. The Future of Religion in America link
4. Religion by Country link

Books

1. Mosques: Splendors of Islam by Leyla Uluhanli link
2. Amazing Churches of The World by Michael Kerrigan link
3. Zen Gardens and Temples of Kyoto by John Dougill link
4. Rose Book of Bible Charts, Maps, and Timelines by Rose Publishing link

* * *

Learn to Play Guitar

Become a campfire entertainer

Set a goal to learn a few guitar songs and unveil your new talent around the campfire with friends! Learning a musical instrument is a bucket list item for many people. Still, somehow, life gets in the way, and it ends up just a far-off fantasy. Finally free from work time restraints, this could be the perfect time to become a musician and live that fantasy.

Set a performance date.

It's easy to get started on something that takes effort and practice, then slowly lose motivation and never really learn the new skill. Setting a goal in the near future to perform in front of others will keep you motivated and provide a sense of accomplishment. Lock in a date, whether it be a camping trip, a holiday get-together, a birthday, or a low-key house party with a few friends, and get started learning your set of songs.

How to learn?

There are free tutorials on YouTube, video courses online, apps that hear your notes and can tutor you as you play, music teachers, and songbooks for learning just about every song.

Learn with Guitar Learning Apps

Forget about trying to figure out how to play from confusing books or even expensive in-person instruction, guitar learning apps are the way to go. You'll have access to hundreds of popular songs to learn, a curriculum with bite-sized video lessons, chord and scale diagrams, background accompanying music, and even the ability to analyze your playing and provide feedback. They'll add a touch of gaming fun as you see your results while playing and challenge yourself to do better.

6 Apps to Learn Guitar

1. **Fender Guitar Tuner (free)-** Gone are the days of needing a tuning fork, a great ear, or a separate device to tune your instrument. This app helps tune your electric guitar, acoustic guitar, bass, or ukulele. It also has 5,000 interactive guitar chords and 2,000 interactive guitar scales showing finger placement diagrams and their sounds.
2. **Fender Play-** Learn guitar, bass, and ukulele.
3. **Ultimate Guitar: Chords & Tabs-** The world's most extensive catalog of guitar, bass, and ukulele chords, tabs, and lyrics to learn your favorite songs.
4. **Gibson: Guitar lessons & Tuner-** Interactive lessons and real-time feedback.
5. **Yousician: Guitar Lessons-** For guitar, bass, and singing lessons.
6. **Simply Guitar-** Step-by-step tutorials.

7 Benefits of Learning Music

1. **Brain growth-** Studies in neuroscience show that music can enhance brain functions. Learning coordinated hand movements, as well as hearing and recognizing notes, stimulates and strengthens the brain.
2. **Enhances memory, attention, and concentration-** Learning music requires a significant level of concentration, attention to detail, and memory—all are important brain functions to keep sharp as we age.
3. **Increased coordination-** Learning music develops motor skills and helps the body and mind work together.
4. **Achievement and discipline-** To learn music, you'll need to work toward short-term goals, develop a routine, and practice self-discipline. Mastering a song leads to a sense of pride and achievement.

5. **Social growth-** Making music with other people brings people closer and provides a social outlet that can be very fulfilling.
6. **Creativity-** Learning the art of music will allow you to experiment with new sounds, create songs, and express your creativity.
7. **Any age fun-** No matter the age, you and the people around you can enjoy the joy of music.

I was in high school with dreams of becoming a rockstar when I started learning electric guitar in my bedroom. Somehow, we pieced together a band among friends and spent many loud nights in the garage having fun and preparing for our big break, my sister's backyard graduation party. The day came, and we performed our set to a few family and friends. Shortly after, someone moved, and the band fell apart. Rockstar dreams drifted away, but fond memories (and now mysterious ringing in my ears) remain.

Go for it! Simple start steps:

1. Go to a music store, try a few guitars, and purchase one.
2. Download a few guitar learning apps and choose the one you like best.
3. Set a "performance" date and start learning to play.

Resources

1. Free online guitar lessons link
2. Beginners Guide to Guitar link
3. Fender Beginners Hub link

Products

1. Fender Dreadnought Acoustic Guitar link

2. Electric Guitar & Amp link
3. Popular Ukulele link

Books

1. Teach Yourself to Play Guitar by David Brewster link
2. Acoustic Guitar Primer Book for Beginners by Bert Casey link
3. 21 Songs in 6 Days: Learn Ukulele by Rebecca Bogart link

Pairs well with: Recording your own song, singing lessons, picnic blankets

You might also like: Visiting the Country Music Awards Show, New Orleans Jazz Festival, learning the piano

* * *

Learn to Surf

Stand on water and connect with the ocean

If you live near the ocean, it's never too late to connect with Mother Nature and enjoy the benefits of surfing. While you may have seen young competitive surfers on short boards aggressively shredding massive waves for the highest scores, the average surfer is in the water for different reasons. Sitting in the lineup waiting for the occasional wave, you'll feel the rhythm of the ocean, see its beauty, and become focused on the moment. Staring out along the watery horizon, free of distracting thoughts, it's easy to feel a great sense of peace followed by the occasional excitement of seeing a great wave heading your way. Frantically paddling into position for what could be the perfect wave, standing up at just the right moment as it breaks, and gliding down the face with sudden speed is thrilling and addicting at any age.

There's a reason there is a subculture of surfers whose only desire is finding the perfect wave. Surf friends enjoy conversation while waiting for waves. The excitement of a few decent waves, exercise, and the extremely relaxed feeling following a great surf session make surfing an ideal hobby.

Longboard Love

The best way to learn to surf is on a longboard. The surf breaks are full of older folks on them. They are more buoyant and thick than shortboards, making them easier to paddle and catch waves with. Floating above the water, there is less drag so that riders can catch smaller and less steep waves. The big boards are more stable to stand on, and as a bonus, the rides will last longer since only a tiny push from the wave is needed to keep surfing.

Did you know?

- Surfing can burn up to 400 calories an hour.
- Surfing is excellent for cardio fitness, muscle strengthening, and balance building.
- Surfing is 95% paddling and waiting.
- Soft-top longboard surfboards are great beginner boards because they are inexpensive, cushioned, forgiving, and perform well.

Go for it! Simple start steps:

1. Search Groupon or local surf shops for longboard surf lessons.
2. Follow the instructor's lessons and catch your first wave.
3. Decide if you'd like to purchase your own surfboard and related gear.

Resources

1. Silver Surfers: A guide to surfing for older adults [link](#)

2. Learning to surf over age 50: 10 tips link
3. Golden Rules for Longboard Surfing link

Products

1. 9-foot Soft Top Surfboard link
2. Longboard soft vehicle rack link
3. Overhead Surfboard Storage Rack link

Books

1. Longboarders Start-up Guide by Doug Werner link
2. The History of Surfing by Matt Warshaw link
3. Surfer Magazine: 1960-2020 by Grant Ellis link

Pairs well with: Sunscreen, wetsuit, Mexican food

You might also like: Stand-up paddle boarding (SUP), snorkeling, kayaking

* * *

Get a Motorcycle License

Find freedom and excitement on two wheels

Perhaps you once dreamt of two-wheel freedom cruising down an open country road, immersed in your surroundings and feeling alive and in the moment. Retirement is the perfect time to reconnect with your old dreams and make them a reality.

First Steps

Experiencing the thrill of motorcycle riding doesn't require a lot of money or even the commitment of purchasing a motorcycle at all. To ride, you'll first need a motorcycle license. Before you can get the license, most areas offer classes that provide beginner motorcycles and instruction in a closed-track parking lot environment. It's a great way to safely build up your riding skills and test out your excitement with motorcycle riding before deciding if you'd like to someday purchase a motorcycle for yourself.

Once you pass your riding and written test and receive a new driver's license with the motorcycle endorsement, you can test ride and rent motorcycles at home or while on vacation. The added excitement of experiencing a new location by rented motorcycle can turn an ordinary vacation into an extraordinary one.

Unlock Future Possibilities

Years ago, a coworker convinced me to take a motorcycle training course with him while he was considering purchasing a bike. I had no intention of buying a motorcycle, but I thought learning would be fun. A local community college offered an inexpensive new rider safety class with about 7 hours of class instruction and 11 hours of skills training. I never used my motorcycle license for several years until my wife's birthday. I rented a Harley and drove around our island of Oahu with her on the back. We took the back roads, cruising through pineapple fields, along windy ocean roads, and around sheer cliffs. Riding out in the open on the motorcycle, feeling the wind, and seeing everything unobstructed was an incredible thrill and made for a wonderful birthday surprise.

Did you know?

- Every year in August since 1938, up to 700,000 motorcyclists from all over the US ride to Sturgis, South Dakota, for the biggest motorcycle rally in the world.
- There is a subtle wave most motorcyclists do to each other when riding by each other from opposite directions.
- Honda is the largest manufacturer of motorcycles in the world, producing about 28% of all motorcycles.

Go for it! Simple start steps:

1. Search for a motorcycle safety training course near you.
2. Enjoy learning to ride.
3. Take the exam with your local Department of Motor Vehicles (or equivalent) and get a motorcycle endorsement on your state driver's license.

Resources

1. Motorcycle Safety link
2. Annual Sturgis Motorcycle Rally link
3. How much does a motorcycle cost link

Products

1. Motorcycle phone mount link
2. Motorcycle gloves link
3. Motorcycle mask link

Books

1. Best Road Trips in the USA by Fodor's link
2. The most scenic drives in America by Readers Digest link
3. Motorcycle Journeys through North America by Dale Coyner link

Pairs well with: Road trips, weekend motorcycle ride groups, travel

You might also like: E-biking, convertible cars, ATV

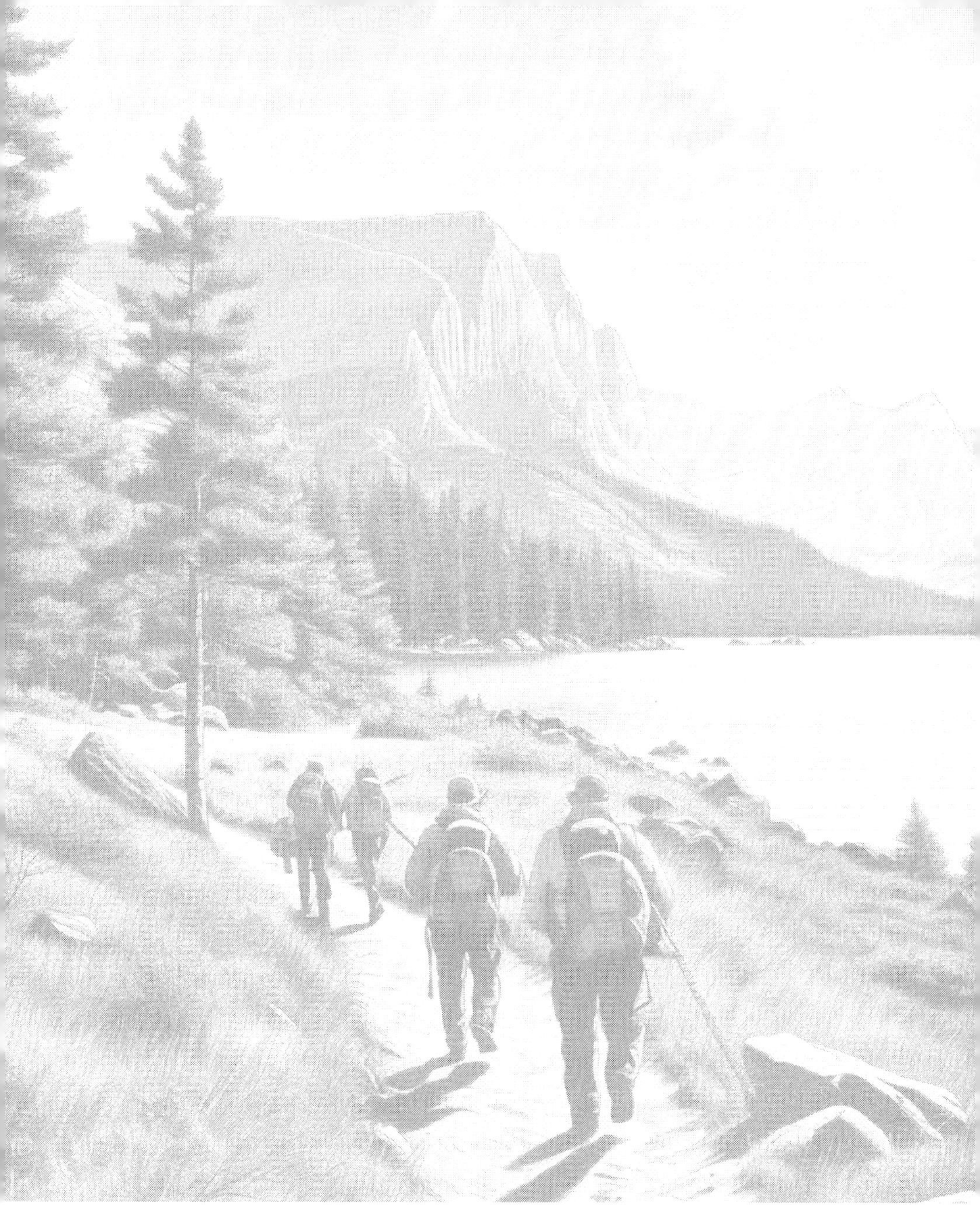

Chapter 5

Social Opportunities

As we age, our social circles tend to shrink. We may retire from our jobs, our children may move away, and our friends may pass on. But this doesn't mean we have to be lonely. In fact, retirement can be an opportunity to expand our social horizons and make new connections that enrich our lives.

Whether through shared hobbies, volunteering, or simply striking up a conversation with a stranger, human connection is an essential part of a fulfilling life. There are countless ways to find social opportunities in retirement, and the key is to find what resonates with you.

Perhaps you find yourself drawn to the arts, and joining a local theater group or attending poetry readings is the perfect way to meet like-minded individuals. Or maybe you have a passion for nature, and joining a hiking or bird-watching group can offer the chance to bond over a shared appreciation for the great outdoors. Whatever your interests may be, there is likely a group or organization that brings together people who share those same passions.

One of the beauties of retirement is the freedom to try new things and explore new interests. This can include joining clubs or groups that are outside of your comfort zone, allowing you to expand your social circle and develop new connections. From salsa dancing to language classes, there are countless opportunities to meet new people and learn new skills. As you continue to connect with others and build new friendships, your retirement can become a beautiful tapestry of social experiences that bring joy to your golden years.

50 Social Opportunities for Retirees

1. Join a local community center.
2. Volunteer at a nonprofit organization.
3. Attend a book club.
4. Join a knitting or sewing group.
5. Take dance lessons.
6. Join a choir or singing group.
7. Attend a cooking class.
8. Join a gardening club.
9. Attend a painting or art class.
10. Join a hiking or walking group.
11. Attend a language class.
12. Join a bridge or card game group.
13. Participate in a local theater group.
14. Join a photography club.
15. Attend a lecture series.
16. Join a bird-watching group.
17. Participate in a local sports league.
18. Join a yoga or meditation group.
19. Attend a film club.
20. Join a writing or poetry group.
21. Attend a music festival or concert.
22. Participate in a community clean-up event.
23. Join a genealogy group.
24. Attend a trivia night.
25. Join a board game group.
26. Participate in a local charity event.
27. Join a debate or discussion group.
28. Attend a craft fair or market.
29. Join a fishing or hunting group.

Chapter 5 151

30. Participate in a charity walk or run.
31. Join a spiritual or religious group.
32. Attend a wine-tasting event.
33. Join a travel group.
34. Participate in a local history group.
35. Join a bowling or bocce ball league.
36. Join a fantasy football or fantasy basketball league.
37. Join a motorcycle or car club.
38. Participate in a local protest or rally.
39. Join a cycling or biking group.
40. Attend a farmers' market or food festival.
41. Join a movie or film club.
42. Participate in a local mentorship program.
43. Join a board of directors for a nonprofit.
44. Attend a political rally or event.
45. Join a theater or drama club.
46. Participate in a local art festival.
47. Join a birdhouse building group.
48. Attend a literary festival or conference.
49. Join a chess or checkers group.
50. Participate in a local talent show or open mic night.

Chapter 5 Website Links

Social Opportunities and Tips from Volume 1:
Activities to Stay Social (43 ideas) - Do Things for Others (20 ideas) - Connect Through Sports and Games (42 ideas) - Make Someone Laugh (20 ideas)

Join a Bowling League
Strike it up with friends

Whether you're a star athlete or have no real competitive drive, joining a bowling league can be a ton of fun for anyone.

7 Benefits of Bowling

1. **Social-** Bowling is a great way to regularly meet up with friends and meet new ones.
2. **Excitement-** Whether by luck or skill, getting a strike or spare feels fantastic.
3. **Scheduled-** Spice up your week with a little something to look forward to.
4. **Exercise-** You're using your body to increase strength and flexibility.
5. **Unwind-** A chance to forget about whatever was on your mind that day and relax.
6. **Stay Sharp-** You'll strengthen your mind while focusing on knocking over pins.
7. **Fun-** Bowling is a game, and games are for fun.

Go for it! Simple start steps:

1. Search online for bowling alleys near you.
2. Visit and ask about leagues.
3. Recruit some friends for a team or sign up to join an open one.

Resources

1. Tips for Senior Bowling Practice link
2. How to Bowl link
3. Bowling Cheat Sheet link

Products

1. Bowling Wrist Positioner link
2. Bowling Shoes link
3. Rolling Bowling Bag link

Books

1. Bowling Fundamentals by Michelle Mullen link
2. Personal Score Book by E. Gijon link
3. Amazing Sports Trivia by Michael Schleuter link

Pairs well with: Beer, trivia and jokes, muscle cream

You might also like: Lawn bowling leagues, shuffleboard leagues, pickleball leagues

* * *

Work at a Sporting Venue

Feel the excitement of your favorite team and make some money

Many retired people choose to take a casual part-time job for social or financial reasons. If you're a sports fan with a favorite local team, consider a job working at the nearby stadium or arena where they play. You'll gain access to the event, feel a part of the excitement, and perhaps gain other behind-the-scenes perks as well.

Retirement flexibility is great for employers looking for available staff at odd times, such as mid-day or evening games. Also, a previous career and more life experience could open up better positions that require a more trustworthy older person.

One of my favorite part-time jobs was in college at the local professional baseball stadium. I worked as a money runner, delivering change from the vault to the food concessions. A retired policeman with a concealed weapon permit accompanied me as I went around to where I was needed. We'd often stop and watch the game with the fans during slow times or when something exciting happened. Our team made it to the World Series that year, and I felt lucky to be there and enjoy the electric atmosphere. The retired police officers I worked with were all big fans and loved the part-time job as well.

Go for it! Simple start steps:

1. Search for jobs at your local stadium or sporting venue.
2. Update your resume to fit the available position(s) and apply.
3. Have fun, meet fellow fans, and make a little extra money to play with.

Resources

1. MVP Event Staffing link
2. Indeed Event Staff Employers link
3. Stadium Jobs link

You might also like: Sports photography jobs, online sports wagering, golf event jobs

* * *

Take Dance Lessons

Move to the rhythm of the night

Whether you have fancy feet or two left feet, it's never too late to learn to dance. In fact, dancing is one of the best activities for seniors to help fight back the effects of aging. With so many dance styles to choose from and more ways than ever to learn, shaking your booty could be the perfect way to strengthen your mind, body, and spirit.

10 Reasons to Learn to Dance

Mind Strengthening:

- **Memory Improvement-** Keeping the mind active and stimulated helps fight against age-related memory loss. Learning dance moves has been shown to improve memory and even prevent the onset of dementia. Cognitive skills such as planning and organizing also improve.
- **Minimize Stress-** Partner dance with music has been shown to relieve stress, increase serotonin levels (the feel-good hormone), and increase mood.
- **Reduce Depression-** A study looking into dance and depression showed patients in a lively dance group had lower levels of depression symptoms, were more upbeat, and had higher energy levels as a result of dance.

Body Strengthening:

- **Improved Flexibility-** Dance movements increase flexibility and reduce stiffness.
- **Weight Loss-** Aerobic dance movements can help you lose as much weight as other activities like jogging or biking.
- **Increased Energy-** A weekly dance program has been shown to increase energy and improve adults' physical performance.
- **Coordination, Strength, and Balance-** Controlling the body through dance helps tone muscles and improve posture and balance.
- **Cardiovascular-** Getting the heart beating faster through dance can lead to a stronger and healthier heart.

Spirit Strengthening:

- **Improved Social & Emotional Health-** Dance classes are a great way to meet new people and get together with friends. Positive relationships have been shown to increase feelings of happiness, reduce stress, and lead to a stronger immune system.
- **Confidence & Self-Esteem-** Dancing has been shown to increase reported levels of confidence and self-esteem.

Popular Senior Dance Styles

- Jazz
- Salsa
- Line
- Waltz
- Tap
- Ballet
- Ballroom
- Belly Dance
- Hula
- Square
- Seated Dancing or Chair Aerobics

Other Dance Styles

- Hip Hop
- Swing
- Video Games
- Tango
- Contemporary
- Famous Dances (Macarena, Thriller, etc.)
- Clogging
- Contra
- Flamenco

- Breakdancing!
- Pole Dancing!

5 Ways to Learn Dance

1. Private dance lessons
2. Group dance lessons
3. Video lessons (purchased or YouTube)
4. Movement tracking video games (Nintendo Switch Just Dance Game, etc.)
5. Practice on your own for fun

5 Free Online Dance Lessons

1. www.movewithcolour.com link
2. "Learn How to Dance" channel on YouTube link
3. www.tapdancingresources.com link
4. www.ballroomdancers.com link
5. "Senior Dance" search on YouTube

Go for it! Simple start steps:

1. Decide the type of dance to learn.
2. Sign up for a dance class or choose to learn by another method.
3. Show up or get started.

Resources

1. Arthur Murray Dance Studios link
2. 11 Fun Online Dance Classes link

158　　　　　　　Social Opportunities

    3. Dance Exercises for Seniors link

Products

    1. Dance Lessons 101 DVD link
    2. Electronic Dance Mat Video Game link
    3. Line Dancing DVD link
    4. Just Dance Nintendo Switch Game link
    5. Chair Dancing DVD link

Books

    1. Dancing with Arthritis at age 86 by H.B. Jones link
    2. Appreciating Dance by Editors of Dance Horizons link
    3. Taking the Lead by Derrek Hough link

Pairs well with: Fun nights on the town, Bluetooth headphones, comfy shoes

You might also like: Music lessons, Tai Chi, art classes

* * *

Become a Beer Judge

Award your good taste

In the 6,000 years or so since humans have been brewing and drinking beer, it's natural that a few different variations have emerged. In fact, over 100 different styles of ales, lagers, and hybrid beers exist. From the typical mass-produced American lager you probably think of as a beer to lesser-known styles such as Geuze and Kvass, you might have never tasted.

The recent proliferation of small breweries has rekindled the art of brewing, and there are now more great beers to explore with your taste buds than ever. Many beer-judging competitions exist throughout the US to separate the best beers from the rest. From professional brewery beers to aspiring homebrewer concoctions, someone has to have the difficult job of sampling and rating them all. It might as well be you!

Too many beer styles?

Are you tired of the same-tasting generic beer? There is a world of different beer styles to explore. Here are a few. Cream Ale, Wheat, Pale, Amber, Dark, Munich Helles, Helles Bock, English Porter, Hefeweizen, Doppelbock, Kolsch, German Pils, Scottish Ale, Oatmeal Stout, Irish Stout, California Common, Lambic, Gueuze, IPA, Double IPA, Triple IPA, Belgian Tripel, Smoked, Barrel Aged, Porter, Gose...

How to become a beer judge?

You'll want to get certified by the Beer Judge Certification Program (BJCP). BJCP was created in 1985 as a way to establish well-rounded judges to improve the quality of homebrew beer. The qualified, unbiased reviews and feedback brewers need to improve recipes help raise the standards of homebrew and commercial beers, as well as mead and cider, in competitions worldwide. Below are the steps to becoming a BJCP beer judge.

1. **Study.** Learn about the examination process and grab a BJCP study guide to become familiar with style guidelines. Each style's overall impression, aroma, flavor, and mouthfeel are evaluated. You'll learn its history, ingredients, vital statistics such as alcohol levels and bitterness, and commercial examples to calibrate your taste buds.
2. **Pass an online entrance exam ($10).** There are 180 multiple-choice and true-false questions over 60 minutes. Once passed, you'll have one year to take the practical tasting exam.
3. **Pass the BJCP judging exam ($40).** You'll taste and evaluate six beers in a competition-like setting. A score of 60+ will earn the entry-level beer judge rank. Later

experience points can be earned through competitions, allowing higher rankings.

Beer Fun Facts To Impress Your Friends

- Considered "the divine drink," beer was first consumed from bowls with straws by the Mesopotamian Sumerians as early as 4000 BC.
- Archaeologists found an ode to Ninkasi, the patron goddess of brewing, which contained the oldest known recipe for making beer using barley from bread.
- In 1040 AD, the monks at Weihenstephan Abbey in Bavaria, Germany, began brewing in what is now the oldest continuously operating brewery in the world.
- McDonald's serves beer in many parts of the world, such as Germany, Spain, and South Korea.
- Beer is the most consumed alcoholic drink in the world and the third most consumed drink after water and tea.
- In 1983, there were 49 licensed breweries in the US. Today there are over 9,000.
- The moon has a crater named Beer.
- California has the most breweries in the United States (about 1,000), twice as much as second-place New York.
- Budweiser, Corona, and 500 other beers are now owned by a Belgian company, AB InBev, the world's largest beer company.
- George Washington and Thomas Jefferson were homebrewers.
- Benjamin Franklin's often-cited quote and popular college dorm poster, "Beer is proof that God loves us and wants us to be happy," is misquoted. He was referring to wine when he said something similar.

Homebrewing and Beer Judging

If you're into homebrewing, becoming a beer judge is a natural progression. I had been cranking out some beers at home of questionable quality and wanted to hone my pallet to understand what a gold medal beer should really taste like. After passing the online exam, I signed up for the judging exam a few months away, and to my delight, there was a "sensory training" course leading up to the test. About 20 of us met in a classroom once a week after work and "studied" the beer styles brought in and led by a current BJCP National Judge. It was a lot of fun and extremely helpful for passing the judging exam. What was also helpful was my background in homebrewing.

Judges are expected to rate the beers in competition and, where necessary, provide feedback to the brewers about flaws usually found because something went wrong in the brewing process. Incorrect fermentation temperatures, oxidation, over-carbonation, improper sanitation, and others can lead to distinct unwanted flavors in the beer. Because of my mediocre homebrewing background, I had an advantage in picking out the flaws in other beers!

Go for it! Simple start steps:

1. Go onto the BJCP website and look for a judging exam near you. Study for the entrance exam.
2. Take the BJCP online entrance exam.
3. Sign up for the BJCP judging exam.

Resources

1. BJCP Certification Program link
2. Beer Styles link
3. Homebrewers Association link
4. BJCP Exam Calendar link

Products

1. Assorted Beer Glasses link
2. Beer Flight Set link
3. All in One Beer Brewing Machine link
4. Portable Breath Alcohol Tester link

Books

1. Beer Bible by Jeff Alworth link
2. Tasting Beer by Randy Mosher link
3. Atlas of Beer by National Geographic link

***

Grow a Relationship

Nurture a friendship

James and Beth had been married for what seemed like an eternity. They had built a life together, raised children, and watched their grandchildren grow up. However, despite all the memories they had created together, James had taken Beth for granted. He was so busy living his life that he never stopped to really appreciate her and the love she had for him.

It wasn't until James got sick that he realized how much he truly needed Beth. He was bedridden and unable to do anything for himself, but Beth was there every step of the way, taking care of him and making sure he was comfortable. She cooked for him, cleaned for him, and never left his side. It was during this difficult time that James realized how truly blessed he was to have such a loving and caring wife.

From that moment on, James promised never to take Beth for granted again. He started putting effort into their relationship, working to build and strengthen it every day. He took her out for romantic dinners, planned surprise vacations, and did little things to show her how much he appreciated her. He never wanted her to feel unappreciated or taken for granted again.

Chapter 5 163

And so, James and Beth continued to build their lives together, making new memories and cherishing each other every day. They laughed, they loved, and they never stopped appreciating each other. James was more grateful for the moments he spent with his wife and how fortunate he was to have her in his life.

28 Ideas to Grow a Relationship

1. Take dance lessons together.
2. Go on date nights, taking turns planning and surprising the other person.
3. Have a trivia night.
4. Go skinny dipping.
5. Attend a local play.
6. Celebrate an unbirthday (a party for no reason).
7. Go fancy picnicking together.
8. Only use candles one night.
9. Leave love notes on the mirror.
10. Walk down fond memory lane often.
11. Grab a list of thought-provoking questions to ask each other.
12. Write a story together.
13. Get to know each other on a deeper level.
14. Learn your partner's love language.
15. Practice active listening.
16. Talk about each other's bucket list dreams, goals, and needs.
17. Pursue a hobby together.
18. Create a list of things you appreciate about the other person.
19. Go to the opera.
20. Practice eye contact with each other.
21. Volunteer together.
22. Plan a trip together.
23. Repair the relationship and apologize if needed.
24. Listen just for empathy and offer no suggestions unless asked.
25. Do something thrilling together.
26. Exercise together.

27. If you're always together, spend some time apart every once in a while.
28. Acknowledge your mistakes and give your partner a break for theirs.

Resources

1. Relationship Building Activities For Couples link
2. 30 Couple Bonding Activities to Strengthen the Relationship link
3. 10 Ways to Create a Strong, Intimate Relationship link
4. A list of Thought Provoking Questions link
5. The 5 Love Languages link

Books

1. The 5 Love Languages: The Secret to Love that Lasts by Gary Chapman link
2. Love More, Fight Less: Communication Skills Every Couple Needs: A Relationship Workbook for Couples by Gina Senarighi PhD CPC link
3. The Couple's Activity Book: 70 Interactive Games to Strengthen Your Relationship by Crystal Schwanke link

Chapter 6

Arts and Crafts

Creativity is like a wildflower, blooming wherever it finds a patch of fertile ground. It is the spark of inspiration that ignites the imagination and the fuel that drives the engine of innovation. To create is to bring something into existence that was not there before, to weave a tapestry of colors and textures from the threads of our thoughts and experiences. Whether painting, writing, music, or any other creative pursuit, it is a way of expressing ourselves and sharing our unique vision with the world.

Like a traveler on a journey of discovery, the creative mind is always searching for new vistas to explore and new horizons to reach. It is a journey that can take us to the furthest reaches of our imagination and the deepest depths of our soul. In retirement, we have the gift of time to devote to these pursuits, to delve into the art of creation, and to explore the boundless possibilities of our creativity. It is a time to discover new talents, unlock hidden potential, and find joy in the act of creating something beautiful.

The benefits of pursuing creative endeavors are many. It is a way to keep our minds engaged to stave off the boredom and restlessness that can sometimes come with retirement. It is a way to connect with others who share our passion for art and creativity, build new friendships, and explore new communities. It is also a way to find inner peace and fulfillment, nourish our spirit, and enrich our lives with beauty and meaning. So, whether it is painting, writing, or any other form of creative expression, let us embrace our inner artist and find the joy and inspiration that comes from creating something new and beautiful.

Chapter 6 Website Links

Craft Ideas and Tips from Volume 1:
Make Crafts to Sell (17 ideas) - Enjoy the Process (16 ideas) - Explore Your Creative Side (28 ideas)

* * *

Tap into the Art of Craft Making

Feel pure in the process of creating

Sometimes, it's not about what you make as much as it's about being fully in the moment and creating. These crafts might not be as detailed as others, but they have old-world artisan pureness.

11 Crafts to Explore

1. **Ancient craft of spinning-** Break out the spinning wheel to create unique, personal, and unusual yarns that

can be used in contemporary weaving, knitting, crocheting, needlepoint, embroidery, and macramé.
2. **Epoxy resin art-** Learn to use epoxy resin to create colorful tabletops, lamps, jewelry, dioramas, and more.
3. **Glass-blowing art-** Create beautiful glass works of art.
4. **Macramè-** A form of textile-making using knotting rather than weaving or knitting. It typically involves knotting cords or strings to create decorative items such as wall hangings, plant hangers, and jewelry.
5. **Soap carving-** A craft that involves shaping and sculpting bars of soap into different forms using tools such as knives, saws, and sandpaper. Some people carve soap as a hobby or a form of creative expression, while others use it to teach children about art and sculpture. Make decorative soaps, ornaments, and other items. Additionally, soap carving can be used as a therapeutic activity. It can help to reduce stress and anxiety, improve dexterity and fine motor skills, and promote a sense of accomplishment.
6. **Screen Printing-** A printing method in which ink is forced through a stencil or mesh screen onto a substrate, such as fabric, paper, or metal. It can be a fun and creative activity at home with some basic materials and equipment.
7. **Pyrography-** The art of decorating wood or other materials with burn marks created by a heated tool, usually a heated pen. The word "pyrography" comes from the Greek words "pur," meaning fire, and "graphos," meaning writing. Pyrography has been around for centuries and has been used to create intricate designs and images on wood, leather, gourds, and other materials. Make a wide variety of decorative and functional items such as wooden boxes, picture frames, plaques, wall hangings, furniture, and kitchen utensils. Pyrographic designs on leather can be used to make wallets, belts, bags, and other leather goods.
8. **Weaving-** A method of textile production in which two sets of yarn or thread, the warp, and the weft, are interlaced at right angles to form a fabric. Weaving can be done by hand or machine and has been used for thousands of years

9. **Essential oil making-** Concentrated plant extracts that contain the natural aroma and beneficial compounds of the plant from which they are extracted. They are typically obtained through distillation, which involves steaming or pressing the plant material to remove the oils. Essential oils can also be obtained through other methods, such as expression, cold pressing, and solvent extraction. They have been used for centuries for their medicinal and therapeutic properties. They are commonly used in aromatherapy, massage, and other alternative healing practices. They can also be used in various household and personal care products, such as soaps, lotions, perfumes, and cleaning products.
10. **Wreath making-** A circular garland or arrangement of flowers, leaves, fruits, twigs, or various materials typically used as a decorative object or a symbol of celebration. They are often hung on doors, walls, or as a centerpiece. Wreaths can be made by hand or with a wreath-making machine, and it can be a fun and creative activity for people of all ages.
11. **Terrazzo Art-** A sculpture or mosaic created by embedding small pieces of colored glass, stone, or other materials into a terrazzo surface. The result is a colorful and unique art piece that can be used as a floor, wall, or table decoration.

Books

1. The Whole Craft of Spinning: From the Raw Material to the Finished Yarn by Carol Kroll link
2. Epoxy Resin Art for Beginners: The Most Amazing Resin Creations with Step-by-Step Instructions and Images to Follow | How to Make Lamps, Tables, Jewelry, Dioramas, and More! by Sarah Smith link

Chapter 6   171

3. The Glass Artist's Studio Handbook: Traditional and Contemporary Techniques by Cecilia Cohen link
4. Macramè For Beginners: A Complete Guide to Learn about the Knots, Techniques, and Creative Projects of Macrame by Rachael White link
5. Complete Guide to Soap Carving: Tools, Techniques, and Tips (Fox Chapel Publishing) 26 Step-by-Step Projects & Comprehensive Guide, from Basic Methods for Beginners to Advanced Techniques for Artists by Janet Bolyard link
6. Beginner's Guide to Screen Printing: 12 beautiful printing projects with templates by Erin Lacy link
7. Learn to Burn: A Step-by-Step Guide to Getting Started in Pyrography (Fox Chapel Publishing) Easily Create Beautiful Art & Gifts with 14 Step-by-Step Projects, How-to Photos, and 50 Bonus Patterns by Simon Easton link
8. Herrschners Learning to Weave by Deborah Chandler link
9. The Beginner's Guide to Essential Oils: Everything You Need to Know to Get Started by Christina Anthis link
10. Wreaths for Every Season: 24 Projects to Make Throughout the Year by Stasie McArthur link

* * *

Use Paper to Make Art

Create with paper

Paper is economical and versatile. It's no wonder it makes an excellent material for creating crafts. Grab some paper and get ready to find your new hobby.

9 Paper Art Projects

1. **Quilling-** When we were in preschool, little did we know our first art projects were probably a thing called quilling. Quilling is the art of creating decorative designs using thin strips of paper rolled, shaped, and glued together. The strips

of paper are often colored or patterned. They can be used to create various designs, including flowers, animals, geometric shapes, and more. Quilling can be used to decorate cards, frames, boxes, and other items and is a popular craft activity for adults and children.

2. **Card making-** Card making offers a creative outlet, an emotional connection to the recipient, and the satisfaction of creating something by oneself.

3. **Calligraphy-** The art of creating beautiful and expressive handwriting using a variety of tools and techniques. The word "calligraphy" comes from the Greek words "kallos" (beauty) and "graphe" (writing), and it is considered a form of visual art. Calligraphy is typically created using a pen or brush and ink. However, it can also be done using other tools such as markers, pencils, or digital devices. The most common types of calligraphy are Western, Chinese, and Japanese, each with its own set of traditional rules and techniques. Calligraphy can be used for creating invitations, addressing envelopes, making posters, or creating artwork. It can also be used to write quotes, poems, or personal messages, making it a unique and thoughtful gift. Calligraphy requires patience, practice, and skill to master. Many people find the practice of calligraphy to be meditative, therapeutic, and relaxing.

4. **Paper monograms-** A design that combines one or more letters, typically initials, to form a decorative symbol or emblem. These monograms are usually made by cutting out the letters from paper, cardstock, or other materials using a craft knife or cutting machine. The letters are then arranged and glued together to form the monogram. The monograms can be used as a personal or family emblem, a logo, or on a wide range of items such as invitations, stationary, home decor, and DIY projects. Paper monograms can be made in different styles, such as traditional, modern, classic, and elegant, depending on the designer's preference or the occasion. Some people use them to personalize items or to give a custom touch to a simple object.

Chapter 6 173

5. **Paper mache clay sculptures-** A sculpture created by molding and shaping layers of paper or paper pulp mixed with glue or paste. Clay is a low-cost, non-toxic, and versatile medium that can create various sculptures, from small decorative items to large, complex pieces.
6. **Origami-** The traditional Japanese art of paper folding. The word "origami" comes from the Japanese words "ori" (to fold) and "kami" (paper). The goal of origami is to create a finished sculpture using only a piece of square paper without glue or scissors. Origami is a versatile art form ranging from simple and uncomplicated designs, such as a paper crane, to more complex and intricate creations, such as realistic-looking animals or detailed geometric shapes.
7. **Pop-ups and novelty cards-** A greeting card with a three-dimensional element that "pops up" or extends out of the card when opened. These cards are often used for special occasions such as birthdays, holidays, and other events.
8. **Collage art-** A form of art that involves arranging and attaching different materials, such as paper, fabric, photographs, or other found objects, onto a surface to create a composition. The word "collage" comes from the French word "coller," which means "to glue." Collages can be made on paper, canvas, or wood surfaces. Collage art is a form of mixed media art, which means that it combines different art forms or mediums. Collage art allows the artist to experiment with different textures, colors, and shapes and create a unique and dynamic composition.
9. **Paper modeling-** A hobby that people of all ages and skill levels can enjoy. It requires good attention to detail, patience, and a steady hand, but it can be gratifying. It is a great way to learn about various subjects such as architecture, engineering, and history. It can be a good form of artistic expression. There are many models to create, such as ships, aircraft, cars, buildings, and more, and paper models can be very detailed and realistic.

Books

1. Quilling Art by Sena Runa [link](#)
2. The Complete Photo Guide to Card-making: More than 800 Large Color Photos by Judi Watanabe [link](#)
3. Origami Extravaganza! Folding Paper, a Book, and a Box: Origami Kit Includes Origami Book, 38 Fun Projects and 162 Origami Papers by Tuttle Publishing [link](#)
4. Practical Pop-Ups and Paper Engineering: A Step-By-Step Course In The Art Of Creative Card-Making, More Than 100 Techniques And Projects, In 1000 Photographs by Trish Phillips [link](#)
5. Extraordinary Things to Cut Out and Collage by Maria Rivan [link](#)
6. The Ultimate Guide to Modern Calligraphy & Hand Lettering for Beginners: Learn to Letter: A Hand Lettering Workbook with Tips, Techniques, Practice Pages, and Projects by June & Lucy [link](#)
7. Paper Monograms: Create Beautiful Quilled Letters by Stacy Bettencourt [link](#)
8. Make Animal Sculptures with Paper Mache Clay: How to Create Stunning Wildlife Art Using Patterns and My Easy-to-Make, No-Mess Paper Mache Recipe by Jonni Good [link](#)

* * *

Craft The Unusual

Create lesser-known things that you enjoy

If you're the kind of person who sees a horseshoe and thinks it would make a great sculpture, then this next group of crafts is for you. They'll give you a chance to express yourself creatively and have something interesting that is just for you.

. . .

15 Unusual Craft Projects

1. **Yarn bombing-** Are you a bit of a rebel and love knitting? If so, yarn bombing, also known as yarn graffiti or guerilla knitting, was made for you! It's a type of street art in which yarn creates colorful and creative decorations on public spaces such as buildings, statues, trees, and other structures. The yarn is often crocheted or knitted into shapes such as flowers, animals, or other designs and is then attached to the surface using yarn or string. It began in the early 2000s as a non-destructive and temporary street art by a group of knitters in Texas looking to bring color and creativity to their community. Since then, yarn-bombing has become a global phenomenon, with yarn-bombers creating unique designs and decorations worldwide.

2. **Arm knitting-** Arm knitting is a fun and easy way to create cozy, chunky blankets and scarves in no time. It's a variation of traditional knitting, but instead of using knitting needles, you use your arms as the needles. It's perfect for beginners because it doesn't require special tools, and the technique is simple. Here's how it works: you take a few skeins of chunky yarn and lay them out on your arm. Then, you loop the yarn around your arm and start knitting by pulling the loops through each other. It's as simple as that. The finished product is a thick, warm, snuggly blanket or scarf that you can use to keep warm on chilly nights.

3. **Whimsey making-** Have you ever wanted to create a miniature world filled with tiny, whimsical scenes and figures? Well, that's precisely what you can do with Whimsey making! It's a fun and unique craft that lets you use found objects to create miniature worlds full of personality and charm. You can make whimsies from almost anything, like buttons, beads, shells, or even old keys. The possibilities are endless, and you can let your imagination run wild. Plus, it's a great way to recycle and repurpose things that might otherwise be thrown away.

4. **Steampunk crafting-** Are you fascinated by the aesthetic of steampunk, a subgenre of science fiction that features Victorian-era technology and steam-powered machinery? Then perhaps you'll love steampunk crafting! Steampunk crafting is all about creating art, clothing, and accessories inspired by the style. You can make goggles, clocks, gears, and other items that look straight out of a Jules Verne novel. The best thing about steampunk crafting is that it's a great way to be creative and express your love for this unique and fascinating genre.

5. **Kintsugi-** Have you ever broken something valuable and felt heartbroken? Well, you don't have to say goodbye to your beloved pottery or ceramics anymore! Kintsugi is the ancient Japanese art of repairing broken pottery using lacquer and gold, making the breaks part of the object's history and beauty. It's a way to turn something broken into something new and give it a new life. Kintsugi teaches us to embrace imperfections and to find beauty in the broken. It's not only a way to fix a broken pot, it's also a way to find a new perspective on the things we own. The process is meditative and therapeutic. It encourages a sense of mindfulness and appreciation for the things we have.

6. **Insect taxidermy-** Are you fascinated by the world of insects and want to learn more about them? Then insect taxidermy might be for you. It's the art of preserving and mounting insects so that you can admire them in a natural and lifelike way. Insect taxidermy is a great way to learn about different types of insects, their behavior, and their habitats. You'll learn about the intricate details of each insect and how to preserve it for display. It's also a great way to appreciate the beauty of insects, many of which are often overlooked or considered pests. The process of insect taxidermy is simple, but it requires patience and attention to detail. You'll need to collect and prepare the insect and mount it using specialized techniques and materials. The finished product is a beautiful, educational display piece you can enjoy for years.

7. **Spoon carving-** Are you looking for a new hobby that combines creativity, craftsmanship, and the great outdoors? Look no further than spoon carving. Spoon carving is the art of taking a piece of wood and transforming it into a functional and beautiful spoon using hand tools. Spoon carving is an excellent hobby for those who enjoy working with their hands and being outdoors. It's a way to connect with nature and to create something useful and beautiful from a natural material.

8. **Bogolanfini-** Are you interested in learning about the traditional textile art of Africa? Look no further than Bogolanfini. Bogolanfini, also known as "mudcloth," is a traditional Malian textile art that involves dyeing fabric using a mixture of mud and other natural materials to create intricate patterns and designs. Bogolanfini is a significant art form in Mali and has a deep cultural history. Creating Bogolanfini is a time-honored tradition passed down from generation to generation. It's a way to connect with the culture and the community and learn about the people's history and customs. Creating Bogolanfini is a multistep process that involves preparing the cotton fabric, making the dye mixture, and applying the dye to the fabric. The finished product is a unique and beautiful textile that tells a story.

9. **Gourd crafting-** Gourd crafting is the art of decorating, carving, and transforming gourds into objects such as bowls, vases, birdhouses, and even musical instruments. Gourd crafting is an excellent hobby for those who enjoy working with natural materials and appreciate the natural beauty of gourds. Gourds come in various shapes and sizes, each with unique characteristics, making each piece one-of-a-kind. The process of gourd crafting is versatile. You can use multiple techniques to create different designs and styles, such as wood burning, painting, carving, and more. The finished product can be functional, decorative, or even a combination.

10. **Bookbinding-** The art of bookbinding creates and repairs books by attaching covers to a text block. Bookbinding is a fantastic hobby for those who enjoy working with paper and want to learn about the history and process of bookmaking. It's also a way to create beautiful, unique books that reflect your style and creativity. The bookbinding process can vary from simple to complex, with different types and techniques you can learn. Each has unique characteristics, from basic bookbinding methods, such as Japanese stab binding, to more advanced techniques, like case binding. Bookbinding is a craft that requires patience, precision, and attention to detail, but the result is a beautiful and unique book that you can use, give as a gift, or even sell.
11. **Pine needle basketry-** The art of creating baskets using the needles of pine trees is an excellent hobby for those who enjoy working with natural materials and appreciate the natural beauty of pine needles. It's also a way to connect with nature and learn about the traditional craft of basket weaving. The process of pine needle basket weaving is relatively simple. It involves coiling the pine needles and binding them together using thread or waxed linen. The finished product is a beautiful and durable basket that can be used for various purposes, such as storage, decoration, or even as a functional piece of art.
12. **Needle felting-** Needle felting uses barbed needles to interlock wool fibers and create a sculpted shape. Needle felting is a great hobby for those who enjoy working with wool and want to learn about the craft of sculpting. The finished product can range from small figurines and ornaments to larger sculptures.
13. **Flower pressing-** Flower pressing is the art of keeping flowers by pressing them flat between layers of paper. It's an excellent hobby for those who enjoy working with natural materials and want to learn about the craft of preservation. It's also a way to create beautiful and unique artworks reflecting flowers' natural beauty.

14. **Horseshoe crafts-** The art of using horseshoes to create various decorative and functional items. Using horseshoes for home decor can be traced to a tradition that goes back to when people believed nailing a horseshoe on your door protects those who pass through from evil spirits. Horseshoe crafting is a superb hobby for those who enjoy working with metal and want to learn about the craft of blacksmithing and metalworking. The process of horseshoe crafts can vary depending on the desired item. It can involve bending, shaping, welding, and painting horseshoes to create wall art, garden decor, candle holders, hooks, and furniture. Today, horseshoe crafts are a popular trend in rustic home decor.
15. **Tie-dye-** Tie-dye is the art of using dyes to create vibrant and unique patterns on fabric. Tie-dye is a sensational hobby for those who enjoy working with color and want to learn about the craft of dyeing. The process of tie-dye is relatively simple. It involves folding, twisting, or bunching up fabric and applying dyes to create various patterns. The finished product is a one-of-a-kind item that is as unique as you are.

Books

1. Yarn Bombing: The Art of Crochet and Knit Graffiti: Tenth Anniversary Edition by Mandy Moore link
2. Arm Knitting: 30 no-needle projects for you and your home by Alpha link
3. Steampunk Your Wardrobe, Revised Edition: Sewing and Crafting Projects to Add Flair to Fashion by Calista Taylor link
4. Kintsugi: Finding Strength in Imperfection by Céline SANTINI link
5. The Beetle and Butterfly Collection - A Guide to Collecting, Arranging and Preserving Insects at Home by Harland Coultas link
6. The Artful Wooden Spoon: How to Make Exquisite Keepsakes for the Kitchen by Joshua Vogel link

7. Bogolanfini Mud Cloth by Sam Hilu link
8. The Complete Book of Gourd Craft: 22 Projects, 55 Decorative Techniques, 300 Inspirational Designs by Ginger Summit link
9. Bookbinding: A How To Guide by E. P. Carter link
10. Pine Needle Basketry: From Forest Floor to Finished Project by Judy Mallow link
11. Needle Felting for Beginners: How to Sculpt with Wool by Roz Dace link
12. The Art of Pressed Flowers and Leaves: Contemporary techniques & designs by Jennie Ashmore link
13. Horseshoe Crafts: More Than 30 Easy Projects to Weld at Home by Barbie The Welder link
14. Tie-Dye 101: How to Make Over 20 Fabulous Patterns (Design Originals) Learn the Secrets of Paper Fold, Tying, and Crumple-Dye for Sunbursts, Strips, Circles, Swirls, & More, for Both Kids and Adults by Suzanne McNeill link

* * *

Use Machines to Make Crafts

Take crafting to the next level

Are you tired of spending hours hand-sewing, cutting, and shaping your crafts? Want to take your crafting game to the next level? Then, it's time to explore the world of consumer crafting machines.

Imagine finishing a quilt in a fraction of the time it would take you to hand-sew it or creating intricate designs and shapes with a press of a button using a Cricut machine. These machines can make crafting more efficient and enjoyable, giving you more time to focus on creating new designs and projects.

But efficiency isn't the only perk. Consumer crafting machines can also give you the ability to create designs and projects that may be impossible or difficult to achieve by hand. Imagine creating a 3D sculpture or a perfect monogram with an embroidery machine. The possibilities are endless. Consumer crafting machines can make your projects look more professional and polished. With precise cuts and detailed designs, your crafts will stand out from the rest.

Give it a try. Many craft stores offer classes on how to use consumer crafting machines, and you can also find many tutorials online. You'll be amazed at the creativity and fun you can have with these machines. So go ahead, embrace technology, and take your crafting to the next level.

7 Crafting Machines

1. **Cricut machines-** These inexpensive machines are used for cutting and shaping materials such as paper, fabric, vinyl, and cardstock to create signs, cards, decals, and other crafts. But what makes Cricut machines so special? First off, they can cut precise shapes and designs with a press of a button, giving your crafts a professional and polished look. Plus, it can cut a wide variety of materials, from thin paper to thick fabrics, allowing you to work with various mediums and giving you endless creative possibilities. Another great feature of Cricut machines is the ability to work with pre-designed projects or create your own designs using Cricut's software, which is easy to use and comes with a wide variety of images, fonts, and shapes. Cricut machines are also great for personalizing gifts, home decor, and clothing. Imagine being able to add a custom monogram to a shirt or creating a one-of-a-kind sign for your home in seconds.

2. **Embroidery machines-** A consumer crafting machine that allows you to create designs and patterns by sewing thread onto a fabric. With an embroidery machine, you can add intricate designs, monograms, and patterns to your fabrics easily and quickly. With the ability to use pre-designed patterns or create your own, the possibilities are endless. Whether you're a beginner or an experienced crafter, an embroidery machine can add a professional and polished touch to your projects.

3. **Laser cutters-** A high-tech, precise, and versatile craft that allows you to create a wide range of items with precision and accuracy. A laser cutter uses a laser beam to cut, engrave, or etch various materials, such as wood, acrylic, and paper. Laser cutting involves using a laser beam to cut, engrave, or etch materials based on a design loaded into the machine. The finished product is laser perfection.

4. **Knitting machine-** A machine that uses needles to create knitted fabrics and garments automatically. Create a wide variety of crafts, such as clothing, home decor, and accessories. They can be an excellent tool for turning your crafting ideas into reality and creating projects quickly and efficiently. A knitting machine can be manual, semi-automatic, or computerized. It can create knits like Rib, Tuck, Slip, and Fair Isle.

5. **3D printer-** 3D printing creates three-dimensional objects using a digital file and a 3D printer. 3D printing is an excellent hobby for those who enjoy working with technology, design, and engineering and want to learn about the craft of creating physical objects. It can create unique home decor, custom figurines, and even replacement parts. 3D printing involves using 3D design software to create a digital model of an object and then using a 3D printer to print it layer by layer using materials such as plastic, metal, ceramics, and more. The possibilities are endless for creators, hobbyists, and professionals.

6. **CNC (Computer Numerical Control) router-** CNC routing uses computer-controlled cutting tools to shape and carve materials such as wood, plastic, metal, and more. CNC routing is a fantastic hobby for those who enjoy woodworking, design, and engineering and want to learn about the craft of creating detailed and intricate objects.

7. **Sewing machines-** Sewing machines can be used to create a wide variety of consumer-made arts and crafts, such as:

Chapter 6 183

- Clothing and fashion accessories: Create custom clothing, including shirts, pants, dresses, coats, and accessories like scarves, hats, and gloves.
- Home decor: Create items such as curtains, pillows, and tablecloths.
- Quilting: Create a layered blanket or bedspread by sewing together multiple layers of fabric.
- Embroidery: Create intricate designs on fabric, adding a personal touch to clothing, home decor, and other items.
- Upholstery: Repair and reupholster furniture, giving it a new lease on life.
- Soft toys and stuffed animals: Create custom soft toys and stuffed animals for children or adults.
- Leathercraft: Create leather goods like bags, wallets, and belts.
- Beading, sequin, and other embellishments: Attach beading, sequins, and other decorations to clothing and accessories, adding a touch of sparkle and shine.

Books

1. Cricut: 11 Books in 1 - A Beginner's Guide to Master Cricut the Quick & Easy Way | Get the Most Out of Your Machine, Draw From +310 Original Projects & Start Your DIY Business by Chloe Ross link
2. The Complete Machine Embroidery Manual by Elizabeth Keegan link
3. First Time Sewing: The Absolute Beginner's Guide by Editors Of Creative Publishing International link
4. LASER ENGRAVING: Engraving at the Speed of Light by J. Stephen Spence link
5. Circular Knitting Machine Patterns | Diana Levine Knits: 25 Patterns for Addi and Sentro Circular Knitting Machines by Diana Levine link
6. 3D Printing Projects by DK link
7. CNC Router Essentials: The Basics for Mastering the Most Innovative Tool in Your Workshop by Randy Johnson link

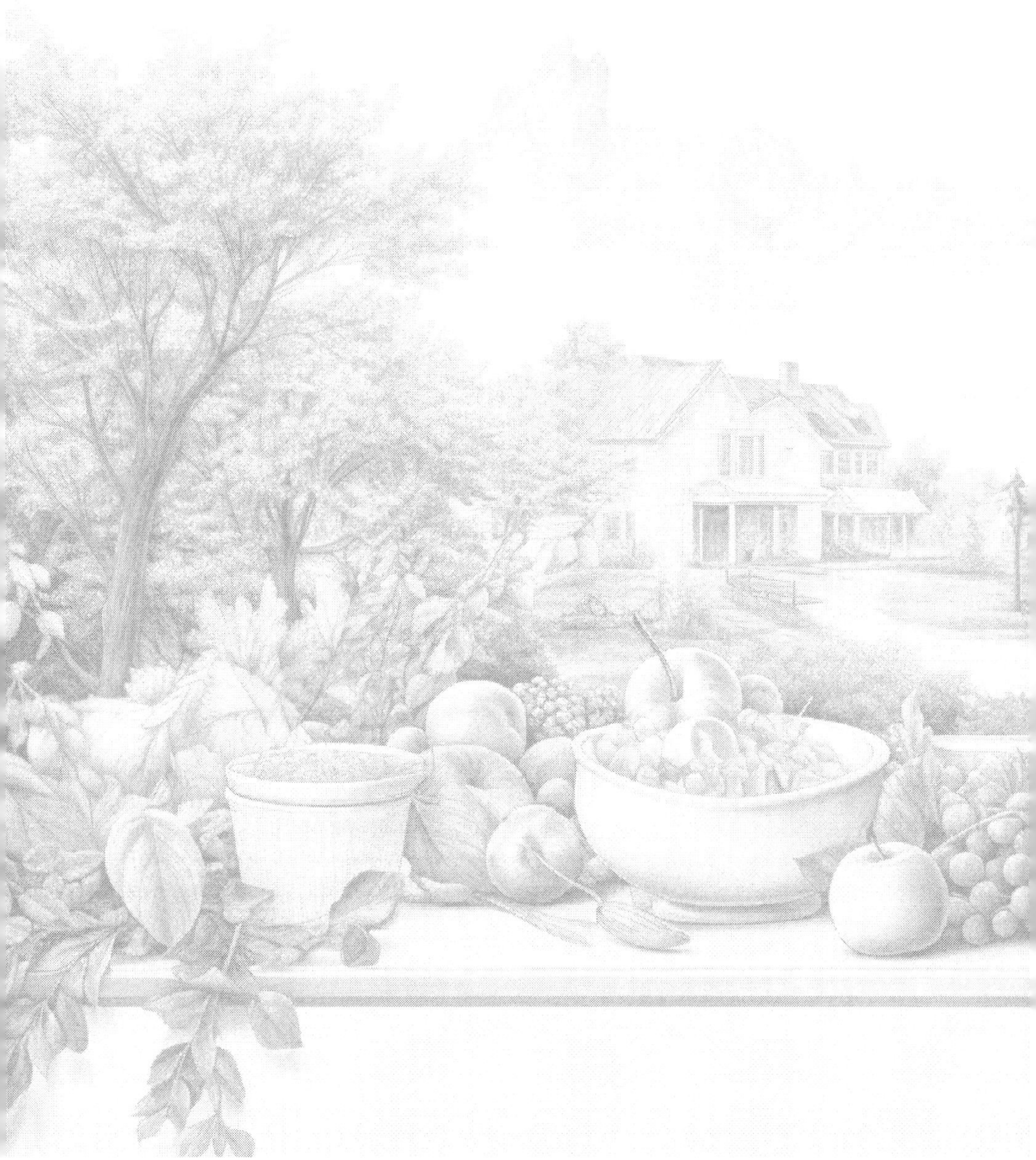

Chapter 7

Cookin' It Up

Ah, the pleasures of food! How they evolve as we age like a fine wine gaining depth and complexity over time. When we are young, we often eat with haste, our minds buzzing with a million distractions. But as we grow older, we begin to savor every bite, to relish the flavors and textures that dance upon our tongues.

We take our time with each meal, no longer in a hurry to move on to the next activity. We gather with friends and family, delighting in the company as much as the cuisine. We linger over our plates, swapping stories and sharing laughter, savoring the camaraderie as much as the culinary delights.

And oh, the flavors that come with age! We develop a taste for the subtle nuances of spice and sweetness, the rich umami of slow-cooked stews, and the tangy bite of fermented foods. We seek out the freshest ingredients, reveling in the earthy aroma of a just-picked herb or the juicy sweetness of a sun-ripened fruit.

As we age, we become more attuned to the connection between food and health, seeking nourishing meals that fuel our bodies and souls. We explore new cuisines, delighting in the exotic flavors of distant lands and cultures. We experiment in the kitchen, creating culinary masterpieces that reflect our unique tastes and personalities.

And yet, for all the sophistication and complexity that comes with age, there remains a childlike joy in the simple pleasures of food. A warm, buttery croissant, a crisp apple picked straight from the tree, a gooey slice of homemade pie – these small delights can bring us as much joy as the most elaborate feast.

Yes, food truly becomes a joyous occasion as we age, a celebration of life and all its richness. So let us raise a glass – or a fork – to the pleasures of the table and savor every moment, every bite, with the fullness of our hearts. Let's sink our teeth into some ideas of how we can savor the food in our retirement.

Chapter 7 Website Links

Food Ideas and Tips from Volume 1:
Savor the Flavor (30 ideas)

* * *

Create Something Yummy

Get creative in the kitchen

If you're looking for a rewarding hobby in retirement, cooking can be a great choice. There are endless avenues to explore, from cooking exotic dishes from different cultures to mastering a challenging recipe. It is a fun way to experiment and challenge yourself and opens the door to socializing with those with the same interests. Not to mention, who doesn't love to eat?

You can start with the basics by mastering a few simple recipes to turn to in a pinch. Perfecting your favorite takeout dish is an easy way to start, and you can practice until you can make it better than your local spot. There are also tons of online resources like blogs, recipe books, and cooking shows that you can use to learn new techniques and recipes.

Once the basics are down and your skills become more advanced, you can experiment with different ingredients and flavors. Trying out exotic and unique dishes from other cultures is a fun option, and you can even invite friends to join. Remember to challenge yourself, too. Taking on a complicated recipe like macarons, souffle, or even homemade pasta can be a personal accomplishment you can be proud of.

Not only can cooking become a fun and calming pastime, but it can also become a hobby you share with others. Taking a cooking class with friends or joining a cooking club is a great way to get together and share recipes and tips. There's also the satisfaction of hosting a dinner party and serving up a delicious meal to your friends and family.

Cooking is a great way to spend some of your retirement, and it is ultimately up to you to decide how far you want to take it. From mastering a few go-to dishes to becoming a master chef, the possibilities are endless.

31 Fun Cooking Ideas

1. **Cake decorating-** A fun and creative way to express your artistic side and make beautiful, delicious masterpieces in the form of a cake.
2. **Charcuterie boards-** Creating a charcuterie board is a fun activity that will make any gathering more special, as you can customize it to your tastes with an array of cheeses, cured meats, crackers, nuts, and other delightful snacks!
3. **Cheese-making-** Exploring the delicious world of cheese-making can be a great way to spend a day as you

learn traditional techniques, experiment with flavors, and create your smelly masterpiece.

4. **Recipe creation-** Creating a delicious new recipe can be an exciting and creative endeavor, bringing the joy of cooking to a new level.
5. **Learn ethnic styles of cooking-** Explore the vibrant flavors of the world by learning and trying out different ethnic cooking styles.
6. **Ayurveda cooking-** Experience the healing power of nature while learning to prepare delicious Ayurvedic recipes that will nourish both your body and soul.
7. **Kettle corn-** Making kettle corn at home is a fun and easy way to enjoy this classic salty-sweet treat.
8. **Bread making-** Why not try making some homemade bread from scratch - you'll be amazed at the delicious smells and flavors from your kitchen.
9. **Chili making-** You can make a delicious chili recipe by experimenting with ingredients like different types of beans, fresh vegetables, and savory spices, creating a unique and tasty flavor that everyone will enjoy.
10. **Cooking your heritage-** Cooking your heritage is a great way to explore the flavors and traditions of your ancestors' cuisine and create meaningful connections with your culture and family history.
11. **Smoking meat-** Delight your taste buds with the slow-cooked smoky flavor of homemade BBQ.
12. **Ice cream making-** Experiment with new flavors, swirls, and toppings to create the perfect homemade ice cream - a scrumptious treat for the whole family.
13. **Hot sauce making-** Experience the fiery delight of crafting your homemade hot sauce with various peppers and seasonings to tantalize your taste buds!
14. **Roasting coffee-** Roasting your coffee beans is an enjoyable, aromatic, and rewarding experience that even the most novice home barista can enjoy.

15. **Canning and preserving-** Canning and preserving is a way to capture the essence of summer by turning your fresh, seasonal produce into delicious jams, jellies, and pickles that can last all year.
16. **Juicing-** You can explore the freshest produce available with juicing, creating a delicious, nutritious, and customized glass of energy to power you through your day.
17. **Brick oven pizza making-** Making brick oven pizza at home is a creative activity that's sure to please the whole family with its delicious smoky flavor, bubbly crust, and delectable topping combinations.
18. **Winemaking-** Making wine can be a satisfying experience, allowing you to express your unique taste and create something you can truly call your own.
19. **Kombucha brewing-** Brew kombucha at home and experience the bubbly, delicious, and tangy thrill of a homemade probiotic beverage like no other.
20. **Brewing beer-** Brewing beer at home can be a rewarding experience, allowing you to experiment with unique flavors, explore the art of beer-making, and impress your friends with a delicious and fresh homebrew.
21. **Cider making-** There's nothing quite like the satisfaction of creating cider from fresh fruit, from the initial juicing to the final bottling and tasting.
22. **Sausage making-** Making sausages at home can be a creative activity that makes you feel like a real culinary artist as you stuff, twist, and tie your way to your homemade sausage masterpieces.
23. **Mead making-** Making mead can be an exciting and delicious adventure as you experience the magic of transforming honey and water into an intoxicating beverage with your hands!
24. **Herbal tea creations-** Experimenting with various herbs to concoct your unique herbal tea blend is a healthy way to explore nature's flavors and aromas.

25. **Tropical cocktail making-** Why not spice up your night and learn to make a delicious tropical cocktail bursting with flavor and the colors of the Caribbean?
26. **Mocktail creations-** Creating mocktails can be fun to experiment with delicious and creative flavors while enjoying your favorite drinks without the booze.
27. **Fermenting-** A delightful way to turn all sorts of ingredients - from fruits and vegetables to grains and even tea - into delicious, probiotic-rich foods and drinks with a range of flavor profiles from sour to sweet.
28. **Barbecuing-** Grilling up delicious burgers and hot dogs on a summer day while basking in the sun and enjoying the company of friends and family is the perfect way to spend an afternoon.
29. **Make a family recipe book-** Create a collection of treasured family recipes that you can share with generations to come by making a beautiful family recipe book.
30. **Take a cooking class in a different country-** Experience a unique and immersive cultural adventure by taking a cooking class in a foreign country and learning to prepare traditional dishes from around the world.
31. **Enter a recipe contest-** Entering a recipe contest is a delightful way to show off your culinary skills and stretch your creativity as you compete to create the most delicious dish or dream up the tastiest concoction.

Books

1. Ayurveda Cooking for Beginners: An Ayurvedic Cookbook to Balance and Heal by Laura Plumb link
2. Project Smoke: Seven Steps to Smoked Food Nirvana, Plus 100 Irresistible Recipes by Steven Raichlen link
3. Ben & Jerry's Homemade Ice Cream & Dessert Book by Ben Cohen link
4. Fermented Hot Sauce Cookbook: A Step-by-Step Guide to Making Hot Sauce From Scratch By Kristen Wood link

Chapter 7 191

5. Mastering Pizza: The Art and Practice of Handmade Pizza, Focaccia, and Calzone by Marc Vetri link
6. Healing Herbal Teas: Learn to Blend 101 Specially Formulated Teas for Stress Management, Common Ailments, Seasonal Health, and Immune Support by Sarah Farr link
7. Tiki: Modern Tropical Cocktails by Shannon Mustipher link
8. Mocktails by Caroline Hwang link
9. The Farmhouse Culture Guide to Fermenting: Crafting Live-Cultured Foods and Drinks with 100 Recipes from Kimchi to Kombucha by Kathryn Lukas link

* * *

Try a New Kitchen Appliance

Get a kitchen helper

Ahh, the delicious possibilities of a new kitchen appliance! Cooking can be one of the most enjoyable and creative activities and anyone can create tasty dishes with the right tools. Sometimes, all it takes is a new appliance to jumpstart your inspiration.

From slow cookers and pressure cookers to toaster ovens and air fryers—the world of kitchen appliances is wide and varied. All of them add convenience to your meal-making process, and they can help you save time and energy while also allowing you to explore unique recipes and ingredients.

For example, a slow cooker is an excellent choice for whipping up a delicious stew or pot roast. You can throw all your ingredients into the pot and let it work its magic. On the other hand, a pressure cooker can help you create amazing dishes quickly.

No matter what kind of cooking machine you choose, it can help you get creative in the kitchen. So don't be afraid to try something new and explore the possibilities. With the right tools, you can create masterful dishes and tantalizing treats full of flavor!

25 Fun Cooking Machines To Try

1. **3 in 1 food processor-** The 3 in 1 food processor is a must-have kitchen appliance that allows you to quickly and easily chop, mix, and blend ingredients to create delicious, homemade meals.
2. **Cocktail Maker Machine**- The cocktail maker machine is perfect for hosting a party, as it can quickly concoct delicious, bar-style drinks for your guests with the push of a button.
3. **Air Fryer-** An air fryer is a great way to enjoy your favorite fried foods without all the added fat and calories, as it uses hot, circulating air to quickly cook your food to perfection.
4. **Fully Automatic Coffee and Espresso Maker-** The perfect way to get your daily dose of caffeine, as it brews perfect cups of coffee and espresso with just the push of a button.
5. **Slow Cooker-** A slow cooker is the ideal kitchen appliance for busy homes, as it can be left unattended to slowly simmer and cook your favorite soups, stews, and casseroles for hours.
6. **Automatic Indoor Herb Garden Machine-** This machine helps you grow fresh herbs right in your kitchen, bringing the taste of the outdoors inside with just the press of a button.
7. **Automatic Pan Stirrer-** This nifty device automatically stirs your food, taking a touch of the mundane out of preparing a delicious meal.
8. **Smart Tea Infuser-** This innovative gadget steeps your tea to the perfect temperature and strength, allowing you to enjoy a unique cup of tea at any time.
9. **Smart Scale-** This high-tech kitchen tool takes the guesswork out of measuring ingredients, giving you perfect results every time.

10. **Smart Meat Thermometer-** This cutting-edge device monitors the internal temperature of your food, helping you get that perfect juicy delight with every bite.
11. **Sous Vide Precision Cooker-** This machine allows users to create restaurant-quality dishes with minimal effort by precisely controlling the temperature and time of the cooking process.
12. **June Oven- 12 appliances in 1-** Innovative and remarkable, this oven is a game changer and the ultimate kitchen time-saver, combining twelve appliances into one machine.
13. **Automatic Can Opener-** An easy-to-use device that quickly and effortlessly opens cans of all sizes, making kitchen tasks a breeze.
14. **Breakfast Sandwich Maker-** Perfect for busy mornings, this machine will craft a custom breakfast sandwich in minutes. It can include any combination of ingredients that tickles your fancy.
15. **Ninja Foodi-** An amazing multi-purpose kitchen gadget that can be used for pressure cooking, air frying, steaming, roasting, and more, this machine will make mealtime more convenient and enjoyable.
16. **Electric Griddler-** The electric griddler is a fantastic kitchen appliance that can transform your cooking by allowing you to make a variety of delicious grilled dishes.
17. **Ice Cream Machine-** The ice cream machine is a great way to make various frozen treats and turn ordinary ice cream into a gourmet treat.
18. **Smart Skillet-** The smart skillet is a fabulous kitchen tool that can help you cook everything from pancakes to stir-fries in a fraction of the time.
19. **Soda Stream Machine-** The Soda Stream machine is a great way to make delicious bubbly drinks quickly and easily, perfect for any gathering or party.
20. **Electric Water Kettle-** The electric water kettle is an essential kitchen appliance that can quickly heat water for

just about any beverage, from coffee and tea to hot chocolate.
21. **Juicer-** A juicer is a perfect way to get your daily dose of fruits and vegetables in a delicious and refreshing drink.
22. **Induction cooktops-** Induction cooktops offer an efficient and convenient way to quickly and evenly cook your favorite meals.
23. **Sushi maker-** A sushi maker is the perfect way to make restaurant-quality sushi rolls at home in no time.
24. **Dehydrator-** A dehydrator is ideal for making healthy, preservative-free snacks, such as dried fruits and vegetable chips.
25. **Shaved Ice Machine-** A shaved ice machine is a terrific way to make snow cones and other frozen treats at home.

Resources

1. 30 of the Most Clever Smart Kitchen Appliances You Can Buy Online link
2. 20 Best Smart Kitchen Appliances That'll Up Your Chef Game link
3. 15 best-selling small appliances that reviewers love link

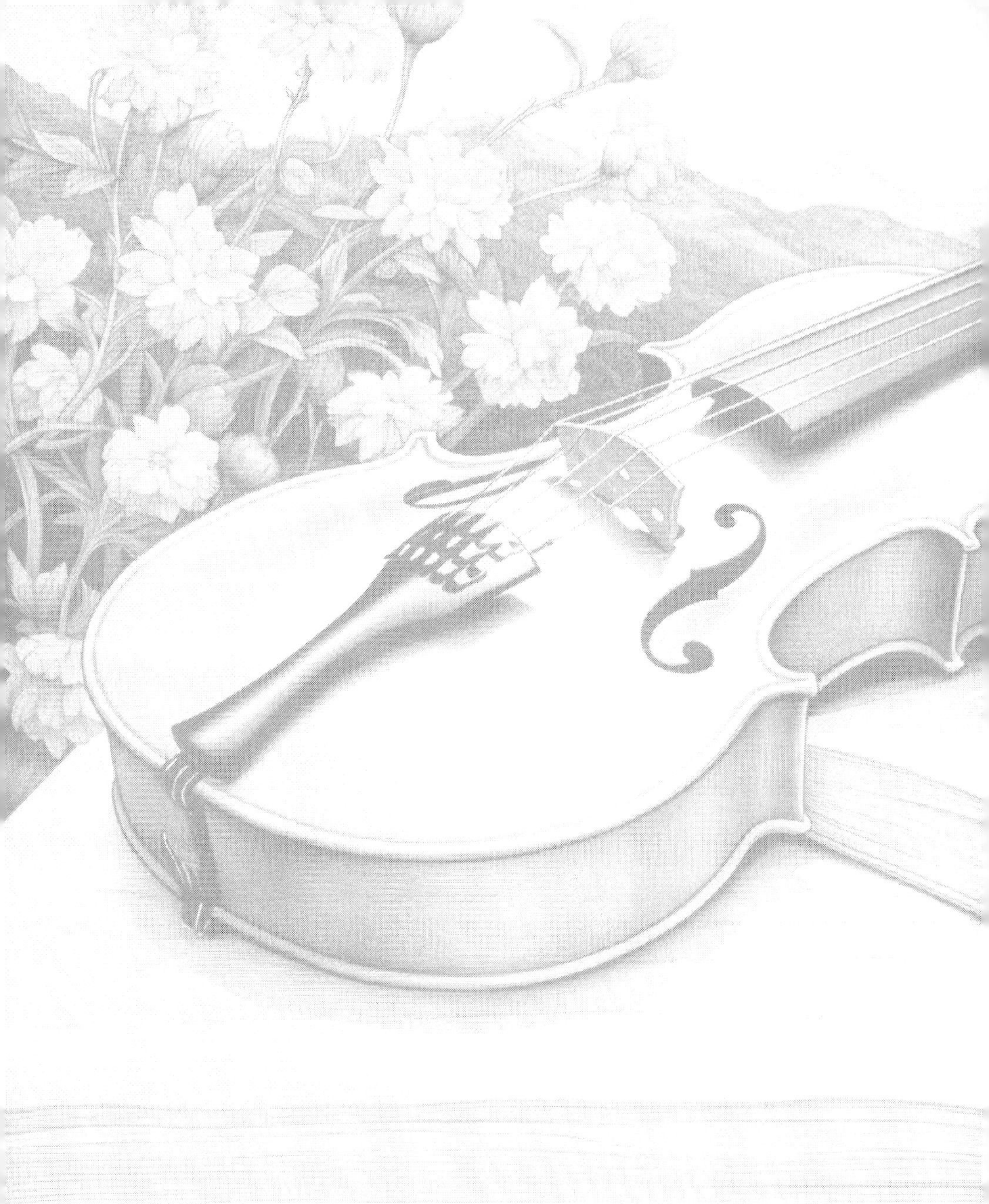

Chapter 8
Games, Music, and Curiosity

Are you ready to add some excitement to your retirement without leaving home? Then buckle up because this chapter is going to take you on a wild ride through the worlds of games, music, and curiosity.

Get ready to unleash your competitive spirit and challenge your brain with some exciting games, or explore your musical talents and learn how to play a new instrument.

And for those curious minds, we'll show you how to explore the unknown and satisfy your thirst for knowledge. But beware, once you open the door to these worlds, you won't want to close it.

So, turn up the volume, grab your favorite snack, and get ready for serious fun. This chapter is all about letting loose and embracing your inner child, so let's jump in and see where the adventure takes us!

Chapter 8 Website Links

* * *

Play a Game

Have some fun and games

Playing games at home can be an enjoyable and fulfilling experience. Games are a great way to pass the time, have fun, and make memories with family and friends.

Playing games at home encourages communication. Whether it's a classic board game like Monopoly or a card game like Poker, you can spend quality time with your family and friends, chatting as you roll the dice, exchange cards, and strategize your way to victory.

Games can help you relax and take a break from the hustle and bustle of everyday life. It can be an escape from the stress of life, relationships, or any other obligations. Who doesn't love a fun night in with a competitive game of Scrabble or a casual game of Uno?

Playing games offers an opportunity to learn and exercise our brains. Whether they're teaching us logic, strategy, or a new language, certain games can help us develop important skills we might not get the opportunity to practice elsewhere.

There is a seemingly endless choice of games to keep busy with, from beloved classics to new strategy games, so take a look at some of the options below, gather up some friends, and start a weekly game night.

. . .

1 6 Types of Games to Play at Home

1. Board games
2. Card games
3. Video games
4. Online video games
5. Virtual reality games
6. Role-playing games
7. Puzzle games
8. Word games
9. Trivia games
10. Sports games
11. Charades
12. Dice games
13. Pinball
14. Party games
15. Karaoke games
16. Table games (pool, table shuffleboard, etc.)

2 7 Popular Board Games

Board games offer a wonderful escape from reality, providing a fun and interactive way to challenge the mind and bond with friends and family. With a vast array of game styles, there's something for everyone, from strategic to luck-based games, making them a perfect source of entertainment and joy.

1. **Monopoly-** A classic game of strategy, Monopoly offers endless hours of fun as players buy, sell, and trade properties, accumulating wealth and attempting to bankrupt their opponents.
2. **Clue-** In this mystery-solving game, players move from room to room, gathering clues and making accusations to determine the culprit behind a crime.

3. **Scrabble-** A word-lover's paradise, Scrabble challenges players to build words from letter tiles, earning points based on the length and complexity of their creations.
4. **Risk-** A game of global domination, Risk requires players to strategically assign their armies, conquer territories and battle for control of the world.
5. **Chess-** A timeless game of strategy requiring players to use critical thinking and cunning tactics to outmaneuver their opponent and capture their king.
6. **Pandemic-** A cooperative game, Pandemic tasks players with working together to cure deadly diseases and save the world from a global pandemic.
7. **Ticket to Ride-** In this railway-themed game, players collect train cards, claim routes, and build the longest railway network, earning points as they connect cities across the map.
8. **Codenames-** A word association game, Codenames challenges players to use their knowledge of words and language to decipher secret codes and solve puzzles.
9. **Trivial Pursuit-** Test your general knowledge with a game of Trivial Pursuit and win the race to answer all the questions correctly.
10. **Sorry-** Steal your opponents' pieces and race to the finish in the ultimate game of Sorry.
11. **Checkers-** Earn the right to crown your pieces and proceed to the king's row in the traditional game of Checkers.
12. **Stratego-** Defend your flag and outwit your opponents in a game of Stratego to become the ultimate victor.
13. **Backgammon-** Put your luck to the test and enjoy a game of Backgammon with friends and family.
14. **Catan-** Compete for resources and strategic settlements to build the most powerful empire in the game of Catan.
15. **Yahtzee-** Roll the dice and prepare for a thrilling round of Yahtzee as you compete to get the best combinations of numbers.

16. **Jenga-** Take turns stacking the blocks and watch the tower grow taller and taller in a classic game of Jenga.
17. **Go-** Challenge yourself and your friends to a game of Go and become the ultimate Go master.
18. **Battleship-** Experience the thrill of sinking your opponents' warships in a classic game of Battleship.
19. **Chinese Checkers-** Outmaneuver your opponents and become the first to reach the star.
20. **Dominoes-** Go head-to-head against your opponents in a game of Dominoes and aim to be the first to empty your hand.
21. **Carcassonne-** Create a mesmerizing medieval landscape as you place tiles and build cities in the game of Carcassonne.
22. **Blokus-** Utilize your strategic thinking and race to fill up the board in the game of Blokus.
23. **Apples to Apples-** Unleash your creativity and compete to make the most entertaining combinations of cards in a round of Apples to Apples.
24. **Ticket to Ride-** Experience the ultimate train adventure and race your opponents to connect the routes in Ticket to Ride.
25. **Cranium-** Test your creativity and knowledge in a fun-filled game of Cranium and become the ultimate team player.
26. **Boggle-** Put your spelling and vocabulary skills to the test in a high-paced game of Boggle.
27. **Scattergories-** An exciting and creative game that will challenge and entertain you and your friends while you compete to think of unique answers to the categories in the game.

14 Popular Card Games

Playing card games helps to challenge your mind, enjoy moments of laughter, friendly competition, and perhaps make a few extra dollars.

1. **Uno-** A deck of 108 cards, red, green, yellow, and blue, with numbers and symbols, that'll leave you feeling lucky and thrilled, all thanks to the ever-changing twists and turns of the classic card game that's sure to get your heart racing - it's Uno!
2. **Skip-Bo-** A joyful game of strategy and luck and is the perfect way to have a thrilling time with friends and family.
3. **Jaipur-** A game of trading and collecting that requires quick decision-making, perfect for those who love a challenge and the satisfaction of outsmarting their opponents.
4. **Exploding Kittens-** A perfect blend of luck and strategy that offers lots of laughs and plenty of surprises, ideal for a lively game night with family and friends.
5. **Sushi Go!-** An adorable card game that is easy to learn and packed with strategic possibilities, perfect for when you're looking for a quick and amusing time.
6. **Hocus Pocus-** An entertaining card game that mixes luck, skill, and strategy for an exciting challenge that will have all players on the edge of their seats.
7. **Joking Hazard-** A hilarious card game that allows you to create raunchy and outrageous comics, great for adding laughter and fun to your game night.
8. **Pokemon Battle Academy-** An exciting and strategic way to battle your beloved pocket monsters with friends. With endless possibilities, you'll never tire of the epic battles you can create.
9. **Arkham Horror-** The card game transports you to a world of horror, mystery, and suspense with its intricate gameplay and immersive storytelling. It's a great way to experience the thrill and action of a horror movie with your friends.
10. **Resistance-** A suspenseful game of deception and deduction, where everyone tries to work together while

determining who is telling the truth and who is lying. It's a great way to challenge your deduction skills and add a little excitement and mystery to your game night.

11. **Gloom-** An excellent game for those looking to experience a unique and darkly comedic twist on the classic card game. With an array of ghoulish characters and the ability to trigger surprising plot twists, this game will keep you and your friends entertained all night.

12. **Marvel Champions-** Marvel Champions lets you become an iconic Marvel superhero and battle against sinister villains in a classic card game format. With plenty of unique characters and immersive role-playing elements, this game is perfect for those looking for a superpowered adventure.

13. **Marrying Mr. Darcy-** A matchmaking card game for those who want to travel back in time to Regency-era Britain. With charming characters, a delightful atmosphere, and plenty of surprises, this game is sure to ignite a spark of romance within your game night.

14. **Agatha Christie's Death on The Cards-** A thrilling game for those who want to solve a murder mystery in a classic card game format. The game will keep you on your toes with its suspenseful storyline and challenging puzzles, making it the perfect game for a night of detective work.

20 Classic Card Games

1. **Poker-** The game of bluffs, bets, and big wins attracts those with a sharp mind, a steely nerve, and a willingness to risk it all - the kind of person who's not afraid to put their chips on the table and see what fate has in store for them.

2. **Blackjack-** A game for the bold, where the thrill-seekers of the card game world gather to test their luck and skill, hoping to beat the dealer and come out on top.

3. **Rummy-** A card game of strategy and luck, perfect for someone who loves a good challenge and has a knack for seeing patterns and making quick decisions.
4. **Bridge-** Bridge is the ultimate game of strategy and skill. In this battleground, your cunning and wits face off against your opponents', attracting those who crave a mental challenge and a taste of victory.
5. **Spades-** The game of wit, strategy, and communication is perfect for those who enjoy both mental stimulation and social interaction and thrive on outsmarting their opponents with a well-placed bid or a clever hand.
6. **Hearts-** Hearts, the game where you try to avoid the Queen of Spades like it's your ex at a party.
7. **Go Fish-** The perfect game for beginner players, with friendly and easy rules where you fish for pairs, trade your catches, and try not to get left high and dry, like a fish out of water.
8. **Gin Rummy-** An exciting game of skill and speed that will surely get your pulse racing.
9. **Canasta-** A thrilling game of cards that offers an immersive blend of luck and strategy.
10. **Texas Hold 'Em-** A classic poker game that gives players the chance to bluff their opponents into a win.
11. **Euchre-** A great game to play with friends, where strategy is vital, and every round can surprise you with a twist.
12. **Cribbage-** Offers hours of strategic fun and the ability to outwit your opponents with your card play.
13. **Pinochle-** A classic game that pits two players against each other in a battle of wits and luck.
14. **War-** An easy game where you can just have fun and watch the cards battle it out for the win.
15. **Crazy Eights-** The perfect game for a wild and fun time, with unexpected moves and lots of laughs.
16. **Solitaire-** A great game to challenge yourself and test your ability to organize and strategize.

17. **500-** A game of bidding and bluffing, where your opponents will never know what you have up your sleeve.
18. **Match Up-** Match Up allows you to show off your memorization skills and challenge yourself.
19. **President-** A game of alliances and betrayal, making it a captivating and thrilling game of strategy.
20. **Slapjack-** Slapjack is full of laughs and suspense as you try to beat your opponents to the jack.

15 Popular Video Games

Video games offer an interactive digital experience that allows players to escape into a world of endless possibilities and adventures. From epic battles and thrilling sports competitions to mysteries to solve and puzzles to conquer, video games offer a chance for players to exercise their minds, bodies, and imaginations in exciting new ways.

1. **Overwatch-** Join a team of diverse heroes and save the world in this fast-paced first-person shooter game with unique characters and abilities.
2. **The Witcher 3: Wild Hunt-** Embark on a thrilling journey through a vast open world filled with magic, monsters, and political intrigue.
3. **Red Dead Redemption 2-** Live life as an outlaw in the American frontier, completing missions and making moral choices in this immersive Western adventure.
4. **Civilization VI-** Build and lead a civilization from the dawn of man to the modern era, making strategic decisions and outwitting rival leaders.
5. **Bioshock Infinite-** Explore the floating city of Columbia and unravel its dark secrets using supernatural powers and cunning tactics.
6. **Fallout 4-** Roam the wasteland, scavenging for resources and making allies or enemies in this post-apocalyptic RPG.

7. **Dark Souls III-** Test your mettle against impossible odds and prove your worth as a warrior in this notoriously challenging action RPG.
8. **Grand Theft Auto V-** Live the high life in Los Santos, pulling off daring heists, racing cars, and causing chaos in this open-world sandbox game.
9. **Doom Eternal-** Rip and tear through hordes of demons using an arsenal of powerful weapons and lightning-fast movement.
10. **The Legend of Zelda: Breath of the Wild-** Explore a vast, beautiful, open world filled with secrets and ancient lore as you become the hero Link.
11. **Minecraft-** Build and explore to your heart's content in this sandbox game, where the only limit is your imagination.
12. **Terraria-** Dig deep into the earth, battle monsters, and uncover treasures in this 2D action-adventure game.
13. **Super Mario Odyssey-** Travel through a variety of kingdoms, collecting power moons and battling bosses as the plumber Mario.
14. **Monster Hunter: World-** Join forces with other hunters and track down dangerous beasts, using strategy and teamwork to bring them down.
15. **Tom Clancy's Rainbow Six Siege-** Plan and execute tactical assaults on enemy fortifications using a variety of operators and gadgets.

15 Immersive Virtual Reality (VR) Games

Virtual reality games are an unforgettable immersive experience where players can enter a digital world unlike anything they have ever seen. With VR headsets, motion controllers, and advanced graphics, players can step into fantastical realms, explore new lands, and interact with digital environments in a way that feels truly real. From battling dragons to solving puzzles, virtual reality games offer boundless opportunities for adventure and excitement, providing an escape from the everyday world that is both engaging and entertaining.

1. **Superhot VR-** A fast-paced, stylish shooter that lets you manipulate time to dodge bullets and take out enemies in slow motion. Feel like a superhero as you take control of the battlefield with your VR headset and motion controllers.
2. **The Climb-** Scale new heights as you explore a stunning virtual world filled with challenging rock-climbing routes. Test your nerves and skills as you make your way up to the summit, taking in the breathtaking views along the way.
3. **No Man's Sky-** Explore an infinite universe filled with procedurally generated planets and alien species. Discover new worlds, trade with other players, and build your custom spacecraft as you navigate this massive sandbox VR game.
4. **Job Simulator-** A humorous and lighthearted VR game that lets you perform everyday tasks but with a fun, futuristic twist. Step into a robotic kitchen or office and complete tasks like cooking food or printing documents, but with a robot's touch.
5. **Beat Saber-** Immerse yourself in a futuristic world where you slash your way through beats and obstacles with laser swords. Experience the thrill of a workout and the excitement of a music-driven action game all in one!
6. **Arizona Sunshine-** A first-person shooter set in a post-apocalyptic world overrun by zombies. Battle your way through hordes of the undead using a variety of weapons and tactical strategies, all while immersively experiencing the fear and excitement of the fight.
7. **Tilt Brush-** Create beautiful, three-dimensional artwork in a virtual world using your VR headset and motion controllers. Choose from a range of brushes and colors, and let your imagination run wild as you sculpt your masterpieces in mid-air.
8. **Raw Data-** A fast-paced, futuristic shooter that tasks you with taking on waves of robots and other enemies. Use your VR headset and motion controllers to duck, dodge, and

shoot your way through intense battles, all while exploring a cutting-edge virtual world.

9. **Space Pirate Trainer-** Battle wave after wave of robotic enemies in a futuristic, laser-filled arena. Utilize your VR headset and motion controllers to dodge incoming fire, shoot down enemies, and prove your worth as a true space pirate.

10. **I Expect You To Die-** A comedic and challenging VR puzzle game that puts you in the shoes of a secret agent. Solve puzzles and complete missions using your wits and gadgets while experiencing the thrill of a James Bond-style adventure.

11. **Robo Recall-** An action-packed, first-person shooter that tasks you with taking on an army of rogue robots. Use your VR headset and motion controllers to blast through waves of enemies, all while immersively experiencing the action.

12. **Eagle Flight-** Soar through the skies of a post-apocalyptic Paris as you explore this breathtaking virtual world. Fly through narrow passages, dodge obstacles, and engage in fast-paced aerial battles as you experience the thrill of flight like never before.

13. **Keep Talking and Nobody Explodes-** A multiplayer VR game that tasks one player with disarming a ticking time bomb while the others frantically search for the instructions. Test your teamwork and communication skills as you race against the clock to defuse the bomb.

14. **Moss-** Explore a magical, fairy-tale world as a small mouse named Quill. Solve puzzles, battle enemies, and uncover hidden secrets as you experience this enchanting adventure from a mouse's perspective.

15. **Fantastic Contraption-** Build and create contraptions to solve puzzles and complete challenges in this imaginative VR game. Use your VR headset and motion controllers to grab and manipulate objects.

5 Fantasy Role-Playing Games (RPG)

A role-playing game, or RPG, is a thrilling adventure where you get to step into the shoes of a character you create and embark on a journey filled with epic quests, challenging obstacles, and dynamic relationships. In this imaginative world, anything is possible, and you can chart your path and forge your destiny. Whether you want to explore a rich, immersive world, flex your strategic muscles, or test your problem-solving skills, role-playing games offer a layered and rewarding experience that will challenge, inspire, and entertain you.

1. **Dungeons and Dragons-** Embark on a thrilling adventure with friends and unleash your imagination, becoming whoever you want to be in a world of your own creation.
2. **World of Warcraft-** Immerse yourself in a fantastical world of magic and monsters, forging alliances, battling enemies, and growing your legend as you quest for glory.
3. **Pathfinder-** Discover a world of epic adventure where you can choose your path and forge your own story, using your cunning and bravery to survive in a dangerous and unpredictable land.
4. **Elder Scrolls-** Explore vast, open worlds filled with mystery, magic, and danger, discovering new lands and ancient secrets as you level up your character and build your legend.
5. **Star Wars: Edge of the Empire-** Join the excitement of the Star Wars universe, taking on the roles of smugglers, bounty hunters, and rogue traders as you explore the galaxy and make your fortune.

The above titles are just a small taste of the nearly endless possibilities of games available to play today. Retirement is the perfect time to dive into the world of gaming and explore the different types of games available. You'll probably find that game nights provide much more stimulation and fun than TV nights.

Resources

1. The Best Adult Board Games on Amazon, According to Hyperenthusiastic Reviewers link
2. 36 Popular Board Games For Adults and Teens link

Products

1. Rummikub - The Original Rummy Tile Game link
2. SEQUENCE- Original SEQUENCE Game with Folding Board, Cards and Chips link
3. Trekking The National Parks Board Game - The Award-Winning Strategy Game for National Park Lovers link

*** * ***

Tap into Your Musical Side

Bring music into your life

Music is the rhythm of the soul, the beat of the heart. From classical symphonies to contemporary pop, it's a universal language transcending borders and cultures, stirring emotions and igniting passion. Music has the power to heal, uplift, and inspire, creating a world of sound where anything is possible. Whether listening to your favorite tunes or creating your own, tapping into your musical side brings joy, relaxation, and a world of fun to life.

Unleashing one's inner musician is a journey of self-expression and creativity, filled with melodic moments. From singing in the shower to playing an instrument, exploring one's musical side can be a beautiful and harmonious adventure that ignites the senses and soothes the soul. Whether you're strumming the chords of a guitar, tapping the rhythm of drums, or belting out a karaoke tune, connecting with your musical side can add a new level of excitement and possibility to your day.

. . .

25 Ideas to Bring Music into Your Life

1. Learn an instrument. Playing an instrument can be an incredibly rewarding experience. From the joy of creating a beautiful song to the pride of mastering a difficult piece, learning to play an instrument can bring you a sense of accomplishment. You can explore the depths of music and discover how to express yourself in ways that are unique to you. Plus, it's an incredibly social and engaging activity that can bring people together from all walks of life. Whether you're learning to play your favorite melodies or creating your own compositions, there's a world of fun that comes from learning to play an instrument.
2. Take singing lessons. A wonderful way to express yourself and tap into your creative side. It can also help to build confidence, enhance self-esteem, and provide a sense of accomplishment.
3. Listen to new music genres. Exploring new musical sounds can open up a world of possibilities and bring you alive with the rhythm and emotion of different cultures. Different musical genres can broaden your mind and take you on an exciting journey of discovery.
4. Go to a concert. An exciting experience that offers the opportunity to immerse yourself in the musical journey of your favorite artists and create lasting memories with friends or loved ones in a lively and energetic atmosphere.
5. Buy a harmonica. An affordable and fun way to begin learning and exploring music.
6. Put your favorite songs together. Make a compilation of your favorite songs and give it to someone.
7. Go Christmas caroling.
8. Challenge yourself to make a rap song in the style of the Hamilton musical.
9. Use Alexa to instantly play nearly any song you ask for.
10. Become a karaoke superstar.
11. Compose and record a song.
12. Listen to slack key guitar.

13. Use an app to learn an instrument.
14. Go to a music tutor.
15. Take an online music course.
16. Watch music documentaries
17. Learn DAW (Digital Audio Workstation) for recording, editing, and producing music files.
18. Learn recording software GarageBand, Audacity, or Ableton.
19. Discover new music with apps like Spotify, Pandora, Soundcloud, Apple Music, and Amazon Music.
20. Read a musician's biography.
21. Find the perfect music for relaxation or meditation.
22. Take a music appreciation online course.
23. Learn the sounds of every instrument.
24. Watch a symphony orchestra.
25. Have a living room dance party.

10 Most Popular Instruments to Play

1. **Piano/keyboard-** With its wide range of musical possibilities, learning to play the piano/keyboard is a delightful journey of creativity and exploration. Its beautiful tones will fill your home with magical and heartfelt music.
2. **Guitar-** Learning to play the guitar allows you to strum along to your favorite songs and create your own music, expressing yourself through its powerful rhythms and soulful melodies.
3. **Violin-** The violin is like the voice of your soul, taking the listener on a captivating journey of emotion and feeling. Its melodic tones will capture your heart and inspire you to create beautiful music.
4. **Drums-** Playing the drums is an exhilarating experience that will get your heart beating and your feet tapping to the

beat. You'll be the star of the show as you bring your unique sound to every song you play.
5. **Saxophone-** Learning to play the saxophone is a joyful experience that will allow you to create soulful solos and improvisations, filling the room with warm and beautiful tones. You'll be amazed at how expressive this instrument can be.
6. **Flute-** Learning to play the flute offers a melodic and gentle journey through the world of music that is sure to bring smiles to the faces of everyone listening.
7. **Cello-** The powerful and soul-stirring sound of the cello will surely bring a wonderful, warm glow to your heart that will linger long after the last note is played.
8. **Clarinet-** With its bright, cheerful tones, it is perfect for providing a rousing, upbeat ambiance to any occasion.
9. **Trumpet-** An exuberant instrument full of personality, the trumpet is a fun and invigorating way to express yourself musically.
10. **Harp-** As one of the oldest instruments in the world, the harp has an ancient, timeless feel to its sound that is sure to inspire and captivate.

Resources

1. The Surprising Benefits of Making Music Your Hobby link
2. What Is the Most Popular Instrument to Play? link
3. Learn Guitar with app and online at Fender Play link
4. Online Music Courses link

* * *

Thirst for Knowledge
Cultivate your curiosity

Tap into your curiosity, and you'll never be bored again. When we tap into our curiosity, we open ourselves to a world of possibility. We become adventurers, explorers, and learners. We can ask questions, seek answers, and challenge ourselves. We can try new things, find new interests, and uncover new passions. We can explore the depths of our imaginations and the limits of our knowledge. We can seek out new experiences and learn from others. We can feed our minds with new information and grow our skills. All of this will help us to stay engaged, inspired, and never be bored again.

Nurturing our curiosity is about taking the initiative to seek out new knowledge and experiences. We can read, listen to podcasts, attend lectures, watch documentaries, or simply talk to people. We can try new hobbies, take classes, and practice activities. We can create and explore, attend events and conferences, or take up a new sport. All these activities can help foster our curiosity and ensure that we stay lifelong learners.

Learning can be challenging as it stretches us out of our comfort zone but also rewarding as we develop new knowledge and deepen our understanding. Learning also helps us increase our understanding of and connection to the world around us, form meaningful relationships, and build empathy for others. All of these skills are essential for leading a successful and content life.

38 Ideas to Explore

Regardless of how knowledgeable we think we are, there is always something more to learn about. Spark your curiosity with the following ideas.

1. **Learn a new language-** It's never been easier to learn a new language. From language apps to interactive websites, learning a language can be as fun as playing a game. Stay dedicated to learning by booking a visit to a country that speaks your new language months in advance.
2. **Unearth your ancestry-** For under $100, DNA test kits (which involve spitting into a tube and mailing it in) will tell you all about where your ancestors were from. They estimate your percentage breakdown of each ethnicity and a

whole lot more. It's an easy and exciting way to start uncovering your story. Leading companies like AncestryDNA or 23andMe are excellent places to begin your search.

3. **Learn magic-** Learn the secrets to amazing your friends and grandkids as you transform yourself into the next David Copperfield.

4. **Architecture-** Learning about architectural styles will provide interest to your neighborhood drives as well as your worldwide travels. You'll start to recognize different architectural influences and understand regional building preferences.

5. **Decorative arts and design-** Learn how to appreciate the objects around us for their artistic and functional uses.

6. **Learn how to hypnotize someone-** Ever wonder if those hypnotized people are just faking it or if there really is a secret to mind control? Perhaps your new skills could be useful for getting a spouse to double down on the chores you wish they would do?

7. **Meteorology-** Just about every day, we're affected by the weather. Learning about what the different types of clouds and weather patterns mean can make our time outside more enjoyable.

8. **Understand the opposite sex better-** Sometimes, it seems like men are from Mars and women are from Venus. Grab a book by that title and learn why men and women act and think differently.

9. **Art appreciation-** Learning about famous artists and their painting styles helps us understand the art around us and makes museum visits much more exciting.

10. **Local plants and geology-** A little time learning about local plants and land formations can go a long way when we're outside and start to recognize and enjoy the nature around us.

11. **Bug hunting-** Bugs are strange little creatures. There is a whole interesting world to discover if we learn about the

types, lives, and struggles of bugs and then seek to find them.
12. **Self-defense-** What would you do if someone grabbed you while walking to your car? Once you know what to do, you'll always know.
13. **Sign language-** Learning sign language can improve cognitive skills, such as memory, problem-solving, and attention to detail. It can also open up new volunteer or job opportunities, such as teaching, interpreting, or working in any field related to the deaf and hard of hearing.
14. **String theory-** String theory is a branch of physics that proposes that all matter is composed of vibrating strings and seeks to reconcile quantum mechanics and general relativity. It postulates that the universe is made up of tiny one-dimensional objects called strings, which vibrate at different frequencies to create the particles and forces observed in nature.
15. **Bird calls-** It can be a hoot to learn about bird calls.
16. **Watch a TED talk-** The mission of TED talks is to "discover and spread ideas that spark the imagination, embrace possibility, and catalyze impact." The brightest minds in their fields give short presentations on ideas that can change how we think for good.
17. **Listen to podcasts-** Podcasts are free audio files on the internet that can be listened to on many devices. They are usually centered around a topic or news event and can be created by anyone from anonymous individuals to professional broadcasters. There are podcasts for every interest.
18. **Take an online course on anything-** Udemy, Masterclass, and other websites have online video courses that teach about anything for reasonable prices.
19. **Inflammaging-** Inflammaging is the chronic, low-grade inflammation that occurs as we age. It is important to learn about inflammaging in order to understand how to prevent it and maintain a healthy life as we age.

20. **Artificial intelligence-** Artificial Intelligence is a branch of computer science that focuses on the development of machines and algorithms to think, reason, and act like humans. Learning about AI is important as it will be an integral part of our future, having the potential to shape our world in countless ways.
21. **Survival preparedness-** Preppers are people who prepare for potential disasters, both natural and man-made, by stockpiling supplies and learning emergency skills. We should learn about prepping to be better prepared for emergencies and protect ourselves and our families.
22. **Music appreciation-** Music appreciation helps us to gain a greater understanding of the various elements of music and can provide us with an enriching cultural experience. It can give us a deeper appreciation of the music we hear and help us to develop a more meaningful connection with it.
23. **History-** Learning history helps us to understand and appreciate the past, as well as to gain a better understanding of the present and prepare for the future. By exploring the successes and failures of the past, we can learn valuable lessons about humanity.
24. **Reciprocity-** Reciprocity refers to the exchange of things of value between two parties, with each party expecting an equivalent return. It is a mutual exchange of favors or privileges, like when you do something nice for a friend, and they do something nice for you in return.
25. **Positive psychology-** Positive psychology is a research-based approach to understanding the strengths and virtues that lead to a more fulfilling life. By understanding positive psychology, we can learn how to cultivate more joy, satisfaction, and meaning in our daily lives.
26. **Longevity-** Longevity is the ability to live a long and healthy life, and it's important to learn about it so that we can make informed decisions about our health and lifestyle that will help us live longer and healthier lives.

27. **Airplane spotting and aviation history-** Airplane spotting is a hobby where people observe aircraft and identify the type of plane they see. There is an exciting world to explore in aviation, from the first aircraft development to the future of humanity in space.
28. **How the stock market really works-** The stock market is a great way to invest money and grow your wealth. Understanding how the stock market works is crucial so you can make informed decisions about your investments.
29. **Philosophy-** Philosophy is the study of fundamental questions about knowledge, reality, and existence. It provides an excellent foundation for understanding the world and how we interact with it.
30. **Religious studies-** Religion is an integral part of our world and history, and understanding it can help us better understand different cultures and people. Learning about religion can broaden our perspectives and lead to more meaningful conversations.
31. **Psychology-** Psychology studies human behavior, thoughts, and emotions. Knowing more about psychology can help us better understand ourselves and others.
32. **Sociology-** Sociology is the study of human behavior and the way people interact with each other in social settings. It looks at how individuals and groups are shaped by their environment and the interactions they have with one another.
33. **Bitcoin-** Bitcoin is a decentralized digital currency that makes it possible for people to transact with each other without the need for a bank or other third-party financial institution. It uses cryptography to secure and verify transactions, and its decentralized nature ensures that it is not controlled by any single entity.
34. **Non-fungible tokens (NFTs)-** Non-fungible tokens (NFTs) are unique digital assets that can be used to represent ownership of unique items like artwork, music, tickets, or game items. They can also be used to create

digital scarcity, allowing people to have exclusive access to digital content and collectibles.

35. **Bible-** The Bible is the holy book of Christianity. Christianity is the world's largest religion based on the teachings of Jesus Christ, who is believed to be the Son of God. The main teachings of the Bible are to love God, to love one another, and to live a life of faith, hope, and charity. Learning about the Bible provides us with an opportunity to understand and explore faith, as well as to develop a relationship with God. It also encourages us to live a life of service to others, thus helping us to lead a more meaningful and fulfilling life.

36. **Gut health-** Gut health is the overall balance of bacteria in the digestive system. Its importance lies in its ability to support a healthy immune system, digestion, and even mental health. Taking care of your gut health is essential for your overall well-being.

37. **Online Safety-** Empower yourself to navigate the digital world confidently while safeguarding your personal information and privacy from potential online threats.

38. **Theory of Relativity-** Proposed by Albert Einstein in 1905, the theory of relativity explains that space and time are not fixed and absolute but rather relative and dependent on the observer's state of motion and gravitational field. This means that time can pass differently for observers moving relative to each other or experiencing different levels of gravity. This theory has led to a deeper understanding of the nature of space, time, and the universe as a whole.

Resources

1. TED Talks 4,200+ talks to stir your curiosity link
2. 210,000+ Online Video Courses link
3. Social Psychology Reciprocity link
4. Become a Positive Psychology Professional link
5. The 4 most accurate DNA test kits link
6. The importance of gut health link

7. 101 New Skills: Learn Something New link
8. 100 Thought-Provoking Questions link
9. 9 Simple and Effective Online Safety Tips for Seniors link

Books

1. The Longevity Paradox: How to Die Young at a Ripe Old Age by Dr. Steven R Gundry MD link
2. Men Are from Mars, Women Are from Venus: The Classic Guide to Understanding the Opposite Sex by John Gray link
3. Art That Changed the World: Transformative Art Movements and the Paintings That Inspired Them by DK link
4. Smithsonian Handbook of Interesting Insects by Gavin Broad link
5. Prepper's Home Defense: Security Strategies to Protect Your Family by Any Means Necessary by Jim Cobb link
6. The Elegant Universe: Superstrings, Hidden Dimensions, and the Quest for the Ultimate Theory by Brian Greene link
7. Stock Market 101: From Bull and Bear Markets to Dividends, Shares, and Margins—Your Essential Guide to the Stock Market by Michele Cagan CPA link

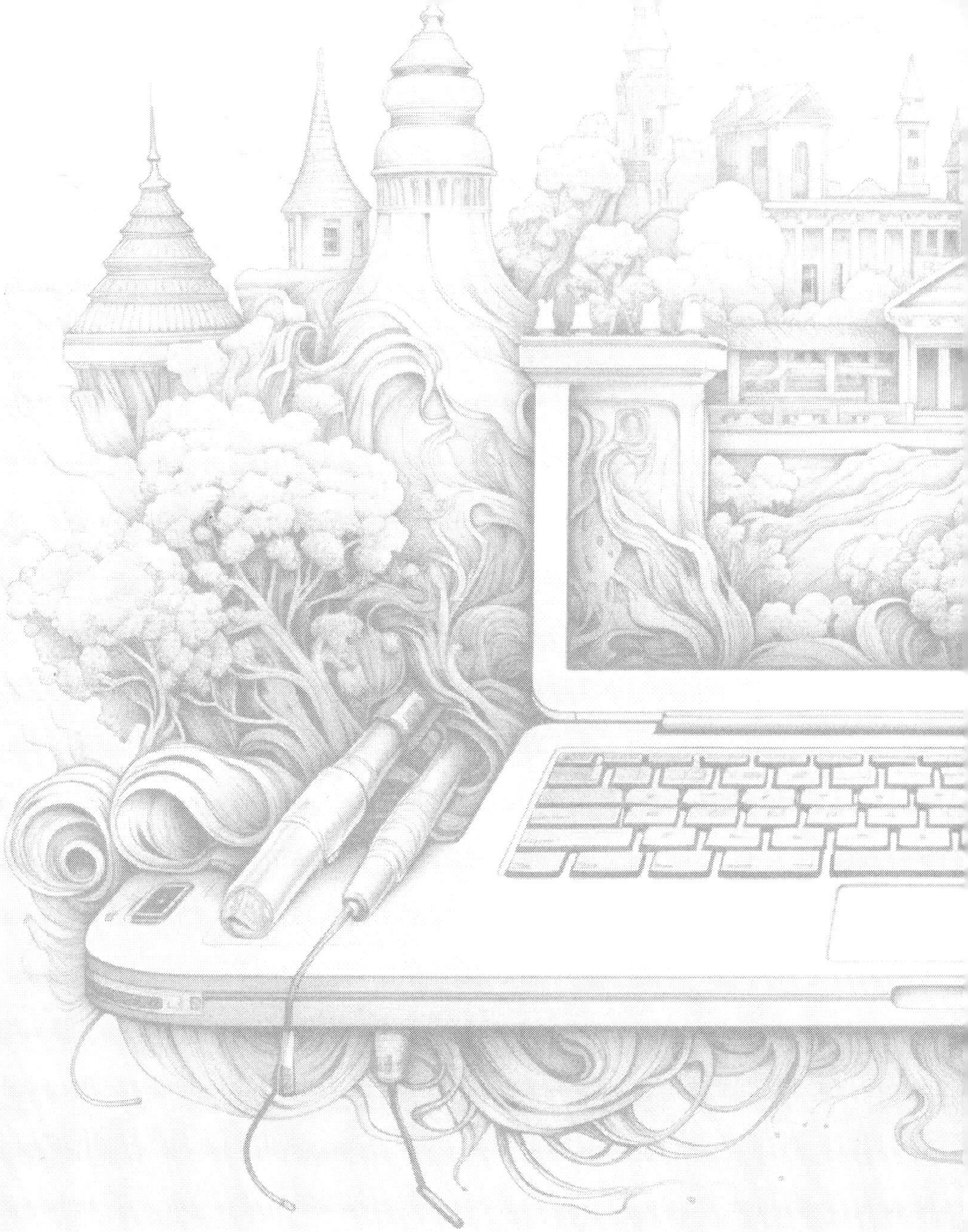

Chapter 9
Use Technology

In a quiet suburban neighborhood, there lived an elderly gentleman named Mr. Jenkins. Retired and living alone, he had always been a bit apprehensive about technology. However, his world changed when his granddaughter gifted him a tablet for his 75th birthday. At first, Mr. Jenkins was reluctant to embrace this newfangled device, but his granddaughter patiently showed him how to use it.

Soon, Mr. Jenkins discovered the wonders of video calling. He had a son who lived across the country, and they hadn't seen each other in years due to the distance. With his tablet, Mr. Jenkins could now have face-to-face conversations with his son and watch his grandkids grow up, even from thousands of miles away. It was like having his family right in his living room.

Over time, Mr. Jenkins also explored other features of his tablet. He learned to use email to keep in touch with old friends, listen to his favorite music, and even read books on the device, which saved him trips to the library. The tablet became his window to the world, connecting him to loved ones and opening up a world of entertainment and knowledge that he never imagined possible.

As Mr. Jenkins continued to explore the digital realm, he not only found joy and connection but also a renewed sense of curiosity and adventure in his retirement. The simple gift of technology had transformed his life, proving that it's never too late to embrace the benefits of the digital age.

In this chapter, we'll explore ideas on how technology can help us. From a smart house that answers to our voice to staying connected, entertained, productive, or fit, technology can serve you in fun and exciting ways. So get ready to plug in and power up your retirement with the many amazing possibilities technology offers!

50 Fun Ideas for How a Retiree Can Use Technology

1. Join social media platforms like Facebook, Twitter, or Instagram to connect with friends and family.
2. Start a blog or vlog to share hobbies and interests.
3. Join online communities related to hobbies or interests.
4. Participate in online courses to learn new skills or hobbies.
5. Play online games with friends and family.
6. Use video chat apps like Skype or Zoom to stay in touch with loved ones.
7. Create a digital photo album to share with family and friends.
8. Explore virtual reality tours of museums, art galleries, or National Parks.
9. Use a fitness app to track your daily exercise routine.
10. Start a virtual book club with friends and discuss books through video chats.
11. Learn a new language through online courses or apps like Duolingo.
12. Listen to podcasts on a variety of topics.
13. Use a recipe app to find and try new recipes.
14. Use video chat apps to connect with grandchildren who live far away.
15. Play brain games and puzzles to keep the mind sharp.

Chapter 9

16. Use a mindfulness or meditation app for relaxation and stress relief.
17. Participate in online fundraising campaigns for charitable causes.
18. Use a weather app to stay up to date on local weather conditions.
19. Use a language translation app when traveling to foreign countries.
20. Join an online knitting or crafting community.
21. Start an online business selling handmade crafts or goods.
22. Create and share playlists on music streaming services like Spotify or Apple Music.
23. Watch movies and TV shows on streaming services like Netflix or Hulu.
24. Use a language learning app to improve communication skills while traveling.
25. Attend online concerts and music festivals.
26. Take online courses on finance and investing to manage retirement savings.
27. Use a genealogy website to research family history and create a family tree.
28. Start a YouTube channel to share hobbies and interests.
29. Join online forums to discuss politics or current events.
30. Use a budgeting app to manage finances and track expenses.
31. Create and edit photos using photo editing apps.
32. Use a dating app to meet new people and find a close friend.
33. Attend online classes to learn new artistic skills like painting or drawing.
34. Use a digital calendar to keep track of appointments and events.
35. Explore virtual tours of historical landmarks and attractions.
36. Use a navigation app when traveling to unfamiliar locations.
37. Use a ride-sharing app for transportation needs.
38. Create and share short videos on social media platforms like TikTok or Instagram.
39. Use a shopping app to make online purchases.

40. Participate in online writing communities and share writing with others.
41. Use a virtual assistant like Alexa or Siri to manage daily tasks.
42. Take virtual cooking classes with a professional chef.
43. Use a weather app to plan outdoor activities like hiking or gardening.
44. Attend virtual wine or beer tastings.
45. Use a language learning app to improve communication with non-native-speaking friends.
46. Participate in virtual political or social activism events.
47. Use a podcast app to listen to audiobooks or storytelling.
48. Use a smart home system to control home devices like lights or thermostat.
49. Join online photography communities to share and learn new techniques.
50. Use video conferencing to connect with former colleagues or professional networks.

Chapter 9 Website Links

Technology Ideas and Tips from Volume 1:
3D Printing - Get a Smart Home Virtual Assistant - Use Online Shopping, Delivery, and Rideshare Apps - Get To Know Your Smartphone - Get Some Cool Gadgets - Read eBooks and Listen to Audiobooks - Build a Fighting Robot - Unlock the Computer and Internet

Turn Your House into a Smart Home

Command and control your space

With minimal effort, you can upgrade your house and become the commander of your domain. Waiting for your orders, an army of appliances is eager to serve.

9 Smart Home Possibilities

1. **Lighting-** Control and schedule the lights in your home and change their color.
2. **Thermostat-** Control and schedule the temperature in your home to save money.
3. **Security-** Arm and disarm security systems, view security cameras, video doorbell, view baby monitors, and get water leak alerts.
4. **Entertainment-** Control and access TV, music, and streaming services.
5. **Appliances-** Control and get alerts on the usage of devices such as washing machines, dryers, ovens, fans, coffee machines, and robot vacuums.
6. **Blinds and curtains-** Control and schedule the opening and closing of blinds and curtains.
7. **Plugs and outlets-** Control and schedule devices plugged into outlets.
8. **Communications-** Announce to the whole house or communicate with rooms by intercom.
9. **Voice Assistants-** Get answers to questions and control everything with your voice.

Installation of most smart devices can be as simple as plugging in a smart switch into an electrical outlet that turns on and off the plugged-in appliance or changing out a light bulb for a smart bulb that can change colors and dim. Even decent smart wireless security systems are now under $300 and battery-operated, so they only need to be placed in the correct locations on doors, windows, or front of the house. Once you see how easy it is to set up and control things like lights and music with your voice, you'll never want to return to a dumb house. You've been warned!

Go for it! Simple start steps:

1. Decide on your artificial intelligence first officer. Google Home, Amazon Alexa, or other smart speaker/display.
2. Look into compatible smart devices, "works with Alexa" etc.
3. Plug the device in and use its app to setup.
4. Learn how to control, schedule, and get alerts from the new device.

Resources

1. The Best Smart Home Devices link
2. 16 Smart Home Assistant Devices For Senior Safety link
3. Smart Home Devices For Seniors link

Products

1. Smart Plugs link
2. Smart Color Changing Dimmable Bulbs link
3. Smart Wireless Home Security System link

Books

1. Alexa For Seniors In Easy Steps by Nick Vandome link
2. Pairs well with: Wireless home internet, wireless speakers, music

* * *

Learn to Use All of Google's Free Resources
Discover more than the search

I'm confident that unless you live under a rock, you know about or are one of the 1 billion users using the world's most popular search engine, Google. You might not know that this trillion-dollar and currently the fourth-largest company in the world has many incredibly useful free resources. They make most of their money selling advertisements to companies, like the top search results that say AD next to them, so they can invest in helpful and sometimes revolutionary tech software and provide them for free. And who doesn't love free things? Here are a few of the Google resources you might want to use.

Google Suite

It's beyond the scope of this book to go over the 80 different apps and tools you can access from Google's website. Go to google.com, click on the square dots in the upper corner, scroll to the bottom, and click on the "More from Google" button to see them all. Then, take a few minutes to learn about each of the tools. Below are a few of the most helpful ones I use on the computer, and many have an app to use on a phone or tablet. Also, because they are cloud-based, meaning the information is stored on internet servers rather than only on your computer, you'll be able to access your information, such as Word documents, on any computer or other device connected to the internet. That's extremely helpful and safer than if your important docs were only on one computer that could be lost forever if it broke.

The Basics:

- Docs- Word processor.
- Sheets- Spreadsheets.
- Drive- Free 15 GB of online storage for anything digital, such as photos.
- Slides- For presentations similar to PowerPoint.
- Calendar

- Contacts
- Photos
- Forms- Custom surveys.

Communications:

- Gmail- Email.
- Chat- Direct messenger.
- Meet- Video calls and group meetings similar to Facetime and Zoom.
- Voice- A free virtual phone number to make, receive, and forward calls on any device.

Travel:

- Maps- Directions to anywhere.
- Street View- 360-degree photos to explore the world.
- Translate- Use the app and camera to translate menus, speech, and more.
- Lens- Search by image, snap a pic, and get information on plants, animals, or buildings.
- Travel- Find the cheapest airfares, find things to do in every city, and save points of interest from the website to your phone's Google map as a pin.
- Earth- View the world in 3D.
- Google Fi- Prepaid mobile phone service with international roaming (phone and data) built in.

Entertainment:

- YouTube- Videos on everything.
- Podcasts
- Games
- News
- Books
- Virtual Field Trips.
- Virtual Reality games and 360-degree videos.

Chapter 9 231

- Art creation
- Photo scan- Old photo digitization tool.

Gadgets and Wearables:

- Chromecast- A streaming media device that allows users to display content from various apps on their television.
- Google Pay- Pay with your phone or send money to people.
- Pixel- A phone made by Google.
- Google TV- Stream content on your TV with a dedicated remote, similar to Amazon Fire TV.
- Wear OS- Smartwatch.
- Google Home- Smart artificial intelligence (AI) speaker to answer questions and control household devices.
- Chromebook- An inexpensive cloud-based laptop.
- Car enabled- AI assistant for your vehicle.

Go for it! Simple start steps:

1. Sign up for a Google account to get a Gmail email and a place to access all your Google resources.
2. Go to the Google Resources link #1 below and learn about what everything can do for you.
3. Open up a few web apps to test, and download the corresponding apps to your phone.
4. Go to Resources link #3 below, Google Training, and learn how to use anything from Google.

Resources

1. Google Resources and Tools link
2. Google Products link
3. Google Training link
4. 50 Google Search Statistics and Facts link

Product

1. Google Pixel Phone link
2. Google Pixel Watch link
3. Chromebook Laptop link
4. Chromecast with Google TV link

Books

1. Gmail Seniors Guide by Jack Hillby link
2. Google Apps Made Easy by James Bernstein link
3. Google Workspace Guide 2022 by Henry Whelan link

Pairs well with: Home productivity, travel planning, backing up important docs

* * *

Exercise at Home With Online Fitness
Join a workout class without going anywhere

It's no secret that exercise is essential to our health and well-being, but going to the gym might not be your thing. Luckily, we can get our heart pumping and muscles working without needing to go anywhere. The internet has brought a "never get bored" supply of workout videos to follow, apps to guide us, and even virtual live classes to join. Intelligent home fitness equipment isn't cheap, but on the other hand, neither are medical bills.

5 Intelligent Home Fitness Equipment

- **Smart fitness mirror-** It's a seemingly ordinary wall mirror with a hidden secret. It transforms into a personal trainer when it's time to get busy. An LCD behind the mirror displays a personal trainer to lead you through a workout while you look at yourself to gauge your form. You

can take a yoga class, work on your cardio, and lift weights in front of a live or AI fitness trainer.
- **Guided smart treadmill-** If the idea of running or walking in place makes you feel like a hamster, consider freeing your mind with a smart treadmill. A large LCD on the front can display scenery like you're running anywhere around the world or live fitness classes with online points leader-type challenges.
- **Stationary smart bikes-** Join a live gym cycle class, or feel like you're racing the Tour De France with the internet-connected front display. During the pandemic, the Peloton Bike and other similar smart bikes sold like hotcakes.
- **Smart stationary rowing-** Row, row, row your machine at home while your mind imagines being on a beautiful glassy lake in Switzerland.
- **Connected weight training-** There are machines with resistance pulley-type handles that are compact and can be great for giving your muscles a workout without needing to store heavy weights. It's a smart mirror with handles extending out and a personal fitness coach guiding you from the mirror right in your living room.

6 Online Workout Videos, Apps, and Courses

1. **Senior Fitness With Meredith** (www.seniorfitness-withmeredith.com)- Free workouts, content, and articles directed towards senior fitness.
2. **Nike Training Club**- Free app with 479+ workout classes for every fitness level, including live instructor-led classes.
3. **Fitness Blender-** Free workouts, recipes, fitness plans, and content. It has a premium section for more perks.
4. **Apple Fitness+-** Subscription-based app (currently $10 per month or $80 annually) with 4,000+ workouts in 12 different categories, including kickboxing, strength, HIIT, Yoga, core,

mindful cooldown, pilates, dance, cycling, treadmill, walk, row, and meditation. There is integration with Apple Watch for heart rate monitoring and other health feedback.
5. **Classpass-** Has paid as well as 4,000+ free on-demand workout videos.
6. **YouTube-** Thousands of free fitness videos. See the #5 resources link below.

Resources

1. The Best Smart Fitness Mirrors link
2. Best Smart Treadmills link
3. The Very Best Smart Home Gym Machines link
4. The 10 Best Online Workout Programs link
5. 28 Free YouTube Fitness Channels to Keep You Moving link
6. 7 Online Workout Classes to Keep Seniors Fit and Healthy link

Books

1. 5-Minute Core Exercises for Seniors: Daily Routines to Build Balance and Boost Confidence by Cindy Brehse link
2. 6-Minute Fitness at 60+: Simple Home Exercises to Reclaim Strength, Balance, and Energy in 15 Days by Jonathan Su link
3. Stretching to Stay Young: Simple Workouts to Keep You Flexible, Energized, and Pain-Free by Jessica Matthews link

***

Take Control of Your Photos

Become a digital memory guru

If you're like most people, you probably have a lot of photos. And rightly so. We remember when getting a film photograph was a costly and slow process. It's so much easier today with digital cameras. But chances are, all your photos are just taking up space on a drive somewhere, and you rarely view them. Well, that's just a shame because they are fun memories of our lives, and it's now so easy to create things that will remind us of these good times.

7 Things to Do With Your Digital Photos

1. Share them on social media platforms like Facebook, Instagram, and Twitter.
2. Print them out and hang them on walls or create photo albums.
3. Use them as backgrounds or screensavers on your computer or phone.
4. Edit them with photo editing software to improve the composition, lighting, and color.
5. Create photo collages or montages.
6. Use them to create custom gifts like mugs, t-shirts, or phone cases.
7. Create videos or slideshows with them.

How To Keep Your Digital Memories Safe

At home or on travel, there's only one way to keep your digital memories safe... redundancy.

If you keep all your photos in one location (like on an external hard drive, computer, or camera phone) and there's an accident (such as the drive mysteriously fails, is dropped and broken, is in a fire, or is stolen), potentially a lifetime of precious memories is gone forever! No bueno.

So always keep at least two copies to lower the risk and preferably keep them in different locations. Keeping a copy online is a great second-copy option. However, the monthly storage fee can get expensive if you take a lot of photos and videos. Perhaps $10+/month indefinitely...

Tip: Did you know that if you're an Amazon Prime member, you currently get unlimited photo (and 5GB video) storage for *free*? Okay, it's not really free since you're paying for the membership, but it's included with other benefits.

If you stop your membership, you'll have six months before your photos are deleted from the cloud.

We use the Amazon Photos app to automatically back up the day's photos. It's a second copy piece of mind if we lose or break our phone before we can adequately back up our pictures/videos onto two external hard drives every few months (usually to free up space on the phone).

A similar Google Photos app or iCloud backup (among others) can store your digital memories on the cloud with some additional benefits we love.

They will reshare your old photos with you in "on this day" photos, quickly search for people or places, and automatically pop into screensavers or slideshows on almost any device. We use the Amazon Fire Stick for streaming on all our TVs, and all our backed-up photos are easily visible and fun to look at on large screens.

How To Digitize Your Old Photo Albums

Old photo albums from film cameras are bulky, not easily shared, can be destroyed and lost forever, and, with time, will fade away. It's a good idea to get them caught up to our modern digital lives and digitize them before it's too late. Hundreds or thousands of years from now, when your great, great, great, great, great, grandchild or distant relative searches for their ancestry DNA in the future internet, your smiling digital face might just pop up.

Digital memories might last forever. Or until the robots take over or we annihilate ourselves. Anyhoo, an easy way to get your old photos digital is to use a free app from Google called PhotoScan. You'll use your phone's camera to snap a photo of your physical photo. The app will automatically crop and make it look digitally purdy. Then you'll have a copy on your phone and can do whatever you want with it like it was a photo you just took. One tip for best results is to ensure the lighting is bright and turn off the anti-glare function in the app if you don't have glare.

Resources

1. Best Way To Store Photo link
2. 8 Cool Things To Do With Your Photos link
3. Google PhotoScan App link

Products

1. 5TB External Hard Drive link
2. Fire TV Stick 4K Max link
3. Echo Show 10 Smart Display link

Pairs well with: Photography, travel, cloud storage

* * *

Fix Anything with the Help of YouTube

Become extremely handy

Chances are I'm singing to the choir when I say YouTube has a helpful video for just about everything. It has saved me thousands of dollars over the years when things break and I have no idea what to do. Without it, I would have unnecessarily hired expensive handypersons, taken my car and RV to the mechanic, and bought new appliances. But more times than not, I'll type in my problem to YouTube, and there will be videos from people who had similar issues and how they fixed them. They will tell you what part you'll need, the tools you'll need, and show you how to fix it step-by-step. Sometimes, it feels easier than following a cooking recipe. I'm not exaggerating.

One example happened just last month when the dishwasher decided to stop working. It wouldn't spray water out with any force to clean the dishes. We tried cleaning everything, thinking it was clogged, with no luck. Then, a YouTube video revealed two possible problems. We bought both parts on Amazon and followed the instructions to replace the first potential problem, the on-off water switch. It worked, and we returned the other unused part. I could go on and on with other YouTube fixes, but I won't. Before hiring someone to fix a problem, search YouTube first; it might be something easy you can do yourself.

Of course, YouTube's help extends beyond troubleshooting problems; it can show you how to do most home improvement things or learn nearly anything new. That may be why it's the #2 most used search engine after Google.

Go for it! Simple start steps:

1. Type your problem into YouTube with as much detail as possible, like the model number.
2. Watch a few promising videos to see if the fix applies to your situation.
3. Order the parts or tools needed online because taking them back is easy if it doesn't work.
4. Follow along with the video while you make the fix.

* * *

Become a Virtual Reality (VR) Gamer

Lose yourself in another reality

The ultimate in high-tech fun is virtual reality, also known as VR. Virtual reality is a computer-generated simulation of a three-dimensional environment that can be interacted with using specialized equipment, such as a VR headset. The user is fully immersed in the experience and can look around and interact with the virtual environment as if it were real.

A VR headset typically includes a head-mounted display with a screen in front of the eyes. It may also include sensors that track the user's head movements and adjust the display accordingly. Some VR systems have hand-held controllers, allowing users to interact with the virtual environment.

VR technology can be used in various applications, such as gaming, entertainment, education, and training. In gaming, players can experience a fully immersive and interactive environment where they can explore and interact inside the game. In education and training, VR can simulate real-life scenarios, allowing people to practice skills, such as surgical procedures or piloting an aircraft, in a safe and controlled environment. In entertainment, VR can create immersive experiences such as being at the movies, theme parks, or other real-life attractions.

Virtual Reality differs from Augmented Reality, which overlays digital content over the real-world environment, creating a blend of the virtual and real worlds.

4 Popular VR Game Systems

1. **Meta Quest 2-** An affordable standalone VR headset that requires no additional hardware or computer to use, it is also compatible with the PC for a more advanced gaming experience. It currently has an exceptional 4.7 out of 5 rating with over 77,000 reviews on Amazon. Meta Quest Pro is a more advanced and expensive upgrade.
2. **PlayStation VR-** A VR headset for the PlayStation 4 and PlayStation 5 consoles.
3. **HTC Vive-** A VR headset that requires a powerful PC to run and offers room-scale VR experiences and motion controllers.

4. **Valve Index-** A high-end VR headset that provides a wide field of view, high resolution, and a high refresh rate. It also offers finger-tracking controllers.

All these VR systems are continually evolving with new technology and updates. They offer a wide range of experiences and support a variety of games and applications, so it's worth researching and comparing the options to find the best fit for your needs and budget.

5 Top Virtual Reality (VR) Games

1. **Beat Saber-** A fast-paced, rhythm-based game where players use virtual lightsabers to slash through blocks representing musical beats.
2. **Superhot VR-** A first-person shooter game where time moves only when the player moves, allowing players to plan and execute complex slow-motion combat sequences.
3. **Job Simulator-** A comedic simulation game set in a world where robots have replaced all human jobs, allowing players to perform various tasks in a virtual office, store, and kitchen.
4. **VRChat-** A social VR platform where players can interact with others in various virtual worlds, play games, and create their own content.
5. **Half-Life- Alyx-** A first-person shooter game that takes place in the Half-Life universe and is set before the events of Half-Life 2.

Resources

1. Best VR Headsets Now link
2. The 51 Best VR Games link
3. Best VR Games: Top Virtual Reality Experiences To Play Right Now link

Products

Chapter 9 241

1. Meta Quest 2 VR Headset link
2. Playstation VR Bundle link
3. HTC Vive VR Headset link

Books

1. The Metaverse: Virtual lands, Avatars, NFTs, VR headsets, Blockchains. A First Insight to This New World Getting Ready For the Next Big Thing by Harrison Boyer link
2. Virtual & Augmented Reality For Dummies by Paul Mealy link
3. Virtual Reality by Samuel Greengard link

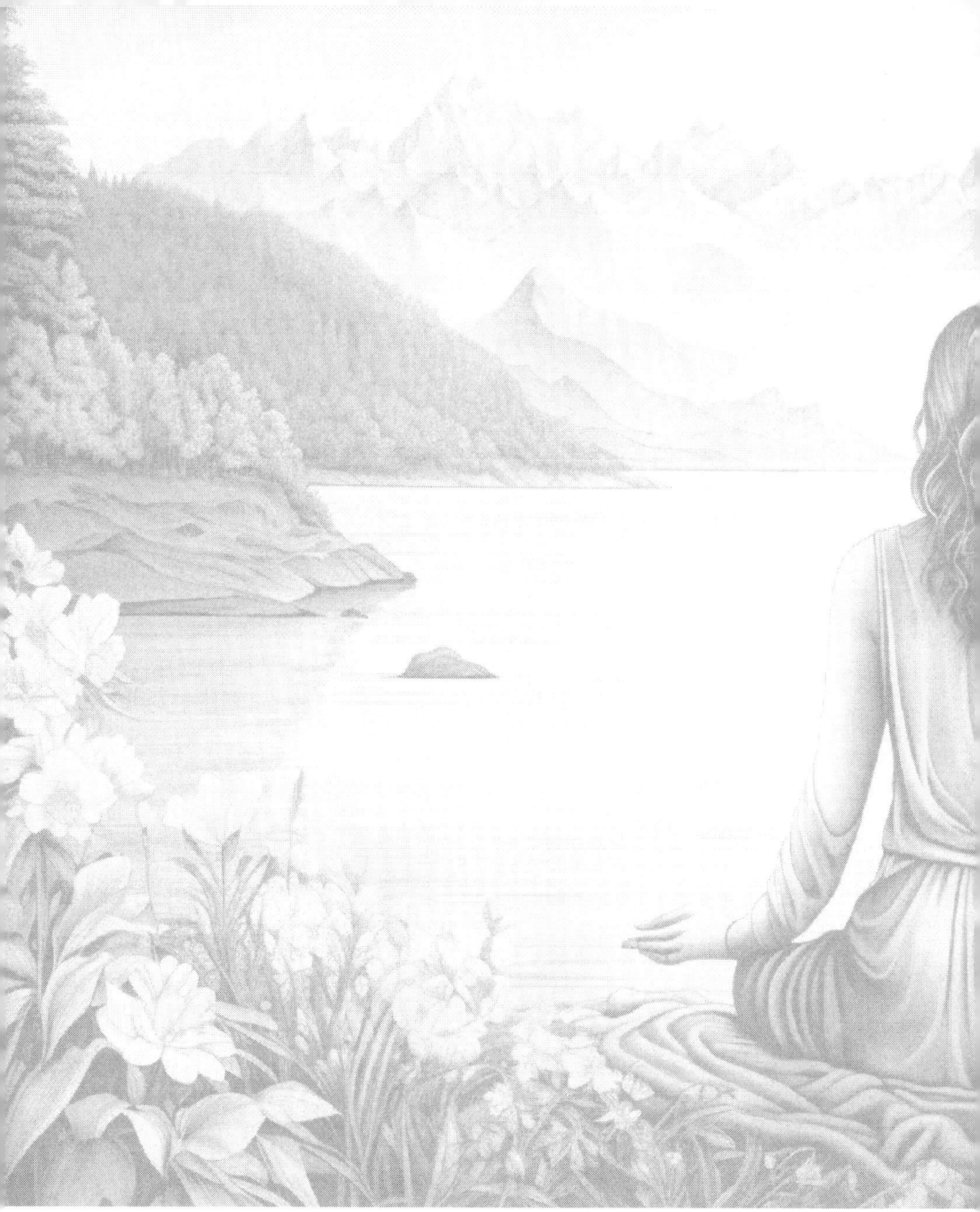

Chapter 10

Healthy Mind

Cultivating a healthy mind is vital for leading a fulfilling and joyful life. Our mental health affects every aspect of our existence, from our relationships with loved ones to our ability to handle challenges and pursue our dreams. When we prioritize our mental well-being by maintaining a positive outlook, engaging in regular exercise and cognitive activities, and finding purpose and joy in daily life, we can unlock a wealth of benefits, such as improved memory, better decision-making, and reduced stress and anxiety. Investing in our mental health is truly an investment in our overall quality of life. Volume 1 of this book goes over physical health and wellness in-depth, so we won't tackle it here, but we'd like to briefly add a few ideas of how to stay healthy before focusing on a healthy mind in this chapter.

25 Ideas to Focus on Physical Health

1. Take a brisk 20-minute walk daily to get the heart pumping and clear the mind.
2. Join a local gym and take a fitness class tailored to your needs, such as yoga, Pilates, or Zumba.

3. Go swimming at the local community pool to strengthen your muscles and improve your flexibility.
4. Take up cycling to get some fresh air, increase your endurance, and explore your surroundings.
5. Stretch regularly to improve your flexibility and prevent stiffness in your joints.
6. Dance around the house to your favorite tunes for a fun and easy way to get moving.
7. Invest in a set of resistance bands for strength training exercises that can be done at home.
8. Do simple exercises like squats, lunges, and push-ups during commercial breaks while watching TV.
9. Take a weekly yoga or tai chi class to improve your balance, flexibility, and overall health.
10. Get a pedometer and aim to walk 10,000 steps per day.
11. Take a dance class with a partner or group for a fun and social way to stay active.
12. Join a local hiking or walking group to explore nature and get some exercise at the same time.
13. Incorporate more vegetables and fruits into your diet to boost your immune system and improve your overall health.
14. Reduce your processed foods and sugar intake to improve your energy levels and reduce inflammation.
15. Take up gardening as a low-impact way to stay active and enjoy the outdoors.
16. Consider a daily multivitamin to ensure you get all the nutrients for optimal health.
17. Try meditation or deep breathing exercises to reduce stress and promote relaxation.
18. Get a massage or practice self-massage with a foam roller to release tension and improve circulation.
19. Take a group fitness class for socialization and accountability, like water aerobics or senior fitness.
20. Practice good posture to prevent back pain and improve breathing.
21. Drink plenty of water throughout the day to stay hydrated and support your bodily functions.

22. Take a hot bath with Epsom salt to soothe sore muscles and promote relaxation.
23. Get a good night's sleep by establishing a consistent bedtime routine and avoiding electronic devices before bed.
24. Spend time outdoors to boost your mood and get vitamin D from sunlight.
25. Laugh often to boost your immune system, lower stress levels, and improve overall health.

Chapter 10 Website Links

Health Inspiration and Tips from Volume 1:
Prioritize Physical Health (37 ideas) - Work on Wellness (37 ideas) - Go Fancy Picnicking - Get in Touch with Your Spiritual Side

* * *

Adopt a Healthy Mindset

Shift your perspective

Having a positive and resilient mindset is essential to our overall wellness because it affects how we perceive and react to life events and challenges. Our thoughts and attitudes shape our experiences and determine our levels of stress, anxiety, and happiness.

Think of your mindset as a lens through which you view the world. A positive lens brings clarity and allows you to see opportunities and growth in difficult situations, while a negative lens clouds your vision and amplifies stress and anxiety.

By embracing a growth mindset, we empower ourselves to see challenges as opportunities for personal growth and development rather than insurmountable obstacles. This positive outlook can help us better cope with stress, as we feel more confident in our ability to handle difficult situations and find solutions.

Furthermore, having a positive mindset can lead to better relationships, improved physical health, and increased success and happiness in all areas of life. So, it's essential to take care of our minds and cultivate a positive and resilient outlook through daily self-care practices like mindfulness, affirmations, and surrounding ourselves with supportive and uplifting people.

In short, our mindset is the foundation of our wellness, and by embracing a positive and resilient outlook, we can live a healthier, happier, and more fulfilling life.

10 Benefits of a Positive Healthy Mindset

1. **Mindset determines our outlook on life-** A positive, optimistic attitude towards life can help us see the best in every situation, even in the most challenging of times. It can keep us engaged, energetic, and passionate, even in retirement.
2. **A positive mindset improves our health-** Positive thinking has been shown to improve our immune system, boost our mood, and lower the risk of chronic diseases such as heart disease and depression.
3. **Increases life satisfaction-** When we approach retirement with a positive mindset, we are more likely to experience greater life satisfaction and well-being. We can focus on what we're grateful for and enjoy life to the fullest.
4. **Helps us adapt to change-** Retirement can bring about big changes in our lives, but with a positive mindset,

we can embrace these changes and make the most of new opportunities.

5. **Reduces stress-** A positive mindset can help us manage stress and avoid becoming overwhelmed. We can learn to focus on the things that matter most to us and let go of those that don't.
6. **Encourages creativity-** We can tap into our imagination and creativity with a positive mindset. We can pursue new hobbies, travel to new places, and enjoy life in new and exciting ways.
7. **Promotes healthy relationships-** A positive mindset helps us build strong, healthy relationships with our loved ones. Even in difficult circumstances, we can be more patient, understanding, and kind.
8. **Increases self-esteem-** When we have a positive mindset, we can feel more confident and proud of who we are and what we've accomplished. We can also feel more comfortable trying new things and stepping outside our comfort zone.
9. **Fosters a sense of purpose-** A positive mindset can help us find meaning and purpose in our lives, even in retirement. We can focus on giving back, pursuing our passions, and making a difference in the world.
10. **Leads to a longer, happier life-** With a positive mindset, we can live a longer, healthier, and happier life. We can embrace challenges, enjoy every moment, and feel fulfilled in retirement.

20 Healthy Attitudes For Success in Retirement

1. **Embrace change-** Instead of seeing change as a threat, view it as an opportunity to grow and learn new things. Embrace it with open arms and be willing to step outside your comfort zone.

2. **Redefine success-** Success in retirement may look different than it did in your working years. Redefine what success means to you and focus on what truly brings you happiness and fulfillment.
3. **Cultivate gratitude-** Take the time to appreciate the little things in life and focus on what you have rather than what you lack. A daily gratitude practice can significantly improve your overall well-being.
4. **Focus on relationships-** Retirement provides an opportunity to strengthen existing relationships and build new ones. Spending time with loved ones and forming new connections can bring immense joy and happiness.
5. **Pursue passions-** Retirement is a chance to focus on your interests and hobbies that may have taken a back seat to work and responsibilities. Find a new passion, or reignite an old one, and dive in with both feet.
6. **Travel-** Seeing new places, experiencing different cultures, and making new memories can bring a sense of adventure and excitement to retirement.
7. **Volunteer-** Giving back to your community can provide a sense of purpose and fulfillment. Find an organization or cause you are passionate about and get involved.
8. **Practice mindfulness-** Take time each day to be present and mindful, whether through meditation, yoga, or simply taking a walk in nature.
9. **Embrace learning-** Retirement is an opportunity to continue learning and growing, whether through taking courses, reading, or simply trying new things.
10. **Let go of perfectionism-** Retirement is not the time to be overly critical of yourself or to strive for perfection. Embrace a "good enough" mindset and focus on enjoying life to the fullest.
11. **Find joy in simplicity-** Instead of focusing on material possessions and external validation, find joy in the simple things in life, like spending time with loved ones, enjoying nature, or reading a good book.

12. **Embrace new experiences-** Don't be afraid to try new things and step outside of your comfort zone. Whether it's a new hobby, travel destination, or adventure, embracing new experiences can bring excitement and fulfillment to retirement.
13. **Find balance-** Retirement is a time to find balance in your life and prioritize self-care. Make time for rest, exercise, and leisure activities that bring you joy.
14. **Focus on physical health-** Regular exercise, healthy eating, and good sleep habits are key components to overall well-being in retirement.
15. **Seek support-** Whether it's through therapy, support groups, or close relationships, seek out support and resources that can help you navigate the challenges of retirement.
16. **Embrace a growth mindset-** Instead of seeing challenges as insurmountable obstacles, embrace a growth mindset and see challenges as opportunities for growth and learning.
17. **Prioritize self-care-** Take care of your physical, emotional, and mental well-being and prioritize self-care in retirement.
18. **Find purpose-** Retirement is a time to explore your sense of purpose and find meaning in your life. Whether it's through volunteering, starting a new hobby, or exploring your spiritual beliefs, finding purpose can bring a sense of fulfillment to retirement.
19. **Focus on positive thoughts-** Practice positive self-talk and focus on the positive aspects of retirement rather than dwelling on the negative.
20. **Embrace the present-** Rather than worrying about the future or dwelling on the past, focus on the present moment and embrace it fully.

Books

1. The Power of Positive Thinking by Dr. Norman Vincent Peale link
2. Get Out of Your Head: Stopping the Spiral of Toxic Thoughts by Jennie Allen link
3. Resilient: Restoring Your Weary Soul in These Turbulent Times by John Eldredge link
4. Keys to a Successful Retirement: Staying Happy, Active, and Productive in Your Retired Years by Fritz Gilbert link
5. You Are the Placebo: Making Your Mind Matter by Dr. Joe Dispenza link

* * *

Stay Mentally Sharp

Give your mind a workout

As we age, it's normal for our bodies to slow down, and that includes our brains. Since our brains are a critical component in our lives, from everyday movement functions to our ability to think and make decisions, it's essential we work to maintain our brain health from age-related decline.

Cognitive skills are a fundamental part of one's life. They enable us to think critically, remember details, and make wise decisions. As the aging process progresses, access to some of these crucial skills can begin to deteriorate. During retirement, actively engaging in activities that stimulate and enhance these skills and following steps to maintain brain health can be one of the keys to a sustained and enjoyable life.

The following steps have been linked to cognitive health through a growing body of scientific research. Adopting these habits as a part of your routine can make a big difference in improving your ability to think, learn, and remember.

. . .

8 Healthy Brain Health Habits

1. **Manage high blood pressure-** High blood pressure affects not only your heart but also your brain health. Midlife high blood pressure increases the risk of cognitive decline, and intensive lowering of blood pressure reduces the risk of mild cognitive impairment and dementia. Blood pressure does not show signs, so routine doctor visits are essential. Your doctor may suggest controlling high blood pressure through exercise, diet changes, and medication to protect both your heart and brain.

2. **Eat healthy foods-** A nutritious diet consisting of fruits and veggies, whole grains, lean protein, low-fat dairy, and limited sugar, salt, and solid fats, may help prevent chronic diseases and preserve brain health. The Mediterranean diet, in particular, may lower the risk of dementia. The MIND diet, a combination of Mediterranean and DASH diets, has also been shown to reduce Alzheimer's risk and slow cognitive decline in observational studies. Eating a healthy diet can help improve cardiovascular health, which in turn, may reduce dementia risk and maintain cognitive function. The typical Western diet, however, increases cardiovascular disease risk and speeds up brain aging.

3. **Be physically active-** Being physically active through exercise, household chores, or other activities has numerous benefits, including improved strength, energy, and balance and reduced risk of heart disease, diabetes, and depression. Studies suggest physical activity also positively impacts the brain and cognition, although a strong link to Alzheimer's prevention has not yet been established. Exercise stimulates brain function and increases the size of brain structures important to memory and learning. Aerobic exercise, such as brisk walking, is more beneficial for cognitive health than non-aerobic exercises, such as weight lifting. Regular physical activity increases brain glucose metabolism, possibly reducing Alzheimer's risk. Guidelines recommend

at least 2.5 hours of physical activity per week. Check with your doctor before starting a vigorous exercise program.

4. **Keep your mind active-** Intellectual engagement can benefit the brain, with people who participate in meaningful activities feeling happier and healthier. Learning new skills has shown some improvement in memory and thinking ability. Studies on engagement in activities such as music, theater, and writing suggest they can improve memory, self-esteem, reduce stress and increase social interaction in older adults. However, strong evidence of the lasting impact on cognition is lacking, and more research is needed. Mentally stimulating activities such as reading, playing games, working, and volunteering have not been proven to prevent cognitive impairment or Alzheimer's but may lower the risk. Some scientists believe these activities establish "cognitive reserve," making the brain more adaptable to age-related changes.

5. **Stay connected with social activities-** Social activities and community programs can keep your brain active, lower health risks, and improve well-being. Engaging in meaningful and productive activities with others, like visiting family and friends or volunteering, can boost mood and provide a sense of purpose. Online groups can also offer a way to connect with others and get support. There's no definitive evidence yet that these activities can prevent Alzheimer's or cognitive decline, but some have been linked to reduced risk of cognitive impairment and dementia.

6. **Manage stress-** Stress is a natural part of life, but chronic stress can harm memory and increase Alzheimer's risk. To manage stress and improve resilience, consider: exercising regularly, writing in a journal, practicing relaxation techniques (mindfulness or breathing exercises), and staying positive by letting go of grudges, practicing gratitude, and enjoying simple moments.

7. **Reduce risks to brain health-** Genetics, environment, and lifestyle all impact cognitive health, with some factors leading to a decline in thinking skills and daily

tasks. Inherited genetic factors can't be controlled, but environmental and lifestyle factors like health problems, brain injuries, medicine use, lack of exercise, poor diet, smoking, excessive alcohol, sleep issues, and social isolation can be managed to lower the risk.

8. **Take control of your physical health**

- Make sure to get regular health check-ups as recommended.
- Control any chronic health conditions you have, such as diabetes, high blood pressure, depression, and high cholesterol.
- Speak with your healthcare provider about your medications and how they might affect your memory, sleep, and brain function.
- Minimize the chances of brain injuries caused by falls or other accidents.
- Avoid excessive alcohol consumption, as some medications can be harmful when combined with it.
- If you are a smoker, quit smoking and avoid other nicotine products like chewing tobacco.
- Get sufficient sleep, around 7 to 8 hours per night.

Resources

1. Cognitive Health and Older Adults link
2. Harvard Medical School on Memory link
3. 11 Methods for Improving Your Memory link

Books

1. The Better Brain Book: The Best Tool for Improving Memory and Sharpness and Preventing Aging of the Brain by David Perlmutter link
2. Grain Brain: The Surprising Truth About Wheat, Carbs, and Sugar - Your Brain's Silent Killers by David Perlmutter link

3. The Fun and Relaxing Adult Activity Book: With Easy Puzzles, Coloring Pages, Writing Activities, Brain Games and Much More by Fun Adult Activity Book link

* * *

Adopt an Animal

Share life with a fur kid

Adopting a furry companion could save its life and enhance yours. Pets give us unconditional love and allow us to become someone they depend on.

Why adopt a pet?

1. **Health-** They'll give you a reason to get outdoors and be active.
2. **Social-** They'll help you meet people and socialize on walks or at the dog park.
3. **Emotional support-** They help you relax and de-stress.
4. **Companionship-** They're great listeners when you're bored and want someone to talk to.
5. **Entertainment-** They're fun to watch, play with, and buy outfits for.
6. **Love-** They don't judge you and are always happy to see you.
7. **Happiness-** Undeniably cute, research has shown that just staring into your pet's eyes can raise your level of oxytocin, known as the love hormone.

Go for it! Simple start steps:

1. Research animal breeds and consider the size and temperament best for you.
2. Consider your lifestyle, daily responsibilities, and pet ownership costs.
3. Search online for nearby adoptable rescue pets and visit a few animal shelters.

Resources

1. Humane Society Adoption Info link
2. ASPCA Adoption link
3. Pet Adoption Websites link
4. Differences between Dog and Cat People link

Products

1. Retractable Dog Leash with Dispenser link
2. Talking Pet Starter Kit link
3. Long Handle Pooper Scooper link

Books

1. Every dog: 450 Breeds by Nancy Hajeski link
2. Zak George's Dog Training Revolution by Zak George link
3. The Complete Guide to Adopting a Cat by Laura Cassiday link

Pairs well with: Walking shoes, pet beds, pet toys

You might also like: Hiking, pet training course, parks

* * *

Practice Happiness Habits

Do what can make you happier

Positive psychology is the scientific study of happiness, well-being, and what makes life worth living. It's a fresh and optimistic approach to psychology that focuses on the positive aspects of human life rather than solely on mental illness and distress. This exciting field of study has uncovered numerous secrets to cultivating happiness and living a fulfilling life.

One of the most enlightening findings of positive psychology is that happiness is not just a feeling that happens to us but rather a result of intentional actions and intentional practices. This means we have a hand in creating and cultivating our happiness rather than just being passive recipients of life's ups and downs.

Their research findings show that our capacity for happiness is set by a combination of three things. 1- 50% genetics such as your heredity and biology. 2- 10% Circumstances such as ethnicity, sex, income, education, geography, etc. 3- 40% intentional activity such as thinking patterns and behavior choices, etc. The intentional activity area is where we can increase our happiness by learning skills and strategies.

The science of positive psychology has revealed many ways to increase happiness and well-being, such as focusing on the present moment, building meaningful connections with others, engaging in activities that bring us joy, expressing gratitude, and doing acts of kindness. The practice of mindfulness, for instance, has been shown to reduce stress, increase feelings of happiness and contentment, and even improve brain function.

So, if you're seeking to live a more joyful and satisfying life, consider learning about and embracing the principles of positive psychology. The findings are overwhelmingly clear - happiness is a choice we can actively cultivate and sustain. So, take the time to invest in yourself and those around you, practice gratitude, and savor life's precious moments. You'll be amazed at the difference it makes.

31 Ways to Increase Happiness (From Positive Psychology Research Studies[7])

1. Practicing self-compassion and kindness.
2. Increasing social interactions and spending time with others.
3. Limiting the expression of anger.
4. Attending religious services or practices.
5. Practicing yoga for physical and mental well-being.
6. Managing alcohol consumption for better mental health.
7. Investing in memorable experiences rather than material possessions.
8. Using "active and constructive" communication methods in relationships.
9. Engaging in regular exercise.
10. Prioritizing quality sleep for improved mood.
11. Building friendships with positive individuals.
12. Practicing mindfulness meditation for mental clarity.
13. Spending money on others to foster happiness.
14. Reflecting on positive memories.
15. Balancing optimism with realistic expectations.
16. Avoiding excessive overthinking.
17. Volunteering for a sense of purpose and joy.
18. Engaging in compassion meditation for empathy.
19. Nurturing deep, meaningful conversations.
20. Maintaining a gratitude journal to appreciate life's positives.
21. Savoring the anticipation of positive events.
22. Finding happiness in small, everyday pleasures.
23. Moderating television consumption.
24. Not relying solely on marriage for happiness.
25. Avoiding settling for less in life.
26. Wearing a genuine smile to boost mood.
27. Avoiding excessive fantasizing.
28. Not obsessing over financial concerns.
29. Incorporating laughter into daily life for happiness.
30. Taking an active, assertive approach to life.
31. Reducing complaints and focusing on positive solutions.

Becoming Even Happier

The final section of this book on *fun* things to do will focus on how we can become even happier. I'm very excited to share it with you because I believe it has the potential to be the most valuable section of this book and add significantly to your well-being. The perspective-shifting ideas below certainly have been invaluable for me. As recently as the pandemic, when others were falling into depression and burdened by stress (largely created by their own minds), the ideas helped me keep a calm and positive perspective.

I've included it not only because happiness is one of my favorite topics but because the word *fun* implies a positive and emotionally rewarding state of engagement that contributes to a sense of happiness and well-being. When we're searching for fun, we're really looking for something enjoyable that could make us happier. So, let's dive deeper into this incredibly important and perhaps universally sought-after mental state of mind and attempt to uncover how a simple change in how we think about happiness can help us become even happier and more resilient.

After all, our country's visionary and philosophical founders felt it was fundamentally important enough to incorporate into our Declaration of Independence. The famous sentence reads, "We hold these truths to be self-evident, that all men are created equal, that they are endowed by their Creator with certain unalienable Rights, that among these are Life, Liberty and the pursuit of Happiness." We may achieve success and fortune, but without happiness, we won't find our lives meaningful. But what exactly is happiness, and why is it so important? Let's look at definitions of happiness and take a few moments to let them sink in.

What is happiness?

"Happiness doesn't depend on any external conditions, it is governed by our mental attitude." - Dale Carnegie

"Happiness is not something ready-made. It comes from your own actions." - Dalai Lama

"Happiness is when what you think, what you say, and what you do are in harmony." - Mahatma Gandhi

"Happiness depends more on how life strikes you than on what happens." - Andy Rooney

"Happiness is the presence of positive emotions and the absence of negative emotions." - Positive Psychology

"Happiness is a sense of fulfillment from pursuing one's passions and values." - "Authentic Happiness," by Seligman, M. E. P.

"Happiness is itself a kind of gratitude." - Joseph Wood Krutch

"Happiness comes only when we push our brains and hearts to the farthest reaches of which we are capable." - Leo Rosten

"Happiness is the ability to live in the present moment." - "The Art of Happiness," by Dalai Lama

"Happiness is not a station you arrive at, but a manner of traveling." - Margaret Lee Runbeck

"Happiness is the ability to savor life's small moments." - "The Myths of Happiness," by Lyubomirsky, S.

"Happiness is the spiritual experience of living every minute with love, grace and gratitude." - Denis Waitley

"Happiness is the pursuit of personal growth and self-improvement." - "Flow: The Psychology of Optimal Experience," by Csikszentmihalyi, M.

"Happiness is a mental habit, a mental attitude, and if it is not learned and practiced in the present it is never experienced. It cannot be made contingent upon solving some external problem. When one problem is solved, another appears to take its place. Life is a series of problems. If you are to be happy at all, you must be happy— period! Not happy "because of." - Maxwell Maltz, M.D.

"Happiness is the meaning and the purpose of life, the whole aim and end of human existence." - Aristotle

Happiness Cure

According to a Harvard Health article[8], happy people tend to have fewer health problems, a lower risk of depression, and longer lives. There is a substantial body of research indicating that happiness and emotional well-being can have a positive impact on physical health and overall functioning. Here are some general findings and themes from such research:

- **Reduced Stress:** Happiness and positive emotions are associated with lower stress levels. Reduced stress, in turn, can have numerous health benefits, such as improved cardiovascular health and a stronger immune system.
- **Better Cardiovascular Health:** Some studies have suggested that happier individuals are less likely to develop heart diseases and have better heart health.
- **Stronger Immune System:** Research has indicated that positive emotions can boost the immune system, making individuals more resilient to illnesses.
- **Pain Management:** Happiness and positive emotions can increase pain tolerance and improve pain management in individuals dealing with chronic pain.
- **Longevity:** Several studies have found a link between happiness and increased longevity. Happier people tend to live longer, healthier lives.
- **Improved Cognitive Function:** Happiness may be associated with better cognitive function, including memory and decision-making abilities.
- **Healthier Lifestyle Choices:** Happy individuals are more likely to engage in healthy behaviors such as regular exercise, a balanced diet, and getting enough sleep.

- **Faster Recovery:** Happier patients often recover more quickly from surgeries or illnesses.

Psychosomatic

The term "psychosomatic" refers to the connection or interaction between a person's mental or psychological state and their physical health or bodily symptoms. It suggests that emotional, psychological, and social factors can have a significant impact on an individual's physical well-being and can influence the onset or progression of physical illnesses or symptoms. Psychosomatic conditions are those in which emotional or mental factors play a role in the development, exacerbation, or management of physical health issues. These conditions highlight the intricate relationship between the mind and the body, emphasizing how emotional and mental well-being can affect physical health.

Happiness does not lie in the future. It lies only in the present.

The idea that happiness resides in the present, not the future, is deeply rooted in the philosophy of mindfulness and the understanding of how our minds function. Here's an explanation:

- **Living on a Deferred Payment Plan:** The concept of "living life on a deferred payment plan" means that some people postpone their happiness to a future date, often conditioned on achieving a specific goal or milestone. They believe that they will be happy "if" or "when" certain conditions are met. This approach can lead to unhappiness because it perpetuates a cycle of anticipation without fulfillment. People continuously set new conditions for their happiness, and each time they reach a goal, they find that it does not bring the lasting happiness they expected.

- **The Illusion of Future Happiness:** Waiting for future events or accomplishments to bring happiness creates an illusion that happiness is somewhere in the distance. This mindset can lead to dissatisfaction with the present moment because it is seen as merely a means to an end. As a result, individuals become preoccupied with what they lack rather than appreciating what they have.
- **Happiness as a Mental Habit:** Happiness is not something external that can be achieved through future achievements; rather, it is a mental habit and attitude. It's a way of perceiving and experiencing life in the present moment. Happiness is a state of mind that can be cultivated through mindfulness, gratitude, and a positive outlook on life.
- **The Importance of the Present:** The present moment is the only time we truly have control over. The past is gone, and the future is uncertain. Therefore, finding happiness in the present is essential for a fulfilling life. When we learn to appreciate and make the most of each moment, we break free from the cycle of perpetual anticipation and disappointment.
- **Mindful Living:** Mindfulness is a practice that encourages us to be fully present and engaged in the here and now. It involves paying attention to our thoughts, emotions, and surroundings without judgment. Through mindfulness, we can learn to find joy and contentment in everyday experiences, no matter how small.
- **The Paradox of Happiness:** The paradox of happiness lies in the realization that it is not dependent on external circumstances but on our internal mindset. Those who continuously chase future happiness often find themselves trapped in an unending pursuit. In contrast, those who focus on cultivating happiness in the present discover that it is always accessible. Don't wait for happiness. Create more happiness.

Internal Happiness Can be Cultivated and Developed

"Most people are about as happy as they make up their minds to be." - Abraham Lincoln

It's been said that happiness is an entirely internal phenomenon shaped not by external objects or circumstances but by our inner world of thoughts, ideas, and attitudes. Consider a few examples that highlight this:

- **The Lottery Paradox:** Imagine winning a massive lottery jackpot, a life-changing external event. At first, the excitement and joy are overwhelming. However, studies show that over time, lottery winners often return to a similar level of happiness they had before winning. Despite the external windfall, their internal state remains unchanged. This demonstrates that even significant changes in external circumstances don't guarantee lasting happiness. It's the individual's internal mindset and how they handle the windfall that determines their long-term happiness.
- **Adaptation and the Hedonic Treadmill:** Research in psychology has shown that humans tend to adapt to new circumstances relatively quickly, both positive and negative. This phenomenon, known as the "hedonic treadmill," suggests that external gains or losses have a temporary impact on happiness. Over time, people tend to return to a relatively stable level of happiness based on their internal disposition.
- **Subjective Nature of Happiness:** Happiness varies significantly from person to person. What brings joy to one individual may not have the same effect on another. This subjectivity suggests that happiness is not solely dependent on external factors but is deeply rooted in one's unique mindset.
- **Contrasting Attitudes:** Imagine two people who face the same job loss. Person A views it as a catastrophic failure and falls into despair, while Person B sees it as an

opportunity for a fresh start and personal growth. Despite identical external circumstances, Person B is more likely to find happiness because their attitude and mindset are geared towards resilience and positive adaptation.

In summary, happiness is not a passive state dependent on external factors; it's an active and internal process that can be cultivated and sustained through the development of constructive thoughts, attitudes, and ideas. While external circumstances may influence our mood temporarily, the enduring and profound happiness we seek lies within our capacity to shape our inner world and perspectives.

Dealing with External Adversity

Let's be honest, simply choosing happiness is easier said than done. Even if we make the simple decision to be happy and think pleasant thoughts most of the time, life finds a way to get on our nerves and try to kick us back into a funk. That's okay.

We can't always be happy and think positive thoughts. No one is happy all of the time.

Just try to deal with life's adversity quickly and aim to be happy more than not! That's an attainable goal for most and will certainly make you a happier person.

Resilience and Coping: Internal qualities like resilience and effective coping strategies are vital for managing life's ups and downs. These skills can be developed and honed over time, enabling individuals to navigate challenges gracefully and maintain their sense of happiness.

Mindset and Perception: Happiness often depends on how individuals perceive and interpret events. Two people facing similar challenges may react differently based on their mindset. Someone with a positive outlook may find opportunities for growth and learning in adversity, while another person with a negative mindset might dwell on the hardships.

Changing our Reactions: Much of our habitual negativity can be traced back to specific events or situations we've interpreted as a blow to our self-esteem. This means that our emotional reactions, especially negative ones, often have roots in how we perceive ourselves and our sense of self-worth. Here's a more detailed explanation:

1. **Event Occurs:** Unhappiness often begins with an event or situation. This could be a failure, criticism, rejection, or any experience that challenges our self-image.
2. **Interpretation:** The key factor in this process is how we interpret the event. If we interpret it as a threat to our self-esteem or self-worth, it can trigger negative emotions like sadness, anger, or anxiety.
3. **Negative Emotional Reaction:** Once we've interpreted the event negatively, we experience emotions associated with it. For example, if we interpret criticism as a sign that we're not good enough, we may feel hurt or defensive.
4. **Habitual Responses:** These interpretations and emotional reactions can become habitual over time. We simply react a certain way without even thinking about it. For instance, a store clerk isn't as pleasant as we expect them to be, and we instantly feel offended by them acting that way. This habitual emotional reaction and negative thinking reinforce our feelings of unhappiness and start to bring us down.
5. **Self-Esteem Impact:** Our self-esteem, which is our overall evaluation of ourselves, can be significantly influenced by these interpretations and reactions. If we habitually interpret events as threats to our self-esteem, it can erode our self-confidence and lead to chronic unhappiness.

Recognizing this pattern and working on our interpretations and self-esteem can be essential for breaking the cycle of habitual unhappiness. It involves developing healthier ways to interpret events, challenging negative thought patterns, and building a more resilient and positive sense of self-worth.

Stop Allowing External Events To Push You Around

No one can decide what your thoughts will be but yourself. Your thoughts trigger your emotions. Only you control your thoughts and emotions. Regaining control over your emotional responses involves making a conscious choice to be happy and refusing to react with unhappiness simply out of habit. By doing so, you assert your autonomy over your emotional well-being.

> *It's not about denying or pretending that something bad didn't happen. We all know crap happens.*

When something bad happens, let's say the fridge broke, you can acknowledge it as a "fact". The fridge broke.

> *But it's only an opinion that it has to ruin your day or bring you down.*

Separate the facts and opinions. **You control your opinions.**

- **Acceptance:** Acknowledge unfortunate events or "facts" but do not assign emotional significance to them. In a cold-blooded ancient Buddhist wisdom sort of way, I like to say to myself, **"It is what it is."** This simple phrase helps keep unfortunate things I cannot control in perspective. It is what it is. Nothing more. Nothing less. Acceptance moves straight forward to resolving the issue internally without assigning negative emotions such as denial, anger, regret, or depression.

- **Empower Yourself:** The solution lies in empowering yourself to resist being swayed by external events. You have the freedom to make a conscious choice to be happy, regardless of what's happening around you.
- **Choose Your Reaction:** Your reactions to events are not predetermined; they are choices you make. Instead of automatically responding with unhappiness out of habit, opt for a different response.
- **Break the Habit:** Habitual unhappiness often stems from reacting the same way to similar situations. By breaking this habit, you can liberate yourself from unnecessary negativity.
- **Mindful Responses:** Practice mindfulness in your reactions to external events. Pause and consider how you want to react, such as in a calm controlled logical way, rather than reacting emotionally. If you feel negative emotions start to creep up, stop and acknowledge them, then think that you have the choice to control your emotions, they don't control you.

Growing Happiness

1. **Selective Focus:** Every day, a mixture of good and bad things happen to you and go on in the world. Deliberately focus your attention on pleasant thoughts and cut out all the negative thoughts. If you're feeling anxious about things you cannot control, stop thinking about them and eliminate consuming negativity. For instance, stop watching the nightly world news, also known as a summary of the worst things that happened in the entire world today. We may live in a fallen world, but why should we focus on the darkness and let it consume us? We can focus on the light and let it shine to the world through our positive thoughts and actions.

2. **Focus on Goals:** Choose some positive goals or projects to focus on and take steps to achieve them.
3. **Gratitude Practice:** Numerous psychological studies have shown that practicing gratitude, a purely internal exercise, significantly boosts happiness levels. By focusing on positive aspects of life, even in challenging situations, individuals can shift their internal perspective and experience greater well-being.
4. **Mindfulness Meditation:** Mindfulness meditation teaches individuals to be fully present in the moment, accepting it without judgment. This practice has been shown to reduce stress and increase happiness. It's a clear example of how one's internal mental activity can influence one's emotional state, irrespective of external pressures or demands.
5. **Personal Growth:** Many people find happiness in personal growth and self-improvement, which are driven by internal motivations. Learning a new skill, pursuing education, or setting and achieving personal goals are activities that can lead to a profound sense of happiness.
6. **Emotional Resilience:** Individuals who develop emotional resilience can bounce back from setbacks and adversity. They see challenges as opportunities for growth rather than insurmountable obstacles. This inner strength enables them to maintain happiness even in challenging environments.
7. **Comparison Trap:** The tendency to compare oneself to others is a common source of unhappiness. Yet, this comparison is often based on external factors like wealth, appearance, or possessions. By shifting focus from external comparisons to internal values and self-acceptance, individuals can break free from the comparison trap and find more lasting happiness.
8. **Recall Happy Moments Often:** Studies have shown that our nervous system cannot tell the difference between an actual experience and an experience imagined vividly in detail. It reacts the same way. So why not make it a point to

frequently think vividly about the small moments in your life when you felt happiest (a great party or small accomplishment)? Your body will react in a similar way to the memory as you relive the event in your mind, making you feel happier.

9. **Act Unselfishly:** Unselfishness, or putting others before yourself, can lead to happiness for several reasons. It gives you a sense of purpose and fulfillment, strengthens positive social connections, reduces stress, and releases oxytocin, which is associated with trust and well-being. Additionally, it broadens your perspective, increases gratitude, and creates a positive feedback loop, fostering happiness through altruistic satisfaction.

Go for it! Simple start steps:

If you've made the conscious decision to be happier regardless of any external circumstance, here are some positive attitudes you can remind yourself of daily to reinforce this new mindset. With practice, they'll become your happiness habits. Today...

1. To the best of my ability, I will maintain a positive and joyful demeanor.
2. I will consciously try to smile a few times throughout the day.
3. I will genuinely compliment or do something to make someone else feel good.
4. I'll make an effort to be a little more warm and friendly towards others.
5. I will aim to be less critical and more tolerant of others, recognizing their imperfections and giving them the benefit of the doubt by assuming positive intent in their actions.
6. I will strive to view facts objectively and avoid interpreting them in a pessimistic or negative light based on my own opinion.

7. I will purposefully disregard and shut out all the pessimistic and negative facts that I have no control over and cannot influence or alter in any way.
8. No matter what occurs, I will be slow to respond with calm composure and thoughtfulness to the best of my ability.

Resources

1. Positive Psychology Strategies for Increased Happiness link
2. What Is Positive Psychology & Why Is It Important? link
3. How to be happy link

A Final Word

As we reach the end of this journey through "The Ultimate Book of Fun Things to Do in Retirement Volume 2," it's my hope that you've found inspiration and ideas that will enrich your retirement years. We've delved into an abundance of exciting activities, from bucket list travel destinations to outdoor adventures, new experiences that bring personal growth, ways to foster social connections, creative pursuits in arts and crafts, culinary ideas, games, music, and the endless pursuit of knowledge. We've explored the role of technology in making retirement even more enjoyable, and we've discussed the importance of health and wellness in this new phase of life.

Now that you've read through all of the ideas in these pages, you may be feeling a bit overwhelmed. That's perfectly normal! With so many options to choose from, it can be hard to know where to begin or how to get started. But remember, there is no right or wrong way to approach retirement. The important thing is to take that first step and find something you're interested in. It could lead to the discovery of your next passion. Our best selves emerge when we're engaged in meaningful pursuits. With the gift of time that retirement brings, it's crucial to fill it with activities that feed your mental and physical well-being. Whether it's exploring a new hobby, traveling to a new destination, or simply spending time with loved ones, the key is to get started.

Moving forward into this exciting chapter of life, I encourage you to focus on what matters most to you. In Chapter 1, we created a personal "things I care about" list, which serves as a guide to help you prioritize your time and energy in retirement. Use this list as your compass, and infuse variety and excitement into your life with the activities we've explored in this book. If you're hungry for even more ideas, consider picking up Volume 1, which offers hundreds more exciting possibilities and useful tips. Also, be sure to leverage some of the 563 website resource links provided throughout this book to gather more information and assistance as you embark on your chosen adventures.

If you found this book has or will add value to your retirement and was worth your hard-earned money, please consider sharing it with others. Your recommendation could make a world of difference to someone searching for a renewed purpose and inspiration in their retirement. Also, leaving a quick review or simply a rating on Amazon and Goodreads would be greatly appreciated.

While embarking on this exciting new chapter in your life, try to cultivate a positive mindset, and focus on the joys of retirement. Yes, there may be challenges and setbacks along the way, but the key is to embrace each day with purpose and intention. Spend your time on meaningful endeavors that bring you joy and fulfillment. Follow your passions and embrace new experiences. Seize the day and make the most of this precious time in your life.

In closing, I want to express my heartfelt gratitude for choosing "The Ultimate Book of Fun Things to Do in Retirement Volume 2" as your guide to living your best life in retirement. I hope this book has ignited your curiosity to explore new horizons, embrace new challenges, and cherish each and every day. Retirement is an exciting journey filled with endless possibilities. Embrace it with open arms and live your life to the fullest!

A Final Word

In retirement, there's much to do
Seize the day, it's up to you!
No more alarms or bosses' calls
Just time to do what you love most of all

You could travel the world, see new sights
Or stay at home and enjoy quiet nights
Catch up on hobbies, read a good book
Or spend time with family, take a second look

The world is your oyster, it's yours to explore
No need to rush, take it slow and adore
Each moment, each memory, each little joy
Life's too short, so seize the day, oh boy!

There's no need to fret, no need to stress
Retirement is a time to feel blessed
To do what you love, to be happy and free
To seize the day, just like you should be!

— Live More

* * *

Please take a moment to leave an Amazon review at the QR below.

Scan the QR to leave a review

To leave a review with **Goodreads,** use the QR below.

For Goodreads Review

Thank you for your support.

Get the free bonus PDF download, The Senior's Quick Guide to ChatGPT, at
www.funretirementbooks.com/v2bonus

Alternatively, scan the QR for the Bonus PDF

Bibliography

1. Wayne, P. M., & Fuerst, M. L. (2013). *The Harvard Medical School guide to Tai Chi: 12 weeks to a healthy body, strong heart, and sharp mind.* Shambhala Publications
2. U.S. Department of Health and Human Services. (2018). *Physical Activity Guidelines for Americans, 2nd edition.* https://health.gov/our-work/physical-activity/current-guidelines
3. Garone, S. (2021, August 10). *5 Health Benefits of Kayaking.* Verywell Fit. https://www.verywellfit.com/health-benefits-of-kayaking-5196341
4. Medical News Today. (2022, August 17). *Benefits of sunlight: Can it improve your health?* https://www.medicalnewstoday.com/articles/benefits-of-sunlight
5. Lindqvist, P. G., Epstein, E., Nielsen, K., Landin-Olsson, M., Ingvar, C., & Olsson, H. (2016). *Avoidance of sun exposure is a risk factor for all-cause mortality: results from the Melanoma in Southern Sweden cohort.* Journal of Internal Medicine, 280(4), 375–387
6. *Brien, S. E., Ronksley, P. E., Turner, B. J., Mukamal, K. J., & Ghali, W. A.* (2011). Effect of alcohol consumption on biological markers associated with risk of coronary heart disease: systematic review and meta-analysis of interventional studies. *BMJ (Clinical research ed.)*, 342, https://www.bmj.com/content/342/bmj.d636
7. Celestine, N., & Neuhaus, M. (2023). *The Science of Happiness in Positive Psychology 101.* Positive Psychology. https://positivepsychology.com/happiness/
8. Solan, M. (2021, November 1). *Health and happiness go hand in hand.* Harvard Health. https://www.health.harvard.edu/mind-and-mood/health-and-happiness-go-hand-in-hand
9. Boehm, J. K., & Kubzansky, L. D. (2012). The heart's content: The association between positive psychological well-being and cardiovascular health. Psychological Bulletin, 138(4), 655-691.
10. Diener, E. (2013). The remarkable changes in the science of subjective well-being. Perspectives on Psychological Science, 8(6), 663-666.

List Index

10 Common Things People Consider Meaningful or Important 2
15 Common "Bucket List" Items 3
10 Popular Things to Do in Retirement 7
30 Ideas to Experience a World of Wonder 12
6 Popular Tropical Destinations 16
5 Popular Wellness Retreat Destinations 17
4 Popular Locations for Hot Springs 18
4 Popular Destinations for Cruising 19
5 Popular National Parks for Relaxation 20
5 Popular All-Inclusive Adult Resort Destinations 21
5 Popular Lake Destinations for Relaxation 22
36 Historic Places to Visit 24
23 Water Experiences Worth Traveling For 29
12 US Amusement Parks Best for Lucky Retirees 34
17 International Amusement Parks Worth Visiting 35
23 International Events and Festivals Worth Experiencing 39
28 US Events and Festivals Worth Experiencing 43
11 Unforgettable Things to Do in Egypt 49
61 Animal Encounters 53
10 Major Sporting Events in the US 57
14 International Sporting Events 58

List Index

12 Disney Theme Parks Around The World 61
14 of Disney's Resort Hotels in the USA 62
13 Exciting Ideas for Visiting Disney 62
50 Outdoor Fun Ideas 66
5 Main Styles of Tai Chi 72
7 Advantages of Powered Paragliding 75
5 Reasons Why Disc Golf is Better Than Ball Golf 77
3 Types of Landscape Paintings 80
4 Steps to Landscape Painting 80
6 Types of Gardens 83
5 Benefits of Gardening 83
5 Benefits of Kayaking 86
5 Talents to Entertain 87
Top 10 Most Popular Things People Collect 88
10 Reasons To Race Remote-Control Vehicles 90
7 Types of Remote-Control Vehicles 91
7 Benefits of Sunlight 95
3 Reasons To Get Your Grill On 98
7 Top Wine Regions in the US 101
4 Reasons To Practice Bushcraft 104
12 Famous Places to Take a Hot Air Balloon Ride 109
5 Main Show Ticket Resources 117
6 Types of All-Terrain Vehicles 118
Top 10 Places in the US for Whale Watching 120
The 14 Most Popular Parades in the US 122
4 Pastries Similar to Beignets to Try 125
The Top 9 Train Journeys in the World 128
The Top 9 Train Trips in the USA 128
15 Eurorail Train Passes 129
3 Istanbul, Turkey Mosques 136
6 Apps to Learn Guitar 139
7 Benefits of Learning Music 140
50 Social Opportunities for Retirees 150
7 Benefits of Bowling 152
10 Reasons to Learn to Dance 155
5 Free Online Dance Lessons 157
28 Ideas to Grow a Relationship 163

List Index

11 Crafts to Explore 168
9 Paper Art Projects 171
15 Unusual Craft Projects 175
7 Crafting Machines 181
31 Fun Cooking Ideas 187
25 Fun Cooking Machines To Try 192
16 Types of Games to Play at Home 199
27 Popular Board Games 199
14 Popular Card Games 201
20 Classic Card Games 203
15 Popular Video Games 205
15 Immersive Virtual Reality (VR) Games 206
5 Fantasy Role-Playing Games (RPG) 209
25 Ideas to Bring Music into Your Life 211
10 Most Popular Instruments to Play 212
38 Ideas to Explore 214
50 Fun Ideas for How a Retiree Can Use Technology 224
9 Smart Home Possibilities 227
5 Intelligent Home Fitness Equipment 232
6 Online Workout Videos, Apps, and Courses 233
7 Things to Do With Your Digital Photos 235
4 Popular VR Game Systems 239
5 Top Virtual Reality (VR) Games 240
25 Ideas to Focus on Physical Health 243
10 Benefits of a Positive Healthy Mindset 246
20 Healthy Attitudes For Success in Retirement 247
8 Healthy Brain Health Habits 251
31 Ways to Increase Happiness 256
9 Essential Happiness Mindsets 267

Also by S.C. Francis

The Ultimate Book of Fun Things to Do in Retirement: Volume 1

Available in ebook, print, and audio. Grab your copy on Amazon here.

Listen FREE with your 1st Audible credit here.

Volume 1 & Audiobook

* * *

Curious Minds Ask: *55 Thought-Provoking Questions for Humanity Answered by Artificial Intelligence*

In the age of Artificial Intelligence (AI) just beginning, where machines can ponder the most profound philosophical queries and offer insights born from vast troves of knowledge, AI will become a partner in our quest for understanding, a tool that amplifies our capacity for exploration and discovery.

We stand at the cusp of revolutionary new breakthroughs in every field, as well as a point where we must be cautious of the dangers that AI poses to our future.

But before we can begin to understand this potential new reality for humanity, we must attempt to understand this Artificial Intelligence. And in the future, when there is superintelligence beyond our own, wisdom will come when Curious Minds Ask the right questions.

We get to know the AI that will shape our world by asking it thought-provoking questions about humanity that span the realms of science, philosophy, ethics, and beyond. The unedited responses provide direct insight into the "mind" of the machine. It's a "first contact" of sorts for many of us, where we're communicating directly with it (ChatGPT). **How intelligent is it, and how well does it know us?**

This is no longer a distant fantasy. This is a real conversation with an Artificial Intelligence.

In asking these questions about humanity, my hope is we'll see the world and ourselves in a different light and have a better understanding of the power of AI to shape our future.

Available in ebook and print. Grab your copy here.

***

Cats Wearing Clothes: *A Photo Journey Through the Ages*

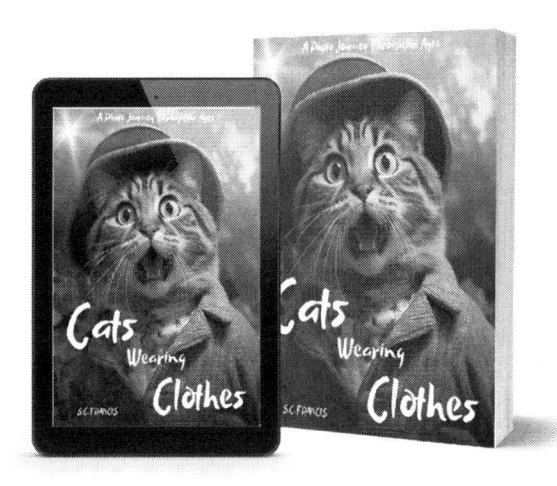

Cats, like you've never seen them before! Journey through the ages with our captivating photobook, where photo realistic AI-generated cats are your guides to the past, modeling the clothing and personality of historical periods. Get ready to be whisked away on an enchanting adventure that's a feast for the eyes and a purr-fect treat for cat lovers and history enthusiasts alike. It's a glimpse into the power, creativity, and beauty of Artificial Intelligence and makes a unique humorous gift!

Available in ebook and print. Grab your copy here.

Cats Wearing Clothes on Amazon

Made in the USA
Monee, IL
10 April 2025

76eecbd7-4926-48d5-8e6e-7b8020be3e80R01